Behold the Lamb of God

Behold the Lamb of God

"Behold the Lamb of God, which
taketh away the sin of the world."
John 1:29

Selections from the Sermons and Writings, Published
and Unpublished, of J. Reuben Clark, Jr.,
on the Life of the Savior

Deseret Book Company
Salt Lake City, Utah

Other volumes in the Classics in Mormon Literature Series:

An Approach to the Book of Mormon, by Hugh Nibley
Articles of Faith, by James E. Talmage
Autobiography of Parley P. Pratt
Essentials in Church History, by Joseph Fielding Smith
The Gospel: God, Man, and Truth, by David H. Yarn, Jr.
Gospel Doctrine, by Joseph F. Smith
Gospel Truth, by George Q. Cannon
Jesus the Christ, by James E. Talmage
Key to the Science of Theology and *A Voice of Warning*
    (in one volume), by Parley P. Pratt
Life of Joseph Smith the Prophet, by George Q. Cannon
Outlines in Ecclesiastical History, by B. H. Roberts
The Spirit of the Old Testament, by Sidney B. Sperry
Why the King James Version, by J. Reuben Clark, Jr.

First printing in the Classics in Mormon Literature Series, April 1991

Library of Congress Cataloging-in-Publicaton Data

Clark, J. Reuben (Joshua Reuben), 1871–1961.
    Behold the lamb of God : selections from the sermons and writings,
published and unpublished, of J. Reuben Clark, Jr. on the life of
the Savior.
        p.   cm. — (Classics in Mormon literature)
    Includes index.
    ISBN 0-87579-536-6
    1. Jesus Christ—Mormon interpretations.   2. Mormon Church—
Doctrines.   3. Church of Jesus Christ of Latter-day Saints—
Doctrines I. Title.   II. Series.
BX8643.J4C42   1991
232 — dc20   91-18679
                                                              CIP

Printed in the United States of America
10   9   8   7   6   5   4   3   2   1

CONTENTS

FOREWORD

An ancient prophet classified men of great worldly learning into two classes:

O the vainness and the frailties, and the foolishness of men! When they are learned they think they are wise, and they hearken not unto the counsel of God, for they set it aside, supposing they know of themselves, wherefore, their wisdom is foolishness and it profiteth them not. . . .

But to be learned is good if they hearken unto the counsels of God.

Rarely from among those of great worldly learning does there emerge one who, though having excelled in eminent scholarship, yet humbles himself and hearkens to the counsels of God.

Among the great scholars of our day was President J. Reuben Clark, Jr. During the earlier mature years of his life, he lived away from the organized units of the Church, in Washington, D.C., and later in Mexico, associated with the State Department of the United States, and then with the diplomatic service.

During these years, the Sabbath Day was observed by him just as sacredly as though he were in full attendance at Church meetings and Church activities. He engaged himself on the Sabbath, when there were very often no other activities available, in the study of the life and teachings of Jesus of Nazareth, the Savior of the world. He procured, over these years, an excellent library on the life of the Master and with painstaking care, set about to work out a "harmony" of the Four Gospels and Third Nephi of the Book of Mormon, to which he referred as the "Fifth Gospel." This treasured work is now compiled under the title *Our Lord of the Gospels*. His study of

the traditions and customs of the Jews at the time of the
Master's birth became public in a small but prized writing: *"Wist Ye Not That I Must Be About My Father's
Business? . . ."* He then set about to point out the gradual
changes which took place following the Master's death, in
the organization of his Church and in his teachings which
led to a complete apostasy after the Apostolic period. This
monumental work is now in published form, under the
heading: *On the Way to Immortality and Eternal Life.* His
studies led him to the conclusion that no modern version
of the Bible surpassed the King James Version. To students, today, who would seek to know why he was so convinced, he has left us a well-documented volume: *Why
the King James Version.*

In his later years, and particularly during the years
he was in the First Presidency, many of his sermons and
writings were drawn from this vast treasure-house of
knowledge and from his profound faith in the Divine
Redeemer, the Savior of the world.

An eminent judge not of the Church, with whom he
was long associated, made a significant statement to the
effect that in all the times they had associated together,
he had never heard J. Reuben Clark speak publicly, when
President Clark had failed to "declare his faith." It was on
one of these occasions in New York City, at a farewell din-
ner in his honor, that again he did "declare his faith" as
he bade his farewell to this non-member audience made
up of business leaders with whom he had been long associated. Here were his closing words:

"For us Christians he is the Christ, the Only Begotten Son of the Living God, the Creator under God, of the
earth, the Redeemer of the world, our Savior, the First
Fruits of the Resurrection, which comes to all born to this
earth, believer and unbeliever alike, the only name under
heaven given among men, whereby we must be saved."

In this volume under the meaningful title, *Behold*

the Lamb of God, the family and intimate friends of President Clark have brought together some of the many sermons and writings of this noble son of God who loved "The Lamb of God" about whom he had studied so deeply. The testimony of John the Baptist who uttered the words in the title now heading this compilation of President Clark's utterances, seems to us now to be almost as a profound injunction to all who read these writings. These words of unquestioned conviction, seem to urge us likewise to see, to believe, and to know, intimately, the Divine Redeemer, the literal Son of God, the Savior of mankind—to know whom, as the Master declared, is to gain eternal life.

Harold B. Lee

PUBLISHER'S PREFACE

"Behold the Lamb of God." That was the phrase used by John the Baptist to identify the Christ. John could so testify, for it was he who had been entrusted with the incomparable privilege of baptizing the Redeemer. This book, which bears that sacred name as its title, breathes the spirit of one who also knew the Christ well. Every aspect of the gospel treated herein is centered in the Lord.

J. Reuben Clark, Jr., the author, made a lifelong study of the life and teachings of the Savior. His was not a casual reading of the scriptures but a deep, thoughtful, analytical, penetrating, and worshipful study. President Clark had the ability to speak and write in a way that causes his readers to realize they are contemplating with him—reflecting, pondering—"wondering," in the sense of being filled with wonder. His words reveal a remarkable closeness to the Lord, an intimacy, a love for him. One has the feeling that the words were written by a dear friend of the Lord, and the sense of reverence is profound.

President Clark unequivocally testified of Jesus' divinity. He knew him as the Savior and Redeemer of mankind, as the Only Begotten Son of God in the flesh, the veritable Son of God. He saw clearly the implications of rejecting or denying that divinity, and he categorically denounced viewing the Lord as only a moralist, ethical teacher, or philosopher. He warned mankind of the consequences of such views for both the individual and society. He made it clear that our thoughts and actions really matter, that one cannot be indifferent to their consequences and hide behind the assumption that they do not count.

Throughout the book there is the implicit, and in many places explicit, theme that the purpose of our existence is to "prove" ourselves and that it is God's work and glory to "bring to pass the immortality and eternal life of man." From his identification of the Christ as the great Creator, the premortal Jehovah, to his stirring remarks on "Kolob, the Governor" and his discussion of the marvelous plan of salvation and its many facets, one obtains a remarkable perspective on the scope of the gospel and Christ's ministry.

As wonderful and unexplainable as the phenomenal miracles the Lord performed to bless people's lives were, President Clark gives us the valuable insight that such miracles were "incomparably simple" for one who was the "Maker and Destroyer of universes."

The gospel itself is not the result of a long and experimental evolutionary process, President Clark teaches, but was given to Adam and Eve in the beginning. Through the exercise of man's agency, the struggle of good and evil brought a series of dispensations and apostasies, including the mortal life and the great atoning sacrifice of the Savior in the meridian of time, followed by "the great apostasy" and the Restoration, in which there was to be a "restitution of all things."

President Clark discusses the nature of ancient sacrifice and ritualistic worship as well as the kind of sacrifice the Lord now expects since he fulfilled the law he gave to Moses. He contrasts the immense difference between the temporal and the eternal, the material and the spiritual, the treasures of the world and the "treasures of the Spirit." He teaches eloquently concerning the personality of God, the power of faith, the potential of prayer *for the one who prays,* the enormous power of the Holy Priesthood, and his tender, merciful, loving concept of God's judgment.

Just as the first chapter, "Jesus Christ, the Son of God," sets forth President Clark's testimony of the Christ, so, near the end of the book, he declares: "We thus believe

Christ to be in the full, true, and most literal sense, the
Creator of the world, one of the Godhead, the Only
Begotten of the Father, the Son of God, the promised
Messiah, the First Fruits of the Resurrection, the
Redeemer of the world." Behold, the Lamb of God.

David H. Yarn, Jr.

AUTHOR'S PREFACE

Jesus Christ, the Son of God

Jesus, the Christ: In the beginning with God; himself God; author of our salvation and exaltation; creator of the world and all that in it is; the light and life of the world; our Savior, dying on the cross for us; our intercessor with the Father, who time and again said: "This is my beloved Son, hear him"; bestower of infinite love and mercy; soul of compassion and forgiveness; healer of sick bodies and broken hearts; friend of the friendless; giver of divine peace, his peace.

God grant to each of us this knowledge, this testimony,

J. Reuben Clark, Jr.

ACKNOWLEDGMENTS

It is the desire of the family of President J. Reuben Clark, Jr., to express its deep appreciation unto all who have assisted in any way in compiling and publishing this volume.

To Elder Marion G. Romney, Chairman of the J. Reuben Clark, Jr., Trust Estate, for his counsel and devoted support of this endeavor, we give thanks. We are grateful to Elder Harold B. Lee for the inspiring foreword which he was kind enough to write.

We acknowledge the interest and helpfulness of Gordon B. Affleck, Executor.

We are grateful to the Relief Society for permission to include the two chapters, "The Journey from Nazareth to Jerusalem" and "Jesus in the Temple Courts with the Doctors," from the book, *Wist Ye Not That I Must Be About My Father's Business?*—copyright to which was assigned to them by the author.

Rowena J. Miller, secretary to President Clark, deserves highest commendation for her untiring efforts and for her superb skill in editing, indexing, and preparing this book for publication.

That the words of our father concerning the life and mission of Jesus Christ, whom he loved so dearly, may touch the hearts of those who read them to the end that they may strive ever more diligently for eternal life, is our humble and prayerful wish.

"And this is life eternal, that they might know thee the only true God, and Jesus Christ, whom thou hast sent."
John 17:3

A Study of the Savior's Ministry Offers a Wealth of Faith, a Wealth of Virtue

AS WE get older, as I get older and become more reflective, I seem to know less and less about the Savior. I seem more and more to grow in wonderment and awe and in deep, heartfelt gratitude for what I understand he did for you and for me, for all of his brothers and sisters, for we all are such.

You know, we all had somewhat the same kind of existence that he had. We had an existence before we came to earth. We have an existence here on earth, and while our time has not yet come, yet when it does come we shall join him and those who have gone before, on the other side.

Two Great Missions

I do not wish to undertake to discuss Adam and the Fall. We shall take that as a fact, and then, knowing the plan as we now know it, we shall know or perceive the two great missions which, as immediately concerning us, we know the Master had. The first mission was a redemptive mission, acting as our Redeemer, making the Atonement for the Fall of Adam, so accomplishing it that the great plan framed in the Grand Council of Heaven might be fulfilled, that we would keep this estate and then in due time go on after our death, finally being resurrected.

Now, the Savior, as I think of him, was both a Creator and a Redeemer, so far as we are concerned. The work of redemption has not been given to us in detail any more than the Fall has been given unto us in detail. I seriously question whether we could understand either the Fall or the Atonement if our Heavenly

Father saw fit to try to explain it to us in detail, as he has not. We know the great facts.

Now so far as that redemption, the redemptive work of the Savior, is concerned, he alone was responsible in that. He did the whole work of redemption himself. We seemingly, so far as we know, had no part at all therein.

But the work of redemption went somewhat beyond just what we know as the Atonement. I often have marveled at the work which the Savior had to do when he came here, and it seems to me that I can sketch it out this way:

First and foremost was his duty to make the atoning sacrifice. None except himself could do this, that is so far as we know.

But he had other things to do, most of which might have been done by someone else duly authorized and empowered thereto by our Heavenly Father. I call your attention to one or two of them.

You will recall that Adam was offering sacrifice to the Lord, and the angel came and asked why he did it, and he said he did not know except the Lord had commanded it. Then the angel told him that the sacrifice which Adam was making was symbolical of the great sacrifice that was to be made by the Only Begotten in due time. From then until the Savior came, the religious service practiced among the people of our Heavenly Father was in good part ritualistic, and the foundation of it was animal sacrifice, although the fruits of the field were also used.

The coming of the Savior did away with sacrifice. He has so stated. His coming was really the end of the ritualistic worship which the people of God had followed up until that time.

Sacrifice of a Broken Heart

Now, I want to read you just a few verses, and I am taking them from Third Nephi 9:18-22. The Lord, visiting here during the time he lay in the tomb, during the time of the great destruction that took place here on this continent at the time of his crucifixion, spoke to the people and said:

I am the light and the life of the world. I am Alpha and Omega, the beginning and the end.

And ye shall offer up unto me no more the shedding of blood; yea, your sacrifices and your burnt offerings shall be done away, for I will accept none of your sacrifices and your burnt offerings.

And ye shall offer for a sacrifice unto me a broken heart and a contrite spirit. And whoso cometh unto me with a broken heart and a contrite spirit, him will I baptize with fire and with the Holy Ghost, even as the Lamanites, because of their faith in me at the time of their conversion, were baptized with fire and with the Holy Ghost, and they knew it not.

Behold, I have come unto the world to bring redemption unto the world, to save the world from sin.

Therefore, whoso repenteth and cometh unto me as a little child, him will I receive, for of such is the kingdom of God. Behold, for such I have laid down my life, and have taken it up again; therefore repent, and come unto me ye ends of the earth, and be saved.

Thus the Lord when he was here on earth, had to begin to teach the people how to live and how to serve him and how to worship him and the Heavenly Father without animal sacrifice. That was one great task that he had to do.

I might return and say that, as you will probably recall, he gave the Gospel to Adam, and I have often thought that these "higher critics" who try to deduce the worship of the Israelites from the pagan nations who preceded them as if God had not himself given his plan of sacrifice to the Israelites—I have often thought that if

they would but consider, if they but knew that Adam had
the Gospel given to him, that he knew all about it, and
that these pagan nations were merely remembering a
part of what was given to Adam, it would put a wholly
different light on their contentions and conclusions.

Now, the Savior, in addition to this task, had to lead
the people to an understanding of the sacrifice which he
was to make, and that he was the Messiah. These "higher
critics" say that this idea of a Messiah was a gradual
growth with him, that he did not understand it at first,
but that gradually he acquired it; that the Apostles in
the years immediately following, amplified the concept,
which was in fact in good part mere myth. But as I read
the record, that is not the fact at all. As I read the record
it was necessary that the Savior should break this news
of his Messiahship, shall I say, gently, gradually to the
people. He began very early declaring his own Messiahship. He did it when he was twelve years old in the temple. He did it again to the woman of Samaria. He did it
to Peter and the Apostles at Caesarea Philippi.

Testimonies of the Messiah

The Father himself gave the testimony at the Lord's
baptism. The Father gave the testimony again at the
Transfiguration. Jesus knew who he was. He knew his
power. He never failed in anything he ever tried to do.
There is no record of any failure on his part. He did
whatever he set his mind to do.

So, to me, this whole record proves without doubt
that the gradual growth of this Messianic concept as
disclosed by his teachings was in order to prepare the
people for their acceptance of it. You will recall that
perhaps the first time it was said by his Apostles was at
Caesarea Philippi, and that after Peter had declared him,
he told them that they should say nothing about it, that

it should be kept secret as among themselves. But like all secrets, it soon got out.

Now, the record testifies that from that time on he began to preach of his death and his resurrection. So he had that task of preparing the people. That was another service he did.

Then still another service that he did was to build a new organization that could carry on his work. The Priesthood of Aaron which had theretofore carried on the work in Israel for over fifteen hundred years, no longer had the authority to perform their earlier functions, and he had to create other agencies to carry on his work; and so he built up his Church.

And time and again, if you will read the record, you will note that he cautioned the people not to talk about him, not to talk about his Messiahship. He was putting off the day (as I read the record) of the crucifixion and resurrection until the people, his disciples, were prepared to follow on after his death. As you know, it was not until then and not until after the Holy Ghost came that they began to go forward fully under the plan which he had taught.

Thus he had to do these two latter things, the subordination of the Aaronic Priesthood in its power and authority, the establishment of the Melchizedek Priesthood, and the building up of his Church.

But he had to go farther than that, he had to teach the principles of the Gospel, his Gospel, which would bring men back into the presence of our Heavenly Father.

All of these things he had to do. They could not be done overnight, they had to be taught gradually. Men had to be brought to see them, and there were very few, relatively, who recognized the Savior in all of these activities and became converted to them.

Actual Personality of the Savior

You know, I am quite a believer in studying the life of the Savior as an actual personality. That is not often done. Our students of the Bible and of the New Testament, seem to refrain from trying to build a biography of the Master out of those four great Gospels which constitute the greatest life of Jesus that ever has been written or ever will be written regarding his earthly ministry until it shall be written by himself or someone appointed by him, that plus what is given in Third Nephi and in the earlier chapters.

So, if I might, I would suggest this to you: Get some good student's Bible that contains a chronological outline of his life, a so-called harmony. It does not make much difference what Bible you take, because I am not impressed with the proposition that the exact order of the events of the Savior's life, of his work among the Saints of that day is of great importance; it is the fact that the things which are narrated did happen. Then try to go along with the Savior, live with him, let him be an actual man, half divine, of course, but nevertheless moving as a man moved in those days.

For instance, I would like, personally, to think of following him after the first Passover, after he had cleansed the temple and after he had had his great talk with Nicodemus, following him when he went on north and came to Samaria and there met the woman of Samaria, the woman who had been many times married, the woman whose life he told; I would wish to realize how she spread the news; how he told her if she had known who he was, she would have asked him for living water; then how she commented about what that meant, and said to him, when he made a little further explanation, that she knew that all these things would be made plain when the Messiah comes. Then I would wish to remember that he

said to her, "I that speak unto thee am he," so, at the
very beginning of his ministry announcing his divinity.

Try to get the picture of that incident. Go along the
road northward from Jerusalem to Samaria, travel with
him, travel with his Apostles, be at the well, Jacob's
Well, learn something about the well.

So I would want to know something about that great
occasion at Caesarea Philippi, when he and his disciples
were there and his questioning of Peter, "Whom do men
say that I am," and so on. I would want to know about
that. I would want to know something about Caesarea
Philippi. Why it was built. Who built it. What kind
of a place it was. I would like to live with the Savior as
he went through that experience, not merely read it as
if it were merely an announcement of some great principle, but read it as if it were a part of a living biography.
I would want to know about that.

I would want to know, too, about the Transfiguration—as much as I could. There is not too much to be
known that we can understand, but I would like to know
something about the mountain on which it took place.
I would like to know something about the conversation
between the disciples who were there and the Savior
afterwards. I would like to remember that there again
the Father bore witness to the Son. Read about it. Live
with it. Live with him. It would be amazing how much
more the New Testament will mean to you if you read
it in that way.

And so on through the rest of his life. Live with
him.

Then when you come to those final days, the days
of the Atoning Sacrifice, follow him as a man, as if you
were going with him; follow him to the Upper Chamber;
then go with him to the Mount of Olives where he gave
that great sermon and uttered that great prayer, "And

this is life eternal, that they might know thee the only true God, and Jesus Christ, whom thou hast sent."

Then follow him into the Garden. I do not believe that you can understand, I know that I cannot understand the kind of agony that he went through in that Garden when he shed drops of blood. I do not know—sometimes I have wondered if anybody who is not a God could understand that. I repudiate, personally, the idea that his agony was caused by any bodily suffering, any fear of death. There was something deep and beyond that, and what it was I do not know.

Follow him to the cross. We can dimly perceive the loneliness which came to him. Apparently only John was present, of the disciples, and the women from Galilee, and the mother. You recall what he said to John and to his mother: "Woman, behold thy son!" ... "Behold thy mother!" Live there with him through that.

Then when you come to his utter loneliness, when he repeated the words of the Psalmist, as he looked down and cried out in his weariness of soul, "My God, my God, why hast thou forsaken me"—be there at the cross with him.

Then take him to the tomb. Go along with Nicodemus and Joseph and bury him. And go back with them after the burial, into Jerusalem. Be with the Apostles that night when all that they had lived with and lived for was seemingly buried in the tomb. He had taught them about his death and his resurrection, but they did not understand. They did not believe it when they saw him a resurrected being.

Mary at the Tomb

Then go with Mary to the tomb that early morning; then later when she with the other women came and looked in, only to find the tomb was empty, but an angel was sitting on the right side, and he said to them, " ... I know that ye seek Jesus . . . He is not here: for he is risen . . . go quickly, and tell his disciples." Try to go with those sisters and with Mary to that tomb.

Live with the Savior and it will give you such a view of him, such an intimacy with him as I think you can get in no other way. And all of those other things that I have mentioned, aside from his redemption, had to do with your exaltation, with my exaltation; they were to teach us how to live. Learn what he did, what he thought, what he taught. Do as he did. Live as he lived, so far as we can. He was the perfect man.

There is a wealth of virtue, a wealth of knowledge, a wealth of testimony, a wealth of comfort, of encouragement, of upbuilding of faith, in getting a real, intimate knowledge of the Savior from the point of view of his mortality.

I bear you my testimony that God lives, that Jesus is the Christ, that, as I have said, he was born, he lived, he was crucified, he lay in the tomb, he was resurrected, and his resurrection, the Atonement which he made for the Fall of Adam, has brought the resurrection to every person born to this earth as surely and truly as he was resurrected. He atoned for Adam's disobedience.

I bear my testimony that the Priesthood was restored after it was taken away from the earth, restored through Joseph and Oliver. I bear my testimony that the principles of the Gospel, some of which had been lost, were re-emphasized, restored. I bear my testimony that Joseph was a Prophet, and that the other brethren who were with him were divinely appointed by our Heavenly Father to do their work.

I bear my testimony that all the keys and the powers that were conferred upon the Prophet Joseph were conferred upon and have been enjoyed by his successors down through and including President David O. McKay.

I bear my testimony that this is the true Gospel,

that we have the true plan of life and salvation. I bear my testimony that there is no other name under heaven given among men whereby we may be saved except Jesus of Nazareth, whom, as Peter said to the Sanhedrin, "ye crucified."

May the Lord be with us always and strengthen our faith and help us to study the life of the Savior so that we may get the most out of it.

"In the beginning was the Word, and the Word was with
                              God, and the Word was God.
"The same was in the beginning with God.
"All things were made by him; and without him was not
                              any thing made that was made.
"In him was life; and the life was the light of men."

John 1:1-4

Who Was This Jesus?

WHO IS this Savior, this man that we worship? We rather localize him and think of him as more or less belonging to us, that he is our Savior and perhaps not known very much.

I want to read you just a few words to begin with. I am going to read from the Book of Moses, from the first chapter, and I am going to begin with the 32nd verse. The speaker declared he was the "Lord God Almighty, and Endless is my name . . . And by the word of my power, have I created them. . . ."

He was showing Moses, as they stood and conversed "face to face," the creation which the Father had made.

And by the word of my power have I created them, which is mine Only Begotten Son, who is full of grace and truth.

And worlds without number have I created; and I also created them for mine own purpose; and by the Son I created them, which is mine Only Begotten. . . .

. . . For behold, there are many worlds that have passed away by the word of my power [which is his Only Begotten Son]. And there are many that now stand, and innumerable are they unto man; but all things are numbered unto me, for they are mine and I know them. . . .

And the Lord God spake unto Moses, saying: The heavens, they are many, and they cannot be numbered unto man; but they are numbered unto me, for they are mine.

And as one earth shall pass away, and the heavens thereof even so shall another come; and there is no end to my works, neither to my words. (Moses 1:2-3, 32-33, 35, 37-38.)

Not a Novice at Creation

It was not a novice, not an amateur, not a Being making a first trial, that came down in the beginning, after the Great Council, with other Gods, and searched

out and found the place where there was "space" (for
so the record tells us in Abraham) and taking of the
materials which they found in this "space" they made
this world.

I want to suggest two or three things to you. I hope
I will not confuse you too much. But we in this galaxy—
and the heavens which we see are the galaxy to which
we belong—we from this point where we stand or float,
can see one billion light-years all around us. A light-year
is the distance which light, traveling at the rate of 186,000
miles a second, will travel in one year. The astronomers
tell us that we now can peer out into space one billion
light-years, we in the center.

Where we are moving, how we are moving, how rapidly we go, we do not know. As you look into the heavens
you do not see the heavens as they are today. You see
them as they were the number of light-years ago when
the light therefrom began to come from them to us. If
it is a hundred million light-years away, it was a hundred
million years ago.

Our Galaxy—Shape and Size

It is said that there are one hundred million galaxies
within this radius that are the same as ours. They say
that this galaxy in which we live, in which we float and
have our existence, is one hundred thousand light-years
in diameter. They say that it is shaped lenticular, as if
two glass watch crystals were put together, ten thousand
light-years through the thickest part, and I repeat, a
hundred thousand light-years through.

Astronomers now yield what they did not formerly
yield, that there may have been many, and probably were,
many worlds like ours. Some say there were in this
galaxy perhaps from its beginning, one million worlds
like unto this one.

"Worlds without number have I created," through "mine Only Begotten Son." I repeat, our Lord is not a novice, he is not an amateur; he has been over this course time and time and time again.

And if you think of this galaxy of ours having within it from the beginning perhaps until now, one million worlds, and multiply that by the number of millions of galaxies, one hundred million galaxies, that surround us, you will then get some view of who this Man we worship is.

Purpose of Our Creation

He was a member of the Godhead—the Father, the Son, and the Holy Ghost. He participated in the Great Council of Heaven which decided that they should build a world, a world to which we might come as mortal beings and work out our salvation. I cannot but think that the same purpose had been present untold numbers of times for our Savior then to work out his world-creative work as he did for us. "Worlds without number have I created," through "mine Only Begotten Son."

From Throne to Manger

There was in Palestine a couple, Joseph and Mary. They lived in Nazareth. They had traveled, evidently, from Nazareth to Bethlehem in order to pay a tax that had been decreed by the Roman Emperor. That was the ostensible purpose. She, heavy with child, traveled all that distance on mule-back, guarded and protected as one about to give birth to a half-Deity. No other man in the history of this world of ours has ever had such an ancestry —God the Father on the one hand and Mary the Virgin on the other.

When they had reached Bethlehem, they could get no place, you remember, in the inn. Everything was

taken. So they were forced to go into a stable, and the
new-born infant, fresh from the throne of God, had to
be laid in a manger, "descending below all things that
he might rise above all things." I have great sympathy
for poor Joseph. He was the husband of Mary, but not
the father of the Son she was to bear. Years afterwards
the Jews twitted him on that fact.

I am not going to try to go through the life of the
Savior except in a most casual way. Here he was, in a
stable in Bethlehem, in a manger. You remember the
story of the Wise Men. We do not know just where they
came from. We do not know how many there were. It
has been assumed there were three, because the gifts
were spoken of as gold, frankincense, and myrrh. You
remember how they came to Herod and inquired about it,
how Herod sent them out to locate the new king of the
Jews and bring word back to him that he might go and
worship, so he said. But true to his nature he was lying
when he said it, for he intended to send back to Bethlehem
and kill all the infants that he might be sure to kill this
king. You know the story. The Wise Men, warned in a
dream, did not return.

Herod, true to his intent, did kill the infants in Bethlehem. But warned of their danger, Joseph and Mary
fled with the newborn King to Egypt. But from that time
until the final scene, the Jews, some among them, sought
constantly to kill him.

Conditions in Palestine

He came into a chaotic condition. Palestine was not
a place of peace and love and brotherhood. It was the
habitation of some of the most terrible passions that
were loose in the world at that time. They were the constant companions of those who were around the Savior.

You remember his trip when he was twelve years
old, when he apparently first indicated, at least, so far

as Mary understood, who he was—where, after three days of search, they finally found him talking to the learned men of the nation and she reprovingly said to him: "Thy father and I . . ." (she meaning Joseph, which indicates that in the household of Joseph and Mary, he was true to his relationship, presumed, to Joseph and to Mary)— she said to him, "Thy father and I have sought thee sorrowing." And he replied in that great disclosure, "Wist ye not that I must be about my Father's business?"

But he went back to Nazareth and dwelt with them, a carpenter, a carpenter's son, until he took on his mission. Thereafter, when they found him doing wonderful things and displaying wonderful information and great knowledge, they said, "Is not this the carpenter's son? . . . Is not this the carpenter?" He lived in a lowly home, the only man born to this earth half-Divine and half-mortal. He dwelt among the most lowly, taught among them, did his works among them.

He went on through life, I repeat, followed day by day by enmity that would have exterminated him, but escaping all because of the great mission which he had to perform.

Jewish Confusion

I can understand, in a way at least, the difficulty which the Jews had. They recognized in his miracles the same sort of miracle that had been done by their prophets all down through their history. He violated the laws of gravity by walking on the water; Elisha had caused an iron axe to float on the water. He raised them from the dead; so had Elisha of old. He fed them the loaves and the fishes; and so had the Prophet Elijah fed a hundred with little and supplied the widow with oil. They had seen all of these great principles manifested, they knew them, and they had hard work recognizing that there was something way and beyond that in Jesus.

Some Miracles of Jesus

I have thought of some of those miracles in the sense of their being the miracle of a Creator, demonstrating his creative power, particularly some that I call creative miracles: the turning of water into wine, how simple that must have been to a Deity who made universes; the feeding of the five thousand, how simple that was.

And I hope none of you will be disturbed by the pigmy-rationalizing which suggests that the multitude was fed on lunches which they brought with them. This Creator of the universe, out of five loaves and two fishes, made food that fed them all. Perhaps, in order to silence the criticism which might be made, or the explanation, that he just hypnotized them and they were all just hypnotized, the record says, "and they took up of the fragments that remained twelve baskets full." Of equal importance and stature was the feeding of the four thousand at a later time.

Other miracles prove he had control of the elements: I am thinking of the night when he was sleeping in the prow of the boat and a great storm arose. The Apostles were terrified. They awakened him. He calmed the storm. And after this feeding of the five thousand, when he journeyed across the water, walking upon it, I recall how frightened were the Apostles in the boat, thinking he was a spirit.

You can almost hear him call to them: "It is I; be not afraid." Peter asked, "Bid me come unto thee on the water." Jesus answered: "Come." Peter stepped out upon the water and started to walk, but his heart and his faith failed him at the sight of the boisterous waves. He started to sink. Jesus stretched forth his hand and saved him, reproving him thus: "O thou of little faith, wherefore didst thou doubt?"

Control of the Animal Kingdom

Jesus had control of the animal kingdom. You remember the miraculous draft of fishes, when he first called Peter and James and John. They had been out fishing all night, but had caught nothing. He asked to get into their boat that he might speak to the multitude; he shoved out from the shore, so that the multitude could not press too much around him.

When he finished speaking he said, "Launch out into the deep, and let down your nets for a draught." They replied they had been fishing all night, and had caught nothing. Nevertheless, at his word they cast their net and it was filled with fish, so much so that the net brake and they had to call for James and John to come out in another boat. Peter, that great Peter, bowed before the Savior. "Depart from me," said he, "for I am a sinful man."

And later, a similar experience, on the shores of the same Galilee, after the resurrection, when Peter and the rest had gone fishing, not understanding there was work in the Lord's service for them to do. They had fished all night and caught nothing. In the early light of the morning they saw a man on the shore; there was a little fire. A voice came from the shore: "Cast the net on the right side of the ship, and ye shall find." They did, and it was filled. John, perhaps recollecting the earlier experience, said, "It is the Lord." Peter, wrapping his cloak about him, for he was naked (he did not want to appear before the Lord nude), cast himself into the sea and waded to the shore. And there they ate, apparently the Savior eating with them. It was there that Peter got his command, "Feed my sheep."

The lowly Jesus thus had control of the animal life.

The Vegetable Kingdom

Finally, the vegetable kingdom came under his dominion, also, for he cursed the barren fig tree as he went
by. Some scholars have a great deal of difficulty in understanding that miracle. It looks rather simple to me,
maybe too simple. But I get from this miracle the principle that he who does not do the things which his Creator fitted him to do, stands in danger of a reprimand.
You cannot be barren with the intelligence, the talents,
which God has given to you.

How great to mortals are these and the other miracles of Jesus, but how incomparably simple to the Maker
and Destroyer of universes. Shall we further doubt the
power of Jesus to do the service he performed on earth?

He Indicates Who He Was

He began very early in his mission to indicate who
he was. As he went north after the first Passover, he
saw Nicodemus and to Nicodemus he indicated that he
was the Christ. Nicodemus did not understand.

He journeyed north until he came to Samaria, and
there he stopped at Jacob's Well and saw the woman of
Samaria. He told her who he was. The Samaritans were
hated by the Jews and the Jews were hated by the Samaritans, and this, I think, was the first time he indicated
in his mission, that he came for all men and not for the
chosen tribes alone. Thereafter from time to time he
indicated that he was the Messiah.

On one occasion when he was attending the Feast
of the Tabernacles in the temple at Jerusalem, he was
being twitted regarding his ancestry. They were talking
about their ancestry; they were the children of Abraham! There came a point in their discussion where they
said, he having said he knew Abraham, "Thou art not yet
fifty years old, and hast thou seen Abraham?" And his

reply to them was: "Before Abraham was, I am." So
he declared his Messiahship.

And so on down through his long course of life, day
after day proclaiming his truths.

His Great Mission

He had a great mission to perform. He had to break
down, to fulfil, as he told us, the Law of Moses. If you
want to know how far he had to go from the laws which
had been given to ancient Israel, read the Sermon on the
Mount, read the Sermon on the Plain, read the sermon
at the second Passover, and see how he had to drive and
drive and drive for the new law.

One illustration—he said:

Ye have heard that it was said by them of old time, Thou
shalt not commit adultery:
But I say unto you, That whosoever looketh on a woman
to lust after her hath committed adultery with her already in
his heart. (Matt. 5:27-28.)

That was the new law.

And so with thousands of other things. Those documents to which I have referred, and a few others, are the
greatest revolutionary documents in the whole history
of the world. They mark the turning away from, the
fulfilment of, the Mosaic Law and the introduction and
operation of the law of the Gospel he restored.

From Cross to Throne

Finally, at the last trial, having been before Annas,
he was taken to Caiaphas, the father-in-law of Annas.
Caiaphas was the high priest installed by the Roman
government. Annas was the man who, under the law of
Moses, should have been the chief priest. At the trial
before Caiaphas and the Sanhedrin, Caiaphas said: "I

adjure thee by the living God, that thou tell us whether
thou be the Christ, the Son of God." And Mark records
that he said unto him, "I am."

But they took him the next day and tried him before
Pilate. Poor Pilate, torn because of his belief in the in-
nocence of this Man, sought to release him, but without
avail! They insisted on the death of the Christ. And so
he was finally condemned and turned over to them.

Then he was taken out on Calvary, and he, a God,
one of the Holy Trinity, he was crucified on a false charge
of treason, between two common thieves. One of the
Fatherhood, one of those belonging to the Godhead, come
to earth, cradled in a manger, fresh from the throne of
God, was crucified like a common criminal between two
thieves!

Resurrected on the morning of the third day, seen
by many, touched by many, he lived here for forty days
as if loath to leave those among whom he had worked so
long. Then, and even before then, he went back to the
Holy Trinity, resumed his seat alongside the Father, sat
again a member of the Godhead.

The Man We Worship

That is the Man we worship. That is the Man who
gave us the law that will enable us to fulfil our destiny
declared from the very beginning. That is the Man who
sacrificed himself. "Behold the Lamb of God," it was
declared anciently, "slain from the foundation of the
world." He died to atone for the sins of Adam.

None of us has been born more lowly; none of us
has died more ignominiously than he. But this he did for
you and for me, that we, when we have finished our
careers here, might be able, after going into the tomb
and paying there whatever penalty there is for us to pay,
we, too, may be resurrected and go back into the presence
of him who sent us, good and bad alike.

That is the Man we worship—not a man of high
degree, world-wise; not a man of power, and yet he said
on one occasion: "Thinkest thou that I cannot now pray
to my Father, and he shall presently give me more than
twelve legions of angels"; never invoking his divine
powers merely for his own selfish good, always for the
benefit of others, for all humanity, always sacrificing,
always trying to obey the will of the Father, telling us
over and over again that he did nothing that he had not
seen his Father do, that he taught nothing that he had
not heard his Father teach.

The mystery of it all is beyond me. I can only take
the record as it stands, and that record tells me that if
I obey his commandments, if I live as he would have me
live, then I shall fulfil and reach the destiny which he
prescribed for me, a destiny of eternal progression, a
destiny of a life in his presence, so far as my work there
will permit, a destiny that knows no limit to the power
which I may receive if I live for it.

May the Lord grant that to each and every one of
us may come a determination to serve him and to keep
his commandments. May the Lord give us a little better
view of him, of who he was, of his great wisdom and experience and knowledge. Said he, "I am the way, the life,
the light, and the truth." Over and over and over again
he said that. They did not believe him then, the world
at large does not believe him now. But it is our right,
our duty, our prerogative to know these truths and make
them part of our lives.

"And I saw the stars, that they were very great, and that one of them was nearest the throne of God; and there were many great ones which were near unto it;

"And the Lord said unto me: These are the governing ones; and the name of the great one is Kolob, because it is near unto me, for I am the Lord thy God: I have set this one to govern all those which belong to the same order as that upon which thou standest."

Abraham 3:2-3

Kolob, the Governor

SCRIPTURES brought forth in this dispensation record that almost four thousand years ago the Lord revealed to Abraham certain great astronomical truths regarding our heavens. The full record recovered was made up partly by personal revelation to Abraham through the Urim and Thummim (those miracles in stone, by which the ancient seers saw the past and gazed into the future), and partly from "the records of the fathers, even the patriarchs, concerning the right of Priesthood, the Lord my God preserved in mine own hands; therefore a knowledge of the beginning of the creation, and also of the planets, and of the stars, as they were made known unto the fathers, have I kept even unto this day, and I shall endeavor to write some of these things upon this record, for the benefit of my posterity that shall come after me." (Abraham 1:31.)

Then Abraham records regarding our heaven:

And I saw the stars, that they were very great, and that one of them was nearest unto the throne of God; and there were many great ones which were near unto it;

And the Lord said unto me: These are the governing ones; and the name of the great one is Kolob, because it is near unto me, for I am the Lord thy God: I have set this one to govern all those which belong to the same order as that upon which thou standest. (*Ibid.*, 3:2-3.)

The Lord said further to Abraham:

. . . that Kolob was after the manner of the Lord, according to its times and seasons in the revolutions thereof; that one revolution was a day unto the Lord, after his manner of reckoning, it being one thousand years according to the time appointed unto that whereon thou standest. This is the reckoning of the Lord's time, according to the reckoning of Kolob. (*Ibid.*, v. 4.)

The Lord added some information regarding the order of planets and their revolutions:

> And thus there shall be the reckoning of the time of one planet above another, until thou come nigh unto Kolob, which Kolob is after the reckoning of the Lord's time; which Kolob is set nigh unto the throne of God, to govern all those planets which belong to the same order as that upon which thou standest.
>
> And it is given unto thee to know the set time of all the stars that are set to give light, until thou come near unto the throne of God. (*Ibid.*, vs. 9-10.)

This revelation came to Abraham in Ur of Chaldea as he was preparing to leave Chaldea to go into Egypt.

> And the Lord said unto me: Abraham, I show these things unto thee before ye go into Egypt, that ye may declare all these words. (*Ibid.*, v. 15.)

Thus the Lord told Abraham, forty centuries ago, that great governing stars, with Kolob as the main one, controlled the rest of the stars of our heavens in their times, revolutions, and courses. What was the force, the intelligence, the wisdom through which this control was exercised over a space of one hundred thousand light-years in diameter and ten thousand light-years thick at its center,—a great whirling disc?

About four and a quarter centuries later (some three thousand five hundred years ago), the Lord gave a great revelation to Moses that opened the Biblical record of the creation and what followed. This revelation is an introductory statement or supplement to the account appearing in the opening chapters of Genesis. The following sublime truths on the structure of the universe, taken from this supplementary statement, were given at the time when Moses was caught up into an exceedingly high mountain and saw God face to face and talked with him:

... And the Lord God said unto Moses: For mine own purpose have I made these things. Here is wisdom and it remaineth in me.

And by the word of my power, have I created them, which is mine Only Begotten Son, who is full of grace and truth.

And worlds without number have I created; and I also created them for mine own purpose; and by the Son I created them, which is mine Only Begotten. . . .

. . . For behold, there are many worlds that have passed away by the word of my power. And there are many that now stand, and innumerable are they unto man; but all things are numbered unto me, for they are mine and I know them. . . .

And the Lord God spake unto Moses, saying: The heavens, they are many, and they cannot be numbered unto man; but they are numbered unto me, for they are mine.

And as one earth shall pass away, and the heavens thereof even so shall another come; and there is no end to my works, neither to my words.

For behold, this is my work and my glory—to bring to pass the immortality and eternal life of man. (Moses 1:31-33, 35, 37-39.)

Modern astronomy seems to confirm fully the basic elemental truths declared in these scriptures.

Within the last quarter of a century, great telescopes and other instruments have enabled astrophysicists to announce new and marvelous facts regarding the universe. They have brought within visual view and radio contact a universe that has as its diameter two billion light-years (Bart J. Bok, "The Milky Way," *Scientific American* (February 1950), p. 31; cited as *Bok I*), that is, the distance light would travel in that many years speeding forth at the astounding rate of 186,000 miles per second.

Two of these telescopes are in Palomar, one with a 200-inch lens—the "Big Eye" which sees far—and the other with a 48-inch lens—the "Big Schmidt" which sees wide. They have uncovered a universe of inconceivable immensity. A third telescope at Mt. Wilson has a 100-inch lens.

Truth-Seeking by Science

Some of the present theories and the facts adduced to support them are of a character that has seemed might be appropriately lined alongside some of the things the scriptures tell us as quoted above.

This is not done with the thought of "harmonizing religion with science"—the problem can never be accurately so stated—the problem must be stated, "harmonizing science with religion." Of course, there is no thought of trying to prove the truths of religion by science. Truth is its own witness. It is merely suggested that the gropings of science for truth (a quest inherent in science which scientists must always and ever make by challenging the accuracy of everything they believe they have come to know), will inevitably come more and more near to the ultimate truth. A courageous, venturesome, modern astrophysicist (Fred Hoyle) quotes approvingly the following from Josh Billings: "It ain't what a man don't know as makes him a fool, but what he does know as ain't so." (Fred Hoyle, *The Nature of the Universe* (Harper & Row, Publishers, New York, 1950), p. 17, cited as *Hoyle*.)

The scientific facts and theories hereinafter stated and quoted, represent what it appears some scientists *presently* believe or feel they know, yet with the further knowledge that many things could be wrong, and with a full and complete reservation to recast seeming facts or best-grounded and settled theories whenever new facts and theories may require. This is the full and undisputed right of science, and true science will die when this basic element of scientific truth-search is given up, short of the discovery of the ultimate truth.

The scientific facts and theories presented herein are stated with the knowledge that they are for the *present, possibly lapping over into the future* for confirmation, for

abandonment, for alteration, for reframing, or for posi-
tive denial.

On this basis, we proceed.

The Extent of the Universe

The Lord said "the heavens, they are many, and they
cannot be numbered unto man." These new telescopes
(the "Big Eye") presently tell us there are one hundred
million galaxies like our own Milky Way, our heavens,
within a diameter of two billion light-years; but they
have not reached the ends of creation. Not even a guess
is made as to what lies beyond the visual out-limits of this
imaginary sphere. Each galaxy in this vast universe is a
"heaven" in its place to its starry inhabitants. Our galaxy—the Milky Way—is our heaven. Many galaxies are
so far away that the "Big Eye" shows only a tiny smudge
of light on our photographic plate to mark their existence.

The Worlds of the Universe in Our Own Galaxy

"Worlds without number have I created," say the
scriptures. (Moses 1:33.) Astrophysicists *now* estimate
that nearly ten million planetary systems, each similar
to our planetary system, must have been formed during
our existence in our own Milky Way; that of these as
many as one million were "possible abodes of life" and
that out of this number as many as one hundred thousand
might have had on them beings with some physical resemblance to ourselves. (*Hoyle,* pp. 102-103.)

Hoyle quotes the distinguished biologist C. D. Dar-
lington as saying:

There are such very great advantages in walking on two
legs, in carrying one's brain in one's head, in having two eyes
on the same eminence at a height of five or six feet, that we might
as well take quite seriously the possibility of a pseudo man and
a pseudo woman with some physical resemblance to ourselves.
(*Ibid.*)

Worlds Outside Our Own Galaxy

The foregoing estimates have to do with our own galaxy. What of the hundred million other galaxies in space, apparently and speculatively like our own?

Some scientists estimate that of the one hundred million galaxies and nebulae in space, there are now upwards of one million planetary systems in each galaxy. (*Hoyle*, p. 109.) Our galaxy appears to be one of the largest. "Worlds without number have I created," the Lord told Moses. "For behold, there are many worlds that have passed away by the word of my power. And there are many that now stand, and innumerable are they unto man; but all things are numbered unto me, for they are mine and I know them."

A Changing Universe

"And as one earth shall pass away, and the heavens thereof even so shall another come; and there is no end to my works, neither to my words." The astrophysicists—the astronomers—do see from time to time what are called supernovae, that is, seemingly exploding stars which thereafter exist in some other form. Whether such supernovae also indicate a new star or orb seems not determined. The Chinese saw a supernova in 1054, since which time two other supernovae have been observed, one in 1572 and another in 1604. These explosions wipe out heavenly bodies previously existing. Hoyle estimates there must have been more than ten million supernovae explosions since the oldest stars were born. Hoyle also theorizes "the Earth actually was at one time a part of a supernova." (*Hoyle*, pp. 102, 84.)

Developing his *theory* that the earth was formed from fragments of the debris of supernovae explosions, Hoyle suggests that in its forming "the Earth moved through a medium consisting partly of gas and partly of comparatively small solid bodies. . . . The rocks of the Earth's crust may well have originated in this way. In particular it is possible that the Earth acquired its radioactive materials during this final stage. Among the gases acquired were probably nitrogen, water, oxygen, and carbon dioxide." (*Hoyle*, pp. 100-101.)

But another theory has been advanced within recent years that seems potentially to offer much in explanation of the origin of our solar system that would fall in with the sacred records.

Dr. Fred Whipple (Harvard Observatory) is reported to have suggested in the recent past a new theory accounting for the creation of our own earth and its solar family associates,—the sun, the earth, and the other planets of the system, and their satellites. ("Birth of Solar System," *Life Magazine* (April 26, 1948), pp. 91-98.)

This new theory would seemingly not consider the whole galaxy (as it would seem some astrophysicists would do) as the result of one great creative act from the explosion of one infinitely great, primordial super-atom bomb from which the whole known universe was created; but rather, as already indicated, the result of an evolving, constantly growing universe to which additions were and are from time to time made.

Following this new theory, our solar system, sun, planets, and satellites would be created out of the great collections of dust, gas, and other debris that drift through interstellar space like enormous clouds in great "puffs," unbelievably light in density with perhaps one tiny frozen particle in as much as five cubic yards of space. However, the clouds are trillions of miles in diameter. (*Ibid.*)

It is said that astronomers have observed many such dust clouds, especially in the Milky Way, many of these of such proportions as would meet the requirements in size that Whipple postulates for this creation of our solar system. (*Ibid.*)

Considering the structure of our galaxy as it is presumed to be—similar to Andromeda (see *Hoyle*, p. 107), it would seem the solar system could be believed to have been formed from gasses and dust which drifted in the space the system now occupies. Such a concept of creation would easily yield itself to the details given in Genesis (see also Abraham and Moses) of the whole plan and order of the creation of the earth and its planetary associates.

Abraham records the sublimely great account of the happenings in the Grand Council and states the precise purpose for which this earth was created. Speaking of and to the vast assemblage of spirits at the Grand Council, the record runs:

> And there stood one among them that was like unto God, and he said unto those who were with him: We will go down, for there is space there, and we will take of these materials, and we will make an earth whereon these may dwell.
>
> And we will prove them herewith, to see if they will do all things whatsoever the Lord their God shall command them;
>
> And they who keep their first estate shall be added upon; and they who keep not their first estate shall not have glory in the same kingdom with those who keep their first estate; and they who keep their second estate shall have glory added upon their heads for ever and ever.
>
> And the Lord said: Whom shall I send? And one answered like unto the Son of Man: Here am I, send me. And another answered and said: Here am I, send me. And the Lord said: I will send the first.
>
> And the second was angry, and kept not his first estate; and, at that day, many followed after him. (Abraham 3:24-28.)

He seemingly spoke of the spirits at the Great Council. The record later runs:

And then the Lord said: Let us go down. And they went down at the beginning, and they, that is the Gods, organized and formed the heavens and the earth. (*Ibid.*, 4:1.)

Our scriptures give in rough draft the blueprint of creation:

First, formless, voidless matter and darkness; the coming of light, its division from darkness into day and night; the division of the waters, below and above the firmament (clouds of watery vapor); the gathering together of the waters below the firmament into the seas; the appearance of the dry land; the coming of vegetable life; the unveiling of the sun and moon and the appearance of the stars as the skies cleared; the full shining of the sun and moon, along with the stars, now showing in their places in the heavens in the great already existing galactic firmament where there was yet space that existed possibly eons before; and so on down to the final creations of all things in orderly progression,—all indescribably glorious, clothed with the eternal beauty of the divine creation, all down where there were space and materials.

Conceived as part and parcel of the creation of the whole universe, Genesis, Abraham, and Moses spoke in poetry that in places seemed only poetry. But conceived as a special creation of our earth, in and of our galaxy, as the account of it tells, the poetry becomes a divinely beautiful anthem, enshrouded in heavenly symphony, glorious beyond measure, speaking with the authority and majesty of the Creator himself.

It should be mentioned here that Einstein declares, and his views seem generally accepted, "that space and time are inseparable and that the universe cannot be understood except in terms of four dimensions, three of space and one of time." For when we look out in space we look back on time. (Claude Stanush, "Geography of the Universe," *LIFE Magazine* (October 9, 1950), p. 108; cited as *Stanush.*)

It is pointed out that the explosion at Hiroshima would not be observed on Sirius (which is *eight light-years away*), for example, by a hypothetical observer until eight years after the event happened here. Visually, what is "past" with us is "future" for the distant observer on Sirius. (*Ibid.*)

As this principle is understood, when we look at a star that is ten light-years away, we are not really looking at the star as it is today but as it was ten light-years ago. Thus, as we now look at the heavens, we do not see them as they actually are now, but as they were the number of light-years ago that represents their light distance from us. In fact, we see the heavens today, not as of today, but as they were sometime in the past, as stated, at a time equal to the time it has taken light to travel (at 186,000 miles per second) from them to us—billions of different times, as many billions as stars with different distances. As we look at a galaxy one billion light-years away, we see it as it looked one billion light-years ago, not as it looks today, and as it then looked in the space where we are now. But at this instant of this day, we do not know how it looks, where it is, whether or not it exists.

It may be interesting to get some concrete idea about the speed of light. It has been computed that traveling at that speed we would be one-seventh of a second in circling the earth. We would go from the earth to the moon in a little over one second, and from the earth to the sun in a little over eight minutes. We could make "a comfortable sight-seeing tour of the whole solar system, visiting all the planets" in about twelve hours and to reach Alpha, the star nearest the sun, we should need more than four years. We would need one hundred thousand years to go from one end of the Milky Way to the other. (*Bok I*, p. 31.)

One other general matter might be mentioned. Two distinguished astronomers (Hubble and Bowen—both of the staff of Mt. Wilson and Palomar Observatories) inform us that some scientists believe (see *supra*) that all matter in the universe was collected in one great primordial "atom" which exploded into the millions of fragments out of which the galaxies have been formed and that those galactic fragments (some of which we see) are still flying off into space. Another theory is that this explosion filled all space with dust and gas, that gradually this dust and gas condensed into galaxies, that stars were formed inside the galaxies, and that this process is still going on. (F. Barrows Colton, "Mapping the Unknown Universe," *National Geographic Magazine*, September 1950), p. 420; cited as *Colton.*)

No appraisal of the definitive value of either of these theories has been noted. Some seriously question the explosion theory. (*Hoyle*, p. 119.)

However, it is affirmed that the only real evidence of such an expanding universe as these theories assume is what is called the "red shift" of light coming from the outer galaxies. This means that lines in the spectrum are "displaced from their normal positions toward the red end of the spectrum." (*Stanush*, p. 106.)

The principle is said to be the same as the Doppler Effect "taught in high school physics," which means that as sound waves moving rapidly toward an observer seem to move toward the blue end of the spectrum and seem to stretch and lengthen when moving rapidly away from the observer, "similarly, light waves from a tremendously fast-moving source may be compressed so that they shift toward the blue (short wavelength) end of the spectrum as the source approaches, or stretched so that they move toward the red end as it retreats." (*Ibid.*)

However, astronomers affirm "there is still some uncertainty about the interpretation of the *red shift* as an indication of motion." (*Ibid.*, italics supplied.) Other explanations are offered for the shift of distant galactic light to the red end of the spectrum. The same author also discusses the possible effect of gravitation on the general problem of light rays.

Some astrophysicists have done some estimating and speculating. They begin:

The greater the distance of a galaxy from us, the faster it is receding. Double the distance, you double speed. Nearby galaxies move onward at several million miles an hour but the most distant ones seen through the "Big Eye" are thought to be receding at over two hundred million miles an hour. The problem is then posed, do they finally exceed the speed of light and, if then, what are the speeds of galaxies out still farther? If the galaxy is far enough away (say the theorists), the light will never reach us. (*Hoyle*, p. 116.)

New Galaxies in the Universe

The scriptures of Moses affirm, "And as one earth shall pass away, and the heavens thereof even so shall another come; and there is no end to my works, neither to my words." While no such phenomenon has seemingly been reported as the destruction of a galaxy, a "heaven," nor has the creation of another galaxy, a "heaven," been observed, yet man's observations cover too brief a time. But both processes seem to be *presently* regarded by some of the astrophysicists as certain of occurrence, though the phenomenon of each seems not now known and the possible physical manifestations that might be incident thereto are *presently* the subject of widely varient theories. The *present* general result seems to be that the universe is an expanding one and will so continue. (*Hoyle*, Ch. 6.) Holy Writ says: "And as one earth shall pass away, and the heavens thereof even so shall another come."

And now we return to the controlling element of this gigantic galaxy of ours, one of the great ones of the observable universe with its infinities of time and space and power—to Kolob of Abraham.

Back to Kolob

Four thousand years ago Abraham made this record:

> And I saw the stars, that they were very great, and that one of them was nearest unto the throne of God; and there were many great ones [the record notes fifteen] which were near unto it;
>
> And the Lord said unto me: These are the governing ones; and the name of the great one is Kolob, because it is near unto me, for I am the Lord thy God: I have set this one to govern all those which belong to the same order as that upon which thou standest.

That we may glimpse, and glimpse we only may, the infinities of time and space involved, the infinities of intelligence, experience, and wisdom that are in constant play, the infinities of force and power employed, the infinities of chance for mistake and error, the infinities of the ruin and chaos that would follow any tragic mishap, the infinities that annihilation would bring to all creation, we may note a few statements about our own galaxy, as presently understood and speculated about by our astrophysicists.

Size of Our Galaxy

Astronomers say our galaxy—our Milky Way—has some one hundred billion stars and could "store a million times as many stars in the present volume of the system without the risk of an undue frequency of stellar collisions." (*Bok I*, p. 31.)

They also now affirm our galaxy is a gigantic disc,
a whirling wheel, lenticular in shape, one hundred thousand light-years in diameter from rim to rim (*Hoyle*, pp.
54, 106, says sixty thousand light-years), ten thousand
light-years thick at the hub or center (another estimate
is twenty thousand light-years [*Stanush*, p. 97]), believed
to lie to the southward of us in America in the direction of
the Great Star Cloud of Sagittarius. We are, say they,
some twenty-five thousand to thirty thousand light-years
from the hub or center of the galactic disc, out towards the
rim. (Bart J. Bok, "The Southern Sky," *Scientific American* (July 1952), p. 47; cited as *Bok II.*) We lie, they
affirm, in or near the central plane of this great whirling disc of one hundred billion stars (*Bok I*, p. 32); and
they also affirm that the galaxy thins out toward the
rims; that very few stars are found out beyond ten thousand light-years from our own sun; that one-half of the
Milky Way is "comparatively thin and dull, the other
dense and vivid"; and that "there are ten times as many
stars per unit area of sky in the Sagittarius cloud as in
the richest part of the winter Milky Way." (*Ibid.*)

At our position in this gigantic whirling wheel
(about thirty thousand light-years from the center), the
earth is credited with four rotary motions: (1) around
its polar axis at a rate, in the United States, of seven
hundred miles per hour; (2) around the sun at about
seventy thousand miles per hour with some slight gravitation disturbances; (3) with the sun around the hub
or center of the galaxy at one hundred fifty miles per
second, or one million miles per hour at the outer rim;
(4) the whole galaxy is moving through space as a unit
(*Colton*, p. 403) at a rate there seems to be no way of
computing.

Neither the why, the whence, nor the whither of this
infinity of universe of mass is known by science, nor
confidently speculated about, nor seemingly is the origin

of the revolutionary movement of the different units that make up the mass.

But the Lord has told us. He knows. He declared to Moses, ". . . For mine own purpose have I made these things. Here is wisdom and it remaineth in me."

It is affirmed it takes two hundred million years for our solar system—sun and planets—to make one complete circuit around the hub or center. (*Hoyle*, p. 56.) This is the whirling affirmed speed of the united galaxy members themselves, all taken together, of which we supposedly know with reference to one another; but, in addition to this movement, the whole galaxy as one unit is moving (as stated) through space while its various elements are so revolving as among themselves, by our measurements in millions of light-years.

While we here have given a few details presently announced of our own galaxy, we must remember there are estimated to be in the universe we see, one hundred million galaxies—ours supposedly among the largest, some smaller, some nebulae. (Hoyle's later estimate is one billion galaxies; see *Saturday Evening Post*, February 21, 1959, p. 38.) Furthermore, there are presently estimated to be as many as one million planetary systems in each galaxy, with billions upon billions upon billions of individual units, numberless, incomprehensible to man. It is now estimated that the average distance apart of these galaxies is rather more than one million light-years. (*Hoyle*, p. 109.) The space occupied by those we know something about is seemingly a spherical space two billion light-years in diameter.

The internal structure of each of these one hundred million galaxies occupying this spherical space is presently assumed to be roughly the same as our own galaxy. The constellation of Andromeda (now estimated to be only about seven hundred thousand light-years away) is spoken of as "practically a twin of our Galaxy." (*Ibid.*,

p. 107.) In regard to its physical shape, structure, proportions, and space it is said we may feel we look at ourselves as in a giant mirror.

In each of the one hundred million galaxies we presently assume the disturbances incident to supernovae,—
thousands of them, in all parts of this infinite universe.

More About the Hub, the Center of Our Galaxy—About Kolob

Apparently by almost, if not quite common consent
(Bok II, p. 50), *the hub or center of our galaxy is assumed
to lie "in the direction of the Great Star Cloud of Sagittarius" in the area (southward from us) of the constellations of Sagittarius and Scorpio. (Bok I,* p. 32, italics supplied.) Between us and this Great Cloud in which lies the
hub, is a distance of from twenty-five thousand light-years
to thirty thousand light-years. (*Bok II,* p. 47.) Astrophysicists now affirm that in this distance between us
and the Sagittarius Cloud in which is the center or hub,
"we can detect a network of dense dust clouds floating
through space within 5,000 light-years of us or less; and
beyond that, up to 25,000 light-years away, we can see
the thickly huddled stars and star-clusters of the hub
itself." (*Ibid.,* p. 57.)   Some say now that this large
Sagittarius Cloud "is estimated to be 80,000 light-years
from us." (*Ibid.,* p. 48.)   One observation is interesting
in connection with this expression "thickly huddled stars"
of the hub.   Colton, speaking of the projected "Sky Survey," holds out some hope for more knowledge by saying:
"But the Sky Survey may reveal rifts in this curtain
through which parts of the 'hub' can be photographed and
studied." (*Colton,* p. 418.)   Hopeful also is Bok's statement *in re* a spiral arm in which he speaks of a "knot of
stars." (*Bok II,* p. 47.)

This hub or central area of the Milky Way (Sagittarius and Scorpio constellations) is extremely brilliant.
As already stated, present photographs show that "there

are 10 times as many stars per unit area of sky in the
Sagittarius cloud as in the richest part of the winter
Milky Way." In short, one half of the Milky Way is
comparatively thin and dull, the other dense and vivid.
(*Bok I*, p. 32.) Evidence is said to show that some of
the stars in the Sagittarius area are "very far away."
(*Ibid.*)

It is declared that the area of the constellations Sagittarius, Aquila, and Cygnus, "seen best in summer, is so
brilliant that parts of it may readily be mistaken for
cumulus clouds when observed near the horizon." (*Ibid.*)

The following statements are interesting: Because
of several considerations,—dust clouds, latitude, and time
of possible observation—"one of the most brilliant sec-
tions in the Milky Way cannot be seen at all from observatories in the U. S.," whereas from the Boyden Station of
the Harvard College Observatory in South Africa, ob-
servers "get the best view of the center of our galaxy,
for as the Milky Way turns in our heavens, the center
passes directly overhead at the latitude of the Boyden
Station." (*Bok II*, p. 47.)

While the language of the astronomers is uniformly
to the point that the hub or center of our galaxy is *in*
the direction of the Sagittarius and Scorpio section of the
Milky Way, their discussions leave little chance for
the layman to question their convictions that the hub or
center is in that area.

The Spiral Arm Theory

There is some speculation as to whether the center
or hub is in a spiral arm of the galaxy and that "the
Large Cloud is a piece of spiral arm broken loose from
our galaxy" (*ibid.*, p. 48), and that probably "here we
are looking along a spiral arm of our galaxy or toward
a knot of stars in such an arm," or whether, according to
another theory, we ourselves are in such a spiral arm of

our galaxy. (*Ibid.*, p. 47; *Colton*, p. 418.) We need not
be troubled about this, as it seems inconsequential to our
purpose.

But the exact location of the hub or center is not
important to our inquiry.   It seems uniformly and presently conceded there is a hub, and that the entire galaxy
revolves around it in determined times and at determined
speeds; that stars in the hub are governing stars that
control the galaxy; that apparently there are several of
these stars working together either in a "huddle," a
"knot," or group. The times of revolution of these is not
suggested.

*But this fact seems reasonably clear that this hub or
center of a galaxy exists and performs, in broad principle,
the functions of Kolob and that Kolob's existence and
function were known about four thousand years before
our day.*

Say the scriptures:

> And I saw the stars, that they were very great, and that one
> of them was nearest unto the throne of God; and there were
> many great ones which were near unto it;
>
> And the Lord said unto me: These are the governing ones;
> and the name of the great one is Kolob, because it is near unto
> me, for I am the Lord thy God: I have set this one to govern all
> those which belong to the same order as that upon which thou
> standest.

As already stated, science obviously has nothing to
offer as to the purpose of the creation of the universe.
This is not the prerogative of science.   Science deals with
facts, not motives.   Indeed it might be said that in one
sense, science does not know motives, while in another
sense it is constantly looking for the purpose, the objective
of this or that phenomenon in things with life.

The Lord began his great theophany to Moses regarding the universe (quoted above), saying: "For mine
own purpose have I made these things.   Here is wisdom

and it remaineth in me. . . . And worlds without number have I created; and I also created them for mine own pur-pose. . . . ." This, for the man of faith, puts the whole mat-ter beyond question.

The Lord then referred to the creation of Adam as the first man but informed Moses he was only going to give Moses an account of this earth and the inhabitants thereof. But immediately followed these words: ". . . For behold, there are many worlds that have passed away by the word of my power. And there are many that now stand, and innumerable are they unto man; but all things are numbered unto me, for they are mine and I know them."

Then Moses immediately followed:

. . . Be merciful unto thy servant, O God, and tell me con-cerning this earth, and the inhabitants thereof, and also the heavens, and then thy servant will be content.

And the Lord God spake unto Moses, saying: The heavens, they are many, and they cannot be numbered unto man; but they are numbered unto me, for they are mine.

And as one earth shall pass away, and the heavens thereof even so shall another come; and there is no end to my works, neither to my words.

Then, seemingly speaking as to all his creations, not of this earth alone, the Lord added:

For behold, this is my work and my glory—to bring to pass the immortality and eternal life of man.

The Lord seems now to leave matters dealing with the universe and to come back to our earth and to Moses' inquiry.

And now, Moses, my son, I will speak unto thee concerning this earth upon which thou standest; and thou shalt write the things which I shall speak.

And in a day when the children of men shall esteem my

words as naught and take many of them from the book which
thou shalt write, behold, I will raise up another like unto thee;
and they shall be had again among the children of men—among
as many as shall believe.   (Moses 1:40-41.)

These were the words spoken to Moses by God on
the Mount.

Then follows in the Book of Moses, Chapter 2, the
opening words of the Inspired Version of the Bible:

And it came to pass that the Lord spake unto Moses, saying:
Behold, I reveal unto you concerning *this heaven,* and *this earth;*
write the words which I speak. . . .   (*Ibid.,* 2:1; italics supplied.)

Then follows the regular text of the Inspired Version.

God largely reserved his purposes for his creations
to himself, save that he disclosed to Abraham as to the
creation of this earth that it was created to see if the
spirits seemingly destined to come here "will do all things
whatsoever the Lord their God shall command them."

So, to the man of faith, there comes out of the Holy
Scriptures, ancient and modern, a testimony that God
had a purpose, as yet only partly disclosed, behind the
making of the universe with all its vastness which he
created; and words from the Book of Moses suggest and
might be interpreted as meaning that other worlds,
numberless to man, were also peopled by the spirits fa-
thered by God himself, his children for whom he has
divine love and concern; that as to them, and all created
and wherever existing, there was to come the opportunity
for which indeed they were created,—of participating
in God's work and God's glory by having brought to pass
for them immortality and eternal life. (See Moses 7:36.)

On the point of other worlds, peopled by God's children, in the great vision vouchsafed to the Prophet Joseph and Sidney Rigdon at Hiram, Ohio, February 16,
1832, after declaring:

By the power of the Spirit our eyes were opened and our understandings were enlightened, so as to see and understand the things of God—

Even those things which were from the beginning before the world was, which were ordained of the Father, through his Only Begotten Son, who was in the bosom of the Father, even from the beginning;

Of whom we bear record; and the record which we bear is the fulness of the gospel of Jesus Christ, who is the Son, whom we saw and with whom we conversed in the heavenly vision. . . .

it is declared:

And we beheld the glory of the Son, on the right hand of the Father, and received of his fulness;

And saw the holy angels, and them who are sanctified before his throne, worshiping God, and the Lamb, who worship him forever and ever.

And now, after the many testimonies which have been given of him, this is the testimony, last of all, which we give of him: That he lives!

For we saw him, even on the right hand of God; and we heard the voice bearing record that he is the Only Begotten of the Father—

That by him, and through him, and of him, the worlds are and were created, and the inhabitants thereof are begotten sons and daughters unto God. (D & C 76:12-14, 20-24.)

This gives the answer to the outcry of the Psalmist:

What is man, that thou art mindful of him? and the son of man, that thou visitest him?

For thou hast made him a little lower than the angels, and hast crowned him with glory and honour.

Thou madest him to have dominion over the works of thy hands; thou hast put all things under his feet. . . .

O Lord our Lord, how excellent is thy name in all the earth! (Psa. 8:4 ff.)

Our faith teaches us that man is potentially a creator.

All this glorious, infinite concept comes to man, layman or scientist, by faith, which is ready for enkindling

in every created soul and which, fanned into flame, will
bring the promised immortality and eternal life.

Science and the scientific urge and spirit will never
alone bring this salvation and exaltation to the soul of
man.

Principal Theories of Creation of Universe

There has appeared in *The Saturday Evening Post*
(February 21, 1959) an article over the signature of
Professor Fred Hoyle dealing with theories concerning
the creation of the universe. The title to the article is,
When Time Began.

Professor Hoyle is Plumian Professor of Astronomy
and Experimental Philosophy at St. John's College, Cambridge University, Cambridge, England. He has been
frequently cited and quoted in the preceding discussion.

However, his observations regarding three principal
scientific theories of the creation of the universe are so
framed that even those of us without scientific training
may seem reasonably to understand them, that it has
seemed that a non-scientist (myself) might (with the
possibility of some interest and value) seek to cover some
of the main points that have bearing on the matters discussed in the "Kolob" memorandum. This feeling gained
some support from a consideration of some expressions in
scripture, ancient and modern.

In this article in *The Saturday Evening Post* Hoyle
seems to reduce the important theories in the matter
to "three different theories which attempt to probe these
mysteries of time and space and matter," which he refers to as "the Explosion Theory, the Expansion-Contraction Theory, and the Steady-State Theory." Noting that
"space is populated with vast galaxies of stars," he comments that "galaxies tend to be distributed in groups,
sometimes in big groups with as many as a thousand
galaxies, sometimes in small groups of only two or three

galaxies," and observes that our galaxy has only two members, our own Milky Way and M-31, "which is seen through the constellation Andromeda—a constellation of Milky Way stars."

He comments further that these galaxies occasionally meet in collision at high speed, but that "the component stars rarely hit each other, because they are small and the distance between them great. But the galaxies also contain huge clouds of gas, and these clouds do collide." (*Ibid.*, p. 38.)

Calling attention to the collision of two galaxies in the constellation Cygnus, he notes the emission from such collision of radio waves and observes that man-made stations having an output of one hundred kilowatts are looked upon as fairly powerful, yet from the Cygnus collision are emitted ten decillion kilowatts. (*Ibid.*, p. 96.) (Is this infinite energy wasted, or is it somewhere made available in the universe?)

"The Explosion Theory"

After noting two different lines of reasoning for determining the age of the universe he observes, speaking of the explosion theory:

It would appear that the universe originated nearly ten billion years ago, and that our galaxy was formed about a billion years later.

The essential concept is that universal matter was originally in a state of very high density, enormously greater than the density of the galaxies today. . . . The whole universe expanded rapidly, its initial state of very high density lasting only a few minutes. In time the continuing expansion produced less and less density. After almost a billion years of expansion and decreasing density, the clusters of galaxies formed. They have since continued to move apart and will go on moving apart throughout eternity.

Thus, according to the Explosion Theory, the universe was born a definite time ago. The state of dispersal caused by the explosion will never cease in this theory. The galaxies will continue to move apart from each other until, in the ultimate limit in the future, space will present a uniform, featureless emptiness. All activity inside the galaxies will ultimately cease. The stars will no longer shine. All sources of energy will be exhausted. (*Ibid.*, p. 98.)

"The Expansion-Contraction Theory"

Arguments and other theories to support this main one, advanced by scientists, have now more gone into discard because of newly discovered, seemingly hostile facts.

One of these new developments is that "we now know that a still higher temperature" (than that heretofore considered and relied upon in support of the "Explosion Theory"), "instead of promoting fusion, prevents hydrogen from fusing to produce complex elements. This realization led to a modification of the Explosion Theory. *It is called the Expansion-Contraction Theory.*" (*Ibid.*, p. 98, italics supplied.)

Some astronomers think that the original explosion of the superdense material may not have been sufficiently violent to produce a complete dispersal. They believe that the clusters of galaxies are moving apart from each other at a markedly declining rate, and that eventually expansion will cease altogether. Gravitational attraction will then cause the clusters to start moving together. This means that the universe will pass into a phase of contraction. The clusters will approach each other at ever-increasing speeds until the galaxies collide. Still further contraction will cause even the stars to collide. As a consequence of the greatly rising temperature that accompanies such a strong compression, the complex atoms will disintegrate and be transformed back into hydrogen. The stage will thereby be set for a reversal of the contraction process, and another universal expansion.

Here, then, is a very different picture—a cyclic universe, with expansion and contraction alternating. During expansion, galaxies and stars are formed. Hydrogen supplies energy inside the stars and is gradually changed into complex elements. During contraction, the galaxies and stars are disrupted, and the complex elements are broken down by the high temperature generated at the stage of greatest compression. Each cycle is similar to the previous one, and there is no limit to the number of cycles. Each cycle lasts roughly thirty billion years. The universe is now about halfway through an expansion phase.

According to the Expansion-Contraction Theory, the amount of matter in the universe is finite. Even the volume of space itself is finite, in somewhat the same way as the area of the surface of a sphere is finite. During expansion, all space swells up like an expanding balloon. During contraction, space collapses literally to a point. (*Ibid.*, p. 98.)

"Steady-State Theory"

The third theory (advanced by Professor Hoyle and some others) is called the "Steady-State Theory." He says it "differs in almost all essentials both from the Explosion Theory and from the Expansion-Contraction Theory." This new theory is both difficult and technical. No attempt will be made to follow it. A few seemingly salient points may be noted. Professor Hoyle makes these in the beginning of his discussion of the Steady-State Theory. They are of a character that some extracts from them will be interesting. We who are neither astronomers nor scientists should read the whole discussion if we are to gain even a cursory knowledge of the subject. However, a few significant paragraphs may be quoted here as an interesting background to certain quotations which may be added from the Book of Moses.

Professor Hoyle's Comments

Professor Hoyle states:

We are thus faced with the alternatives of creation plus expansion or of annihilation plus contraction. In theory we must weigh both these alternatives, because every physical hypothesis considers two possible ways of viewing the direction of time—the case where time runs forward into the future in the usual sense, and the case where time runs backward into the past. . . .

The maintenance of a constant average density of matter in space leads to the Steady-State Theory, first discussed by Prof. Hermann Bondi, Prof. Thomas Gold and myself some ten years ago. . . .

In the Steady-State Theory the clusters of galaxies expand apart, but as they do so new galaxies are born, and at such a rate that their average density in space remains unaltered with time. The individual clusters change and evolve, but the universe itself, viewed on the large scale, does not change. Thus the old problem of the beginning and end of the universe does not arise at all in the Steady-State Theory, for the universe did not have a beginning and it will not have an end. Every cluster of galaxies, every star, every atom, had a beginning, but the universe itself did not. . . .

If new galaxies are being formed, the Explosion Theory and the Expansion-Contraction Theory would be suspect because they do not provide for such creation. If new galaxies are not being formed, the Steady-State Theory becomes untenable. . . .

The Explosion Theory gives us the picture of the universe as an explosion from a superdense state of matter. Many people are especially attracted to this hypothesis because it requires a definite moment of creation for the whole universe. According to this theory, the universe is not a self-operating concern. It has to be started, much as one might switch on a huge machine. There are many questions relating to this hypothesis that we can never hope to answer, for many of the present-day characteristics of the universe depend on the precise manner of the 'switching on' process. There is also a philosophic undercurrent of an existence outside the universe that touches on religion, a feature that seems attractive to some and unappealing to others.

The Expansion-Contraction Theory and the Steady-State Theory are similar in that they both present the universe as a fully self-operating system. There is no moment of origin, time extends backward into the past as far as we care to consider it. Otherwise these two theories are very different, the one depending on permanence and the other on impermanence of particles in the gravitational field.

Space and time play very different roles in the three theories. In the Explosion Theory, space is infinite, while time is finite toward the past and infinite toward the future. In the Expansion-Contraction Theory, time is infinite in both the past and the future, but space is finite. In the Steady-State Theory, space and time are both infinite. Moreover, space and time have a still deeper connection in the Steady-State Theory. This is a point of such considerable interest as to be worth a short diversion. . . .

This wider interpretation of equivalence provides one of the strongest aesthetic reasons for preferring the Steady-State Theory. Moreover, the whole progress of modern physics has been closely bound up with the discovery of relations that are independent of the special position of the observer. For this reason alone, I feel that it would be most surprising if the Steady-State Theory, with its compelling space-time equivalence, should turn out to be wrong. . . .

In the Expansion-Contraction Theory we are asked to think of expansion and contraction following each other in a never-ending series. During expansion, matter becomes organized into galaxies, stars, planets, living creatures. During contraction the galaxies, stars, and so on are entirely disintegrated in preparation for the succeeding phase of expansion. Each cycle is exactly similar to the preceding cycle. Nothing new ever happens from cycle to cycle, and it is just this that seems uninspired and inelegant. This is an aesthetic rather than a scientific objection, but it may be worth adding that scientists are more concerned with aesthetics than is commonly supposed! . . .

. . . Are there any ultimate final laws of physics? Might it not be that however deep one digs, there are always still deeper levels of subtlety to be uncovered? Nowadays the trend is to answer the last question affirmatively, to believe that no end will be found to the intricacy of the laws of physics.

Such a point of view makes sense in the Steady-State Theory, but not, I think, in the other theories. In the Expansion-Contraction Theory, for instance, we have a universe that is entirely finite—a finite amount of matter, finite space, a finite time of cycling. It seems to me most doubtful whether such a universe could possibly accommodate laws of an infinite complexity. The situation is better in the Explosion Theory. Here we could possibly have an infinite universe with infinite laws—but one in which only a finite fragment of the laws was discoverable. For in the Explosion Theory there is but one single generation of galaxies. The stars and the living creatures in these galaxies live only for a finite time of a few tens of billions of years. Hence any understanding gained by living creatures must always remain finite. Digging beyond a certain finite depth would manifestly be impossible.

The situation is otherwise in the Steady-State Theory. Here it is possible to accumulate knowledge indefinitely, to dig to any depth, however deep. Here we have an unending series of generations of galaxies. When a particular galaxy dies, the knowledge that has been gained by creatures in it can (in principle!) be passed to a nearby younger galaxy. This process can be repeated without end, so that in the long run knowledge can be piled up to any required degree. Here we have a universe that is infinite, not only in its obvious physical characteristics but also in its intellectual possibilities. (*Ibid.*, pp. 99-100.)

Ancient and Modern Scriptures

We shall conclude by adding a few quotations of scriptures, ancient and modern, that deal with matters treated upon in some of the theories advanced by Professor Hoyle in his presentation of the subject, with especial reference to the Steady-State Theory.

Isaiah

The great Prophet-poet Isaiah (Nephi said, ". . . my soul delighteth in his words. . . ." [2 Nephi 11:2]), in a burst of divine inspiration concerning the "day of the Lord" declared:

Behold, the day of the Lord cometh, cruel both with wrath and fierce anger, to lay the land desolate: and he shall destroy the sinners thereof out of it.

For the stars of heaven and the constellations thereof shall not give their light: the sun shall be darkened in his going forth, and the moon shall not cause her light to shine.

And I will punish the world for their evil, and the wicked for their iniquity; and I will cause the arrogancy of the proud to cease, and will lay low the haughtiness of the terrible. (Isa. 13:9-11; see also *ibid.*, 24:23; Mal. 4:1.)

Ezekiel

Ezekiel voiced the same thoughts:

And when I shall put thee out, I will cover the heaven, and make the stars thereof dark; I will cover the sun with a cloud, and the moon shall not give her light.

All the bright lights of heaven will I make dark over thee, and set darkness upon thy land, saith the Lord God. (Ezek. 32:7-8.)

Joel

The same conditions were made known to Joel:

The sun shall be turned into darkness, and the moon into blood, before the great and terrible day of the Lord come. . . .

The sun and the moon shall be darkened, and the stars shall withdraw their shining. (Joel 2:31, 3:15.)

While these passages seem not to contemplate destruction of galaxies, nor indeed total destruction of worlds, they do seem to be a prophet's visualization of cataclysmic disturbances and darkness.

However, in the great Olivet discourse, the Savior in instructing his disciples, seems to push the words of the prophets to their ultimate conclusion, and at least to concede the destruction of galaxies and worlds. All three of the Synoptists make the same record. The whole discourse should be read. (Matt. 24:1-51; Mark 13:1-37; Luke 21:5-36.)

Each of them says, in essence, as voiced by Matthew who, after listing the terrible tribulations of the last days, records Jesus as declaring, "Heaven and earth shall pass away, but my words shall not pass away." (Matt. 24:35; Mark 13:3; Luke 21:33.)

The tribulations preceding the second coming are told in Matthew (the translation in the Pearl of Great Price is better arranged as to the period and chronology of the incidents covered in the chapter as appearing in the King James Version), by Mark, and by Luke. (Matt. 24:35 ff.; Mark 13:9 ff.; Luke 21:10 ff.)

It may be well, however, to quote from each Gospel as to what shall happen after the tribulations recounted.

Matthew says:

Immediately after the tribulation of those days shall the sun be darkened, and the moon shall not give her light, and the stars shall fall from heaven, and the powers of the heavens shall be shaken:

And then shall appear the sign of the Son of man in heaven. . . . (Matt. 24:29-30.)

Mark says:

But in those days, after that tribulation, the sun shall be darkened, and the moon shall not give her light.

And the stars of heaven shall fall, and the powers that are in heaven shall be shaken.

And then shall they see the Son of man coming in the clouds with great power and glory. (Mark 13:24-26.)

Luke's record reads:

But when ye shall hear of wars and commotions, be not terrified: for these things must first come to pass; but the end is not by and by.

Then said he unto them, Nation shall rise against nation, and kingdom against kingdom:

And great earthquakes shall be in divers places, and famines, and pestilences; and fearful sights and great signs shall there be from heaven. . . .

And there shall be signs in the sun, and in the moon, and in the stars; and upon the earth distress of nations, with perplexity; the sea and the waves roaring. . . .

. . . for the powers of heaven shall be shaken. (Luke 21:9-11, 25-26.)

In each record, the recounting of these and other tribulations (not quoted here) is followed by the solemn declaration: *"Heaven and earth shall pass away: but my words shall not pass away."* (Mark 13:31; Matt. 24:35; Luke 21:33; italics supplied.)

We should note here some of the more direct and clear statements made by the Prophet Joseph, either as inspired instructions to the Saints or as revelations from the Lord.

First, the Prophet, at Ramus, May 16 and 17, 1843, made the following comments:

It is impossible for a man to be saved in ignorance.

There is no such thing as immaterial matter. All spirit is matter, but it is more fine or pure, and can only be discerned by purer eyes;

We cannot see it; but when our bodies are purified we shall see that it is all matter. (D & C 131:6-8.)

At this point we might recall that Moses, when telling of his great interview with one who declared himself, "Behold, I am the Lord God Almighty, and Endless is my name; for I am without beginning of days or end of years; and is not this endless" (Moses 1:3), recounted some of the things the Lord God Almighty showed him:

But now mine own eyes have beheld God; but not my natural, but my spiritual eyes, for my natural eyes could not have beheld; for I should have withered and died in his presence; but his glory was upon me; and I beheld his face, for I was transfigured before him. (*Ibid.*, 1:11.)

In a revelation given through Joseph Smith the Prophet, in the presence of six elders, the Lord, after commenting upon the sinfulness of the world, the Millennium and the scenes of judgments, declared:

And again, verily, verily, I say unto you that when the thousand years are ended, and men again begin to deny their God, then will I spare the earth but for a little season;

And the end shall come, *and the heaven and the earth shall be consumed and pass away, and there shall be a new heaven and a new earth.*

For all old things shall pass away, and all things shall become new, even the heaven and the earth, and all the fulness thereof, both men and beasts, the fowls of the air, and the fishes of the sea;

And not one hair, neither mote, shall be lost, for it is the workmanship of mine hand.

But, behold, verily I say unto you, before the earth shall pass away, Michael, mine archangel, shall sound his trump, and then shall all the dead awake, for their graves shall be opened, and they shall come forth—yea, even all.

And the righteous shall be gathered on my right hand unto eternal life; and the wicked on my left hand will I be ashamed to own before the Father:

Wherefore I will say unto them—Depart from me, ye cursed, into everlasting fire, prepared for the devil and his angels. (D & C 29:22-28; italics supplied.)

This comes directly to the point,—our heaven and our earth shall pass away and a new heaven and new earth shall come.

In a revelation given to the Prophet Joseph at Kirtland, Ohio, March 7, 1831, the Lord comments upon a variety of matters and also false doctrines. Turning his attention particularly to the Jews, the Lord said:

And it shall come to pass that this generation of Jews shall not pass away until every desolation which I have told you concerning them shall come to pass.

Ye say that ye know that the end of the world cometh; ye say also that ye know that the heavens and the earth shall pass away;

And in this ye say truly, for so it is; but these things which I have told you shall not pass away until all shall be fulfilled. (*Ibid.*, 45:21-23.)

This is another affirmation that ". . . the heavens and the earth shall pass away; and in this ye say truly. . . ." (See Sec. 67 for a statement that ". . . heavens and the earth are in mine hands, and the riches of eternity are mine to give"; and see for a general discussion of kingdoms, their governing laws and like matters, Sec. 88.)

We turn now to the Pearl of Great Price scripture— the "Book of Moses." These have already been quoted, but it seems desirable to quote them again as they may have a particular significance from the point of view of the Steady-State Theory advanced by Professor Hoyle.

Before considering the scriptures from Moses, it will be useful to have in mind some of the words of the vision of Abraham (Abraham 3:22 ff. and 4:1, also already quoted above). These scriptures read:

> Now the Lord had shown unto me, Abraham, the intelligences that were organized before the world was; and among all these there were many of the noble and great ones;
>
> And God saw these souls that they were good, and he stood in the midst of them, and he said: These I will make my rulers; for he stood among those that were spirits, and he saw that they were good; and he said unto me: Abraham, thou art one of them; thou wast chosen before thou wast born.
>
> And there stood one among them that was like unto God, and he said unto those who were with him: We will go down, *for there is space there,* and we will take of these materials, and we will make an earth whereon these may dwell;
>
> And we will prove them herewith, to see if they will do all things whatsoever the Lord their God shall command them;
>
> And they who keep their first estate shall be added upon; and they who keep not their first estate shall not have glory in the same kingdom with those who keep their first estate; and they who keep their second estate shall have glory added upon their heads for ever and ever.
>
> And the Lord said: Whom shall I send? and one answered like unto the Son of Man: Here am I, send me. And another answered and said: Here am I, send me. And the Lord said: I will send the first.
>
> And the second was angry, and kept not his first estate; and, at that day, many followed after him.
>
> And then the Lord said: Let us go down. And they went down at the beginning, and they, that is the Gods, organized and formed the heavens and the earth.
>
> And the earth, after it was formed, was empty and desolate, because they had not formed anything but the earth; and darkness reigned upon the face of the deep, and the Spirit of the Gods was brooding upon the face of the waters. (Abraham 3:22-28; 4:1-2; italics supplied.)

Note should be taken of Chapter 3, verse 24, and Chapter 4, verses 1 and 2 (just cited) as to the creation

of a new earth in a place where ". . . there is space . . ."
and that in their creative work ". . . we will take of
these materials, and we will make an earth whereon these
may dwell"; and in Chapter 4, verse 1, it is recorded that
". . . they went down *at the beginning*, and they, that is
the Gods, organized and formed the heavens and the
earth." (Italics supplied.)

The whole tenor of what follows in this account
leaves the impression that, at most, the use of the word
"heaven" in this account refers not to our whole galaxy.
If so, there could, it would seem, be no question about
"space" in which to build (Abraham 3:24), and possibly
no question about materials in the place chosen. If a
galaxy were to be formed, it would seem no question
need be made about materials for one little earth. Finding "space" suggests, at any rate, that there were neighboring creations to be considered. Finally, the provisions
of verses 14 to 18 (Chapter 4) suggest that at most, even
if so much, the question of our solar system was directly
involved. However, this obviously conjecture, based on
fragmentary allusions, might easily be wrong.

Leaving here these preliminary matters about the
creation of this earth, we return to the great vision of
Moses when the "Lord God Almighty" showed Moses
some of ". . . the workmanship of mine [the Lord God
Almighty's] hands; but not all, for my works are without
end, and also my words, for they never cease." (Moses
1:3-4, italics supplied.)

First announcing to Moses:

And behold, the glory of the Lord was upon Moses, so that
Moses stood in the presence of God, and talked with him face
to face. And the Lord God said unto Moses: For mine own purpose have I made these things. Here is wisdom and it remaineth
in me. . . .

the Lord continued:

And by the word of my power, have I created them, which is mine Only Begotten Son, who is full of grace and truth.

And worlds without number have I created; and I also created them for mine own purpose; and by the Son I created them, which is mine Only Begotten. . . .

But only an account of this earth, and the inhabitants thereof, give I unto you. For behold, there are many worlds that have passed away by the word of my power. And there are many that now stand, and innumerable are they unto man; but all things are numbered unto me, for they are mine and I know them.

And it came to pass that Moses spake unto the Lord, saying: Be merciful unto thy servant, O God, and tell me concerning this earth, and of the inhabitants thereof, and also the heavens, and then thy servant will be content.

And the Lord God spake unto Moses, saying: the heavens, they are many, and they cannot be numbered unto man; but they are numbered unto me, for they are mine.

And as one earth shall pass away, and the heavens thereof even so shall another come; and there is no end to my works, neither to my words.

For behold, this is my work and my glory—to bring to pass the immortality and eternal life of man. (Moses 1:31-39.)

It is unnecessary to point out the similarities in certain respects between the Lord's words and the speculations of the Steady-State Theory of the Hoyle school of thought in the creation of the universe.

The Contribution from Job

There is one scripture not usually dealt with in connection with problems hereinabove discussed to which, in conclusion, it would seem attention might be called —the final chapters of Job.

Whether or not this is the oldest book in the Bible and whether or not, as some contend, it was written before the Law was given to Israel—that is, was pre-Mosaic—yet it is a very ancient scripture and may be taken fairly to represent the knowledge of the universe which existed at the time of its writing.

It is generally conceded by scholars to be a great

dramatic poem and that, "The poetical descriptions con-
tained in the book are unequalled elsewhere." (*The
Queen's Printers' Aids to the Student of the Holy Bible,
Variorum Edition* (Eyre & Spottiswoode, 1893), p. 26.)

It is not written as a text book on astronomy or on
the creation of the earth or the biological and mineralog-
ical history thereof. But some of its expressions indicate
that in them is more than poetic imagery.

"Where wast thou when I laid the foundations of
the earth. . . ." (Job 38:4) refers to the beginning of
the creation of the earth. Man has more information
now than then, but it is still mystery.

"Who hath laid the measures thereof . . . or who
hath stretched the line upon it," and again, "whereupon
are the foundations thereof fastened" and ". . . who laid
the corner stone thereof" surely contemplate the interrelation of the earth with other members of the solar
system, the interrelation of the billions of members of our
galaxy, the interrelation of the billions of galaxies that
the Palomar telescopes bring within our vision. (*Ibid.*,
38:4-6.) God knew the infinity and the space thereof.

God's questions regarding light and darkness, and
the separation of the waters, the problems of life and
death, and so on, with a myriad of matters leading up
to the constellations and galaxies as we now know them,
some bearing the names that have come down to us in
our time, even as to certain stars named; these questions
are underlain with matters that are still mysteries. God
then pushes his enquiry into the habits of created things.

All this at least shows that in the time of Job these
matters were troubling men who were pushing their
search for knowledge into regions that still are in the
unknown to us.

"When the morning stars sang together, and all the
sons of God shouted for joy" (*ibid.*, 38:7), could well
have been the acclaim that came in the Grand Council

when the decision was reached to create an earth where
those assembled might come and prove themselves willing
to keep their second estate that they might ". . . have
glory added upon their heads for ever and ever." (Abraham 3:26.)

This search by Divinity of the mind of Job, suggest-
ing the depth of human ignorance upon matters that man
must have been then concerned with and are still so
largely unsolved, begins in the dignity of the Infinite
and follows thus:

Then the Lord answered Job out of the whirlwind, and said,
Who is this that darkeneth counsel by words without knowledge?

Gird up now thy loins like a man; for I will demand of thee,
and answer thou me.

Where wast thou when I laid the foundations of the earth?
declare, if thou hast understanding.

Who hath laid the measures thereof, if thou knowest? or
who hath stretched the line upon it?

Whereupon are the foundations thereof fastened? or who
laid the corner stone thereof;

When the morning stars sang together, and all the sons of
God shouted for joy?

Or who shut up the sea with doors, when it brake forth, as
if it had issued out of the womb?

When I made the cloud the garment thereof, and thick darkness a swaddlingband for it,

And brake up for it my decreed place, and set bars and
doors,

And said, Hitherto shalt thou come, but no further: and
here shall thy proud waves be stayed?

Hast thou commanded the morning since thy days; and
caused the dayspring to know his place;

That it might take hold of the ends of the earth, that the
wicked might be shaken out of it?

It is turned as clay to the seal; and they stand as a garment.

And from the wicked their light is withholden, and the high
arm shall be broken.

Hast thou entered into the springs of the sea? or hast thou
walked in the search of the depth?

Have the gates of death been opened unto thee? or hast thou seen the doors of the shadow of death?

Hast thou perceived the breadth of the earth? declare if thou knowest it all.

Where is the way where light dwelleth? and as for darkness, where is the place thereof,

That thou shouldest take it to the bound thereof, and that thou shouldest know the paths to the house thereof?

Knowest thou it, because thou wast then born? or because the number of thy days is great?

Hast thou entered into the treasures of the snow? or hast thou seen the treasures of the hail,

Which I have reserved against the time of trouble, against the day of battle and war?

By what way is the light parted, which scattereth the east wind upon the earth?

Who hath divided a watercourse for the overflowing of waters, or a way for the lightning of thunder;

To cause it to rain on the earth, where no man is; on the wilderness, wherein there is no man;

To satisfy the desolate and waste ground; and to cause the bud of the tender herb to spring forth?

Hath the rain a father? or who hath begotten the drops of dew?

Out of whose womb came the ice? and the hoary frost of heaven, who hath gendered it?

The waters are hid as with a stone, and the face of the deep is frozen.

Canst thou bind the sweet influences of Pleiades, or loose the bands of Orion?

Canst thou bring forth Mazzaroth in his season? or canst thou guide Arcturus with his sons?

Knowest thou the ordinances of heaven? canst thou set the dominion thereof in the earth?

Canst thou lift up thy voice to the clouds, that abundance of waters may cover thee?

Canst thou send lightnings, that they may go, and say unto thee, Here we are?

Who hath put wisdom in the inward parts? or who hath given understanding to the heart?

Who can number the clouds in wisdom? or who can stay the bottles of heaven. (Job 38:1-37.)

God then challenged the knowledge and wisdom of Job regarding the life and habits of certain animals and birds that were important in Job's world, pointing great characteristics thereof of deep importance to them, and affecting Job and his life of all of which Job seemed ignorant. The description of the war horse and of the hunting hawk found herein rivals anything in literature.

God then challenged Job still further and with reference to specific animals and besought Job's knowledge about them and Job's ability to control and direct them, to which Job declared, realizing his ignorance and lack of power:

"Behold, I am vile; what shall I answer thee? I will lay mine hand upon my mouth," and added in abasement, "Wherefore I abhor myself, and repent in dust and ashes." (*Ibid.*, 40:4, 42:6.)

The Planets and the Solar System

Name of Planet	Dist. from Sun in Miles		Approx. Dist. from Earth Millions of Miles	
	Maximum	Minimum	Max.	Min.
Mercury	43,355,000	28,566,000	136	50
Venus	67,653,000	66,738,000	161	25
Earth	94,452,000	91,342,000	....	....
Mars	154,760,000	128,330,000	248	35
Jupiter	506,710,000	459,940,000	600	367
Saturn	935,570,000	836,700,000	1028	744
Uranus	1,866,800,000	1,698,800,000	1960	1606
Neptune	2,817,400,000	2,769,600,000	2910	2677
Pluto	4,600,000,000	2,760,000,000	4700	2670

Jupiter has 4 large and 8 small satellites, or moons, revolving around it; Saturn has 9; Uranus, 5; Neptune, 2; Mars, 2; the Earth, 1.

(*The World Almanac* (New York World-Telegram, 1959), p. 428.)

"And there stood one among them that was like unto God, and he said unto those who were with him: We will go down, for there is space there, and we will take of these materials, and we will make an earth whereon these may dwell;

"And we will prove them herewith, to see if they will do all things whatsoever the Lord their God shall command them."

Abraham 3:24-25

The Great Plan of Salvation and Exaltation

AT THE Grand Council, "The Council of the Eternal God," a plan was framed under which the spirits assembled might take on mortality to "prove" themselves "to see if they will do all things whatsoever the Lord their God shall command them." (Abraham 3:25.) Spirits keeping their first estate were to be permitted to take on mortal bodies and gain the experiences of mortality, those 'who kept not their first estate should not have glory in the same kingdom with those who kept their first estate'; and those who kept their second estate should "have glory added upon their heads for ever and ever." (Abraham 3:26.)

Gospel in World from Adam till the End

Since to "prove" themselves 'to see if they would do all things whatsoever the Lord their God should command them,' it was necessary that the Lord should make his commandments known to them, "the Gospel began to be preached, from the beginning, being declared by holy angels sent forth from the presence of God, and by his own voice, and by the gift of the Holy Ghost. And thus all things were confirmed unto Adam, by an holy ordinance, and the Gospel preached, and a decree sent forth, that it should be in the world, until the end thereof; and thus it was. Amen." (Moses 5:58-59.) "And Adam and Eve blessed the name of God, and they made all things known unto their sons and their daughters." (*Ibid.*, 5:12.)

Perversion of the People by Satan

But with the Fall came sin. Satan came among the people declaring he was a son of God, and they should

not obey the teachings of Adam and Eve. Many of the
people believed and followed Satan, "and men began from
that time forth to be carnal, sensual, and devilish." The
Lord through the Holy Ghost called upon men to repent,
promising that those who obeyed should be saved and
those who "believed not and repented not, should be
damned." (*Ibid.*, 5:12 ff.)

But Satan intruded himself into the very household
of Adam himself, and Cain, Adam's son, murdered his
brother Abel in cold blood. Unrighteousness spread. The
work of the Lord languished among the people. So the
Lord established the Adamic dispensation, which is a
period during which there was on the earth the "power
and authority to dispense the word of God, and to administer in all the ordinances thereof." (*A Compendium
of the Doctrines of the Gospel*, Franklin D. Richards and
James A. Little, compilers and publishers (Salt Lake
City, second stereotyped edition, 1884), p. 143.)

The Two Plans

The plan of the "Council of the Eternal God" required that every spirit falling within the plan should
have opportunity to "prove" himself. Satan had proposed
to save all these spirits, denying them their agency; not
one soul was to be lost. The Only Begotten had proposed
to give each spirit an opportunity for salvation, opportunity to "prove" himself in the exercise of his free
agency. God chose this plan.

Thus each and all of the spirits, entitled to the blessings of the plan, must be given the opportunity to take
on a mortal body, if he desired to do so, and have the
experiences of mortality. He could do good or evil.

The Lord's Solicitude

So all along the way of mankind's march towards
the end of mortality on the earth, the Lord has, at inter-

vals, intensified his efforts to save God's children under
the plan by sending some of the great ones, who were
chosen at the beginning, as Abraham was chosen (Abraham 3:23), to reestablish his work and service. Each such
occasion has carried with it a reemphasis of the Priesthood, its duties and powers, for the Lord has always
sought to bring salvation to his children, no matter how
wayward they might be. He has always fixed upon periods
for setting up his work anew, either when there was
some special purpose to be worked out, as with the Mosaic dispensation and the Messianic, or when the peoples
of the earth reeked in unrighteousness, as in the dispensation of Noah when the people had become "carnal,
sensual, and devilish." (Moses 5:13; 6:49.)

The Gospel Dispensations

Thus other dispensations followed the first dispensation, that of Adam, the Lord in each trying to bring
his children to his way of life that he might "bring to
pass the immortality and eternal life of man." (*Ibid.*,
1:39.)

The Prophet Joseph has told us of the dispensations
from Adam to Enoch, from Enoch to Noah, from Noah
to Abraham, Abraham to Moses, Moses to Elias, Elias
to John the Baptist, and from then to Jesus Christ, and
from him to the Apostles, Peter, James, and John. (*Compendium*, p. 143; see Paul's statement as to his personal
dispensation, 1 Cor. 9:17; Eph. 3:2; Col. 1:25.)

The End from the Beginning

God in his infinite knowledge saw the end of all
things even from the beginning. Isaiah declared the
words of the Lord:

Remember the former things of old: for I am God, and there
is none else; I am God, and there is none like me,

Declaring the end from the beginning, and from ancient times the things that are not yet done, saying, My counsel shall stand, and I will do all my pleasure. (Isa. 46:9-10; see also Isa. 41:26.)

Thus God knew men in the beginning not only *en masse*, but each individual and what each would do, when tested by the trials and temptations of mortality.

Limitations upon Achievements of Early Dispensations

So God knew from the beginning that the dispensations of Adam and Enoch and Noah and Abraham and Moses and Elias, and even of the Messiah himself, could not bring man to that culmination of earth-life for which the grand plan provided—the birth, the death, the resurrection, the exaltation of men in the presence of God in the eternities.

The pre-Messianic dispensations could not do so, because at their times the Messiah had not yet received his body, lived, died, and been resurrected—man had not been redeemed from the Fall, and this must be done to reunite the spirit and body, overcoming the mortal death. The Messianic dispensation could not do so because in Christ's time—the Meridian of Time—there were still multitudes of those hosts that Abraham was shown, who had not yet had opportunity to receive mortal bodies and "prove" themselves and show whether they should "have glory added upon their heads for ever and ever." This opportunity must be given them under the plan.

Purposes of Various Dispensations

Recalling the purpose of mortality as disclosed in the great plan, the "proving" of men "to see if they will do all things whatsoever the Lord their God shall command them" (Abraham 3:25), one can gather, at least in part, an understanding of the Lord's course over the ages.

The Dispensation of Adam

To Adam the Gospel was given that he might "prove" himself and try to lead his children in paths of righteousness. But they began to stray; the Lord warned: "My spirit shall not always strive with man" (Gen. 6:3) ; man became so wicked it "grieved him [the Lord] at his heart." (*Ibid.*, 6.) The people died in their wickedness.

The Dispensation of Enoch

Then came the dispensation of Enoch who vindicated the grand plan by showing men could keep God's commandments if they had a sincere desire thereto. Enoch led his people into a state of translation. (Heb. 11:5.)

The Dispensation of Noah

But the earth's people who were not of Enoch so increased in wickedness, became such a stench in the Lord's nostrils, that he resolved to destroy mankind and to begin all over again, and bring a new race through Noah and his posterity. Then came the Flood. The antediluvians likewise died in their wickedness, rejecting the truth.

The Dispensation of Abraham

But Noah's posterity did no better than the immediate descendants of Adam. Wickedness and corruption, and a pervading spirit of apostasy again cursed the peoples of the earth. Finding a righteous strain in Abraham—whose father apostatizing from the true faith, was a 'worshiper of the gods of the heathens' (Abraham 1:5), the Lord founded an elect family with Abraham at

its head, so opening the dispensation of Abraham. The
Lord made a solemn covenant with Abraham and declared:

> I will multiply thy seed as the stars of the heaven, and as
> the sand which is upon the sea shore; and thy seed shall possess
> the gate of his enemies;
>
> And in thy seed shall all the nations of the earth be blessed;
> because thou hast obeyed my voice. (Gen. 22:17-18.)

The Lord repeated this blessing upon the head of
Jacob. (*Ibid.*, 28:13-14.) And Abraham's seed kept for
generations the knowledge and worship of the only true
God. Yet the other peoples of the earth were in spiritual
darkness; they lived and died heathens.

The Dispensation of Moses

In due time, as the result of a long residence in Egypt,
begun to save themselves in a famine and finally ending
in grievous bondage, Abraham's seed, now called Israel,
for God had so christened Jacob at Peniel (*ibid.*, 32:28),
became so inclined to idolatry that later during the ex-
odus when Moses left them so he might commune with
God at Sinai, they had Aaron make them an Egyptian
golden calf to worship. So to preserve his true worship
and to save his chosen seed, the Lord raised up the great
statesman, leader, lawgiver, prophet, Moses, who led
the Children of Israel out of the bondage of Egypt. The
Lord reestablished his Priesthood, attempting to give
them the Melchizedek Priesthood, but they refused to
accept it (D & C 84:25), and were left with the Aaronic
Priesthood only. Thus the Mosaic dispensation was set
up to reestablish the worship of the true God, and to
gather all Israel into one place, separated from the heath-
enish influences of the idolators of the world. But all
the while these idolators themselves continued in their

blind wickedness, and continued, as was the rule during all the long centuries since Adam, to die in their sins.

The Dispensation of Elias

But the neighboring tribes in Palestine, themselves idolators, soon began to corrupt even Israel. The Lord raised up mighty prophets to try to lead back to the worship of the true God, the apostates from his true worship. Elijah vindicated before them, the power of the true God in his contest with the priests of Baal. (1 Kings 18.) Yet the Lord having granted to Elijah this proving miracle, Elijah was forced to flee for his life to Mount Horeb, to escape the wrath and revenge of King Ahab's wife, Jezebel. Elisha followed Elijah, and other great prophets followed him, Isaiah, Jeremiah, Ezekiel, Daniel, and the others down to Malachi, living through the division of Israel into two kingdoms, the two captivities, the return to Jerusalem, through the period of the Maccabees, even down to the days of John the Baptist. All these sought to preserve Israel in the true worship. But there was a great falling away to idolatry among Israel. Abraham's seed in part perished in sin, while the world still wallowed and died in wickedness.

The Dispensation of John the Baptist and the Christ

John the Baptist, coming in the spirit of Elias as a forerunner, began turning Judah back to the worship of the true God and the practice of the true ordinances. The ten tribes of Israel had been lost for generations. John could reach but a few of Judah. The rest of Judah followed in a corruption of the true worship, with venal priests and a priesthood wandering from the order and principles given to them in the wilderness by the Lord through Moses.

But John's dispensation seems among all up to that

time to have been truly successful—he prepared the way
for One who was to come after, "the latchet of whose
shoes I am not worthy to unloose" (Luke 3:16; Matt.
3:11-12; Mark 1:7)—the Christ, who in turn fully consummated his dispensation. He was born, he lived, he
performed his ministry, he was crucified, buried, lay in
the tomb, was resurrected on the third day—the First
Fruits of the Resurrection—and ascended into heaven.
His dispensation came to a perfect fruition.

The Dispensation of the Apostles

Then followed the dispensation of the Apostles.

But, as had been foreseen from the beginning and
proclaimed by the ancient prophets, on this hemisphere
and in Palestine, the dispensation of Christ's Apostles
did not bring the earth-culmination of the grand plan.
The Savior had said this plainly enough in his great
prophetic discourse to the Apostles on Mount Olivet on
the third day of the week of the Atoning Sacrifice. But
the Apostles did not understand and, at least at first,
seem to have anticipated that this earth-culmination of
the plan, with the second coming of the Christ, was in
the immediate future.

The Apostasy

But such was not the plan. Already during the lives
of the Apostles the apostasy from the true faith had
begun. The writings of James, Peter, John, Paul, and
Jude abundantly show this. The world progressively
twisted and turned away from and finally abandoned the
pure principles and ordinances of the Gospel—they 'trans-
gressed the laws, changed the ordinance, and broke the
everlasting covenant' (Isa. 24:5); they became wicked
and corrupt, again "carnal, sensual, and devilish"; the
Priesthood was taken from them. The apostasy was finally complete.

Sectarian Estimate of the Post-Apostolic Centuries

A learned sectarian divine—writing about the condition of the world at the close of the first Christian century (which he marks as the time of the death of the Apostle John) indicts the condition of the people of the eastern hemisphere, in these brilliantly eloquent words:

The age of inspiration is over,—that peerless century which began with the birth of Christ, and closed with the death of John—and the course of the ages descends once more to the ordinary level of common time.

It was with the Church now as with the disciples at Bethany, when the last gleam of the Savior's ascending train had passed from their sight, and they turned their faces, reluctant and sad, to the dark world again. The termination of the age of inspiration was in truth the very complement and consummation of the ascension of the Lord. The sun can then only be said to have fairly set, when his departing glory has died away from the horizon, and the chill stars shine out sharp and clear on the dun and naked sky.

That time has now ful'y come. The last gleam of inspired wisdom and truth vanished from the earth with the beloved apostle's gentle farewell, and we pass at once across the mysterious line which separates the sacred from the secular annals of the world,—the history of the apostolic age from the history of the Christian Church. (Islay Burns, *The First Three Christian Centuries* (T. Nelson and Sons, London, 1884), p. 49; see also p. 63.)

Once more the people of the earth (other than Israel) were finally left, as they had been left in each dispensation before, down to the dispensation of John, without the Priesthood of God, without his Church, without the true faith and its saving principles and ordinances.

Hosts Dying without Opportunity to "Prove" Themselves

All those myriads upon myriads born to mortality all over the earth during the dark ages of all the dispensations had not the opportunity to "prove" themselves

and show "they will do all things whatsoever the Lord
their God shall command them." (Abraham 3:25.) They
could not, without further opportunity, "have glory
added upon their heads for ever and ever."

Furthermore, not all principles and ordinances of the
Gospel of Christ, so far as the scriptures show, had been
in the Church during each of these various dispensations
(D & C 128:18), though certain of them were present in
every "dispensation of the priesthood." (*Ibid.*, 128:9.)
Yet an opportunity for a full knowledge of the complete
Gospel by every spirit coming to mortality on this earth,
was necessary under the grand plan.

Salvation for Those Dying without the Gospel

So to these countless hosts of the dead, so dying in
spiritual poverty, must come the full message and op-
portunities of the Gospel of Christ. He himself began
this work while his mortal body lay in the tomb, by going
to, and preaching "unto the spirits in prison; which sometime were disobedient, when once the longsuffering of
God waited in the days of Noah," and "for this cause was
the gospel preached also to them that are dead, that they
might be judged according to men in the flesh, but live
according to God in the spirit." (1 Peter 3:19-20; 4:6.)

Forecasting his visit to the imprisoned spirits and
his preaching to them, Jesus, attending his second Passover during his active ministry and speaking to the multitude assembled at the pool of Bethesda (where he
healed a man "which had an infirmity thirty and eight
years"), said:

Verily, verily, I say unto you, The hour is coming, and now
is, when the dead shall hear the voice of the Son of God:
and they that hear shall live.

For as the Father hath life in himself; so hath he given to
the Son to have life in himself;

And hath given him authority to execute judgment also, because he is the Son of man.

Marvel not at this: for the hour is coming, in the which all that are in the graves shall hear his voice,

And shall come forth; they that have done good, unto the resurrection of life; and they that have done evil, unto the resurrection of damnation. (John 5:5, 25-29.)

Dispensation of the Fulness of Times

That these myriads dying in darkness and it seems, still existing in darkness and ignorance, might have an opportunity to hear, and, believing, live the Gospel, it was necessary that a new dispensation should be set up, another period when there should be on the earth the "power and authority to dispense the word of God, and to administer in all the ordinances thereof."

Paul envisaged this, though perhaps not too clearly nor entirely (see Gal. 4:4; and as to Peter also, see Acts 2:17), when, having first spoken of our redemption through Christ and his making known his will, he said to the Ephesians:

That in the dispensation of the fulness of times he might gather together in one all things in Christ, both which are in heaven, and which are on earth; even in him. (Eph. 1:10.)

In the very early days of the Church our people were advised as to "what the fulness of times means":

Now the thing to be known is, what the fulness of times means, or the extent and authority thereof. It means this, that the dispensation of the fulness of times is made up of all the dispensations that ever have been given since the world began, until this time. (*Millennial Star,* vol. 16, p. 220.)

And Peter speaking with John to the people in the temple, after performing his first miracle, declared:

Repent ye therefore, and be converted, that your sins may

be blotted out, when the times of refreshing shall come from the presence of the Lord;

And he shall send Jesus Christ, which before was preached unto you:

Whom the heaven must receive until the times of restitution of all things, which God hath spoken by the mouth of all his holy prophets since the world began. (Acts 3:19-21.)

And here it may be recalled that after Christ ascended into heaven leaving his Apostles dazed and bewildered, looking "stedfastly toward heaven as he went up . . . two men stood by them in white apparel; which also said, Ye men of Galilee, why stand ye gazing up into heaven? this same Jesus, which is taken up from you into heaven, shall so come in like manner as ye have seen him go into heaven." (*Ibid.*, 1:10-11.)

The Age of Spiritual Darkness

So during the long centuries that followed the apostasy from the Gospel of the Primitive Church and the loss of the Holy Priesthood of God, men wandered in spiritual darkness. Priestcraft was rife. Men again died in spiritual poverty. They had much of the letter of the law, but the vivifying spirit which gives life to the law, the Holy Ghost which bears record of the Father and of the Son (D&C 20:27), were not among men; ". . . the letter killeth, but the spirit giveth life." (2 Cor. 3:6.) There were in the earth, during all these spiritually turbulent centuries, millions of good men. They lived as best they knew. But not having the Gospel in its fulness nor the Priesthood with its powers and authorities, they could not "do all things whatsoever the Lord their God shall command them." (Abraham 3:25.)

Thus was the condition of men at the beginning of the last century. The people must have the light. The Fulness of Times was drawing nigh as predicted by the prophets and by Jesus himself. Another dispensation must be introduced to bring salvation to the living and dead, and under the prophecies this would be the last dispensation, with its tremendous responsibilities to the countless living and the innumerable dead. This was to be the time declared by Peter, "the times of restitution of all things, which God hath spoken by the mouth of all his holy prophets since the world began." (Acts 3:21.)

The Opening of the Dispensation of the Fulness of Times

Pricked with an inspired longing to serve God properly and bewildered by the conflicting claims of sectarian ministers, the young boy Joseph, not yet fifteen years old, read the sovereign formula:

If any of you lack wisdom, let him ask of God, that giveth to all men liberally, and upbraideth not; and it shall be given him. (James 1:5.)

In the faith which James prescribes—"faith, nothing wavering. For he that wavereth is like a wave of the sea driven with the wind and tossed" (*ibid.*, 1:6), Joseph went into the woods and prayed. The Father and the Son came to him, in a glorious vision, following an almost life and death personal, physical struggle between Joseph and the powers of evil. The Father introduced the Son with essentially that same solemn presentation he used at the baptism of the Son by John (Matt. 3:13-17; Mark 1:9-11; Luke 3:21-23), at the time of the Transfiguration with Peter, James and John (Matt. 17:1-15; Mark 9:2-13; Luke 9:28-36), and at the time Christ visited the Nephites after his resurrection (3 Nephi 11:1-7)—"This is My Beloved Son. Hear Him!"

The boy as soon 'as he got possession of himself' asked the question on which he wished wisdom—which of the contending sects should he join.

I was answered that I must join none of them, for they

were all wrong; and the Personage who addressed me said that
all their creeds were an abomination in his sight; that those
professors were all corrupt; that: "they draw near to me with
their lips, but their hearts are far from me, they teach for doctrines the commandments of men, having a form of godliness, but
they deny the power thereof."

He again forbade me to join with any of them; and many
other things did he say unto me, which I cannot write at this
time. (P. of G. P., Joseph Smith, 2:19-20.)

The Father and Son thus appeared together on earth
for the first recorded time since the day of the visitation to the ancient Nephites. The door had opened on the
last dispensation, the Dispensation of the Fulness of
Times.

Nine years from the time of the First Vision, the
Holy Priesthood of God was restored, first the Aaronic
and then the Melchizedek.

Ten years after the First Vision (the Book of Mormon having meanwhile been translated and printed) The
Church of Jesus Christ of Latter-day Saints was organized.

The Dispensation of the Fulness of Times was now
ushered in.

The Restitution of All Things

The young boy Prophet, taught by the experience of
the First Vision, went again and again to the Lord for
wisdom and guidance, and beginning in 1829, revelation
after revelation poured in upon him, giving minute direction, admonition, commendation, reproof when necessary.
The Lord was squaring away his Church for the great
burdens it must carry.

There are certain ordinances and blessings indis-
pensable to the salvation of man in the celestial kingdom.

Baptism

Jesus came to the Jordan to be baptized of John; but John forbade him, saying: "I have need to be baptized of thee, and comest thou to me?" And Jesus answered: "Suffer it to be so now: for thus it becometh us to fulfil all righteousness." (Matt. 3:13-15; Mark 1:9-11; Luke 3:21-23; and see for full discussion, 2 Nephi 31:4 ff.)

Later Jesus declared to Nicodemus:

Except a man be born of water and of the Spirit, he cannot enter into the kingdom of God. (John 3:5.)

Christ, giving his final charge to his Apostles, directed:

Go ye into all the world, and preach the gospel to every creature.

He that believeth and is baptized shall be saved; but he that believeth not shall be damned. (Mark 16:15-16.)

All power is given unto me in heaven and in earth.

Go ye therefore, and teach all nations, baptizing them in the name of the Father, and of the Son, and of the Holy Ghost:

Teaching them to observe all things whatsoever I have commanded you: and, lo, I am with you alway, even unto the end of the world. Amen. (Matt. 28:18-20.)

Thus baptism is essential for entry into the kingdom of God. (D & C 76:50 ff.) It must obviously be performed by those having authority. None are exempt, even the Christ himself being baptized. The authority to baptize was conferred upon Joseph and Oliver on the banks of the Susquehanna River, by John the Baptist; the precise formula to be used in this ordinance (one of the three formulae which the Lord has given to us in this day, the other two being the blessing on the bread and on the wine) had been given shortly before. (*Ibid.*, 20:73 ff.)

Baptism for the Dead

Then came a clarification on baptism that had been wanting since Paul had put his rhetorical question to

the Corinthians, in his great sermon on the resurrection:
"Else what shall they do which are baptized for the dead,
if the dead rise not at all? why are they then baptized
for the dead?" (1 Cor. 15:29.)

The Lord now again revealed the principle of vicarious work for the dead—a principle lost since the early
Christian days. He made clear that the ordinance of
baptism should be performed vicariously for the dead
(D & C 127:4 ff.; 128), in order that they might enter the
celestial kingdom. (*Ibid.*, 76:50 ff.)

For, as the Prophet declared:

> . . . we without them [the dead] cannot be made perfect;
> neither can they without us be made perfect. Neither can they
> nor we be made perfect without those who have died in the gospel
> also; for it is necessary in the ushering in of the dispensation of
> the fulness of times, which dispensation is now beginning to
> usher in, that a whole, complete and perfect union, and welding
> together of dispensations, and keys, and powers, and glories
> should take place, and be revealed from the days of Adam even
> to the present time. And not only this, but those things which
> never have been revealed from the foundation of the world, but
> have been kept hid from the wise and prudent, shall be revealed
> unto babes and sucklings in this, the dispensation of the fulness
> of times. (*Ibid.*, 128:18.)

The Holy Ghost

The conferring and reception of the Holy Ghost,
which bears record of the Father and the Son must be
again provided for. The Holy Ghost was promised to
the Apostles by the Savior in the Passover chamber (John
14), but he explained that "if I go not away, the Comforter will not come unto you." (*Ibid.*, 16:7.) Just before
his ascension, Jesus again promised them the Holy Ghost,
which was to come to them, "not many days hence."
(Acts 1:5.) On the day of Pentecost, the Holy Ghost
came with a sound like the "rushing mighty wind," and
"appeared unto them cloven tongues like as of fire, and

it sat upon each of them," and miraculous manifestations followed. (*Ibid.*, 2:1 ff.)

As to how necessary the power of the Holy Ghost is, may be gathered from the following scriptures which speak of his functions. Discoursing on the Comforter to his Apostles in the Passover chamber Jesus said:

> But the Comforter, which is the Holy Ghost, whom the Father will send in my name, he shall teach you all things, and bring all things to your remembrance, whatsoever I have said unto you. . . .
>
> But when the Comforter is come, whom I will send unto you from the Father, even the Spirit of truth, which proceedeth from the Father, he shall testify of me. (John 14:26, 15:26.)

In this dispensation the Prophet Joseph, under divine inspiration, declared, after calling brief attention to the crucifixion and resurrection of the Savior:

> That as many as would believe and be baptized in his holy name, and endure in faith to the end, should be saved—
>
> Not only those who believed after he came in the meridian of time, in the flesh, but all those from the beginning, even as many as were before he came, who believed in the words of the holy prophets, who spake as they were inspired by the gift of the Holy Ghost, who truly testified of him in all things, should have eternal life,
>
> As well as those who should come after, who should believe in the gifts and callings of God by the Holy Ghost, which beareth record of the Father and of the Son. (D & C 20:25-27.)

The power to confer the Holy Ghost and its gifts was again given to men (*ibid.*, 20:43; 39:23; 49:14); it was a part of the restitution of all things prophesied by Peter. (Acts 3:21.) This essential part of the plan of salvation is again provided for.

The Sealing Power

On the occasion of Peter's testimony of the Christ in the region of Caesarea Philippi, Jesus promised him the keys of the kingdom of heaven, that "whatsoever thou shalt bind on earth shall be bound in heaven: and whatsoever thou shalt loose on earth shall be loosed in heaven." (Matt. 16:19.) A little later in Capernaum, speaking to his disciples, he affirmed:

> Verily I say unto you, Whatsoever ye shall bind on earth shall be bound in heaven: and whatsoever ye shall loose on earth shall be loosed in heaven. (*Ibid.*, 18:18.)

On this hemisphere, the Lord conferred the same power upon Nephi, the son of Helaman:

> Behold, I give unto you power, that whatsoever ye shall seal on earth shall be sealed in heaven; and whatsoever ye shall loose on earth shall be loosed in heaven. (Helaman 10:7.)

The Prophet Joseph declared as to the sealing power:

> Nevertheless, in all ages of the world, whenever the Lord has given a dispensation of the priesthood to any man by actual revelation, or any set of men, this power has always been given. (D & C 128:9.)

The Lord expressly conferred the power on the Patriarch Hyrum Smith:

> That whoever he blesses shall be blessed, and whoever he curses shall be cursed; that whatsoever he shall bind on earth shall be bound in heaven; and whatsoever he shall loose on earth shall be loosed in heaven. (*Ibid.*, 124:93.)

Upon the Prophet himself the Lord conferred this power in these words:

> Whatsoever you seal on earth shall be sealed in heaven; and whatsoever you bind on earth, in my name and by my word, saith the Lord, it shall be eternally bound in the heavens; and whosesoever sins you remit on earth shall be remitted eternally in the heavens; and whosesoever sins you retain on earth shall be retained in heaven.

And again, verily I say, whomsoever you bless I will bless, and whomsoever you curse I will curse, saith the Lord; for I, the Lord, am thy God. (*Ibid.*, 132:46-47.)

Thus the sealing power has been restored, a part of the restitution of all things which were to come in this, the last dispensation.

Eternity of Family Relationship

In connection with this sealing power, the eternity of the marriage covenant and of the family relationship should be noted.

During the last day Jesus spent in the temple before his crucifixion, the Sadducees, who denied the resurrection, came to him questioning which of seven brothers each of whom a woman had married in succession, following the death of the one preceding, should have this woman as a wife in the resurrection. This colloquy is usually cited to the point covered by the reply of Jesus that they erred, "for in the resurrection they neither marry, nor are given in marriage, but are as the angels of God in heaven." (Matt. 22:23-33; Mark 12:18-27; Luke 20:27-38.)

But the incident may also be understood as showing that the Sadducees recognized by their question that they who believed in the resurrection believed also in the continuation of the relation of husband and wife after death, and that the reply of Jesus went merely to the point that this post-resurrection relationship of man and wife must be perfected before the resurrection.

And the perpetuation of this family relationship of man and wife in eternity connotes the relationship there of parent and child also, as between them and their children.

First quoting the final recorded words of Malachi, "Behold, I will send you Elijah the prophet before the coming of the great and dreadful day of the Lord: and he shall turn the heart of the fathers to the children, and the heart of the children to their fathers, lest I come and smite the earth with a curse" (Mal. 4:5-6), the Prophet Joseph said:

> I might have rendered a plainer translation to this, but it is sufficiently plain to suit my purpose as it stands. It is sufficient to know, in this case, that the earth will be smitten with a curse unless there is a welding link of some kind or other between the fathers and the children, upon some subject or other—and behold what is that subject? It is the baptism for the dead. For we without them cannot be made perfect; neither can they without us be made perfect. (D & C 128:18.)

And with reference to the work for the dead, referring to the recording of baptisms, the Prophet made the following record:

> Verily, thus saith the Lord unto you concerning your dead: When any of you are baptized for your dead, let there be a recorder, and let him be eye-witness of your baptisms; let him hear with his ears, that he may testify of a truth, saith the Lord;
> That in all your recordings it may be recorded in heaven; whatsoever you bind on earth, may be bound in heaven; whatsoever you loose on earth, may be loosed in heaven. (*Ibid.*, 127:6-7.)

Thus the sealing power conferred upon the Prophet Joseph and passed from him down through his successors as Presidents of the Church (and the Lord said, "there is never but one on the earth at a time on whom this power and the keys of this priesthood are conferred" [*ibid.*, 132:7]), enables husband to be sealed to wife, parent to child and child to parent, in a union of a family relationship that shall last through time and all eternity, in a never ending existence of joy and bliss divine.

This sealing power with its vast and multiple uses, is thus brought to earth as part of the restitution of all things prophesied by Peter.

Restoration of the Keys of Former Dispensations

In the great vision to the Prophet and Oliver in the Kirtland Temple, the Prophet records, after picturing the glorious vision of the Christ:

After this vision closed, the heavens were again opened unto us; and Moses appeared before us, and committed unto us the keys of the gathering of Israel from the four parts of the earth, and the leading of the ten tribes from the land of the north.

After this, Elias appeared, and committed the dispensation of the gospel of Abraham, saying that in us and our seed all generations after us should be blessed.

After this vision had closed, another great and glorious vision burst upon us; for Elijah the prophet, who was taken to heaven without tasting death, stood before us, and said:

Behold, the time has fully come, which was spoken of by the mouth of Malachi—testifying that he [Elijah] should be sent, before the great and dreadful day of the Lord come—

To turn the hearts of the fathers to the children, and the children to the fathers, lest the whole earth be smitten with a curse—

Therefore, the keys of this dispensation are committed into your hands; and by this ye may know that the great and dreadful day of the Lord is near, even at the doors. (*Ibid.*, 110:11-16.)

Finally, we may add the great testimony of the Prophet Joseph and Sidney Rigdon at Hiram, after which the Lord revealed to them the three great glories to which men might go in the hereafter:

And while we meditated upon these things, the Lord touched the eyes of our understandings and they were opened, and the glory of the Lord shone round about.

And we beheld the glory of the Son, on the right hand of the Father, and received of his fulness;

And saw the holy angels, and them who are sanctified before his throne, worshiping God, and the Lamb, who worship him forever and ever.

And now, after the many testimonies which have been given of him, this is the testimony, last of all, which we give of him: That he lives!

For we saw him, even on the right hand of God; and we heard the voice bearing record that he is the Only Begotten of the Father—

That by him, and through him, and of him, the worlds are and were created, and the inhabitants thereof are begotten sons and daughters unto God. (*Ibid.*, 76:19-24.)

Thus principle after principle, ordinance after ordinance (not only those named, but others) dealing with the children of God and their destiny in the hereafter have been restored in this restitution of all things in this the last dispensation, the Dispensation of the Fulness of Times.

As we ponder these great truths, we are burdened with the thought of how vast is the service and how great is the responsibility of this Dispensation of the Fulness of Times that carries in it the salvation and exaltation of billions of spirits who during the ages since Adam, have come to the earth and taken mortal bodies, and have died without the opportunity to "prove" themselves, that they might "have glory added upon their heads for ever and ever"; and how vast also the service and great the responsibility of bringing the Gospel to the billions now on the earth, and still coming in multitudes, that they may "prove" themselves likewise.

For to us in our day has come the same commandment and commission that was given to Christ's own Apostles on the day of his ascension. The Lord has said to us:

Go ye into all the world, preach the gospel to every creature, acting in the authority which I have given you, baptizing in the name of the Father, and of the Son, and of the Holy Ghost.

And he that believeth and is baptized shall be saved, and he that believeth not shall be damned.

And he that believeth shall be blest with signs following, even as it is written.

And unto you it shall be given to know the signs of the times, and the signs of the coming of the Son of Man;

And of as many as the Father shall bear record, to you shall be given power to seal them up unto eternal life. Amen. (*Ibid.*, 68:8-12.)

God give us the strength, the wisdom, the power and his inspiration and revelation, which we need to obey this command of the Almighty to us.

"And she brought forth her firstborn son, and wrapped him in swaddling clothes, and laid him in a manger; because there was no room for them in the inn."

Luke 2:7

The Nativity

BROTHERS and sisters, all, brothers and sisters of our Elder Brother, Jesus, the Christ: Into what a world of meaning and relationship reaching back into the eternities, and reaching forward into the eternities to come, does that statement of fact, which has been revealed to us, take us. I realize, more fully than you, how hopelessly inadequate I am to try to develop the eternal truths of life behind this relationship. My words are wholly inadequate. I shall not even attempt it. I come back to the simple fact that I can somehow understand, merely the birth to Mary the Virgin. The Divine Conception I do not understand. But I know it existed and I take it on faith and the knowledge which has come to me from it.

At the Christmas Season of the year, the air, the churches will be filled with expressions of adoration, of reverence, and of worship. It is for us to see that in the days and the months and the years to come these do not become, as I fear sometimes they do in the world, mere hollow memories, hollow reverence, hollow worship, as we go about our daily tasks. We must live with these eternal facts and with the eternal relationship to which I have already referred. From that lowly cottage on the outskirts of Jerusalem under the circumstances which the Holy Writ tells us about, came him who was to be and was the Savior of the world.

Judgment by the Father in Mercy

As I get older and come nearer to the day when I shall go to meet him, I become more and more impressed with his boundless, eternal love, and mercy, and charity. Those great qualities, to me, almost absorb all else that I know and can think about him. I have come to feel that

there are two great principles which shall govern our
meeting with him and the Father, hereafter. In his
mercy, in his tenderness, in his love, in his experience
which came to him as a mortal being, out of all of this
there will come his judgment. We shall have all of the
reward that love and mercy and tenderness and divine
relationship can give for our services here on earth. We
shall receive the punishments, and those only, which infinite justice require as they are tempered by the love
and by the mercy and by the charity and by the experience
not only of the Christ, but of the Father who, if we
understand correctly, passed through those experiences
which Christ, himself, lived through.

I become more and more impressed with the great
truths expressed by Peter, facing the synagogue, on a
charge of having healed a cripple. He was to be penalized
for restoring health and when asked, as you all know, by
what name he did this, he stated, "By the name of Jesus
Christ of Nazareth, whom ye crucified. . . ," and added,
"for there is none other name under heaven given among
men, whereby we must be saved."

We must never forget that. We must cling to the
knowledge we have of the Master. We must hold him in
reverence and in worship, knowing that we can come to
the Father only through his Son.

Reflect Upon His Love

May God increase this testimony to us day by day,
the testimony that I bear witness to you; help us to live,
day by day, as he would have us live; help us to reflect,
truly, upon him and his work, his love, his mercy, his
charity—that consistent with our humility we may day
by day grow more nearly like him. I bear my witness
that Jesus of Nazareth is Jesus the Christ, born in the
lowly cottage in the humblest of circumstances, to go for-

ward and be the Savior of mankind; that he lived, he
taught, he suffered, he endured crucifixion, was martyred,
was buried in the tomb, and the morning of the third day
rose, a resurrected Being, having lived out the full measure of the mission for which he came to this earth. I bear
my testimony that the great truths and the Priesthood
which he left on the earth disappeared, and that these had
to be restored.   I bear my testimony that this restoration
was made through the Prophet Joseph.

I pray again that our lives may be so lived that
when we get to the other side we may join our loved ones
who have gone before, loved ones faithful in the Lord,
and that we may meet there, as the plan provides, with
our Master, our Savior, our Elder Brother and with our
Heavenly Father.

"... And it came to pass in those days, that there went out a decree from Caesar Augustus, that all the world should be taxed...."

Luke 2:1

Palestine at the Time of the Savior's Birth

A S ONE approaches the life and teachings—the service and work of the Master—one moves towards the fountain from which mortals drink the truths of eternity that never change nor alter however much men's concepts, men's understandings, may change.

The All-Wise may find it necessary in one period of the existence of mortality on this earth, in order to reach us humans, to cause us to view, as it would seem he might, eternal truths now through one facet, so to speak, of the eyes of our understanding, now through another. But while the human so viewing may at one time gather into his mind one impression regarding a truth, its composition it may be, its substance, its dimension, its value, its meaning, and while man may at another time view, so to speak, the truth through another facet of his understanding, yet the ultimate truth remains always the same, never changing, never growing, never shrinking. The difference to the human results, so to speak, only from the different facet through which he looks at the moment.

Of the doubters among us some seem natural doubters requiring little doubting stimulation from others, and others are doubters who are so stimulated by someone else. Both sorts find difficulties in the Gospel that Jesus taught, running from real and fundamental doubts that become almost denials. Others have shadowy doubts which they would like to put out of their minds but have not the strength so to do. These latter doubters particularly, seek (if they search the Holy Scriptures at all, or if they seize upon things which they hear) to find, frequently, small and unimportant matters in order to justify the doubts which they have.

Among the principles which some of these doubters seize upon in their doubting excursions in the teachings of the Savior, is that principle set out in the Gospels about the peace which the Savior may afford to those who believe in him. They recall that those who heralded the birth of the Savior announced:

And there were in the same country shepherds abiding in the field, keeping watch over their flock by night.

And, lo, the angel of the Lord came upon them, and the glory of the Lord shone round about them: and they were sore afraid.

And the angel said unto them, Fear not: for, behold, I bring you good tidings of great joy, which shall be to all people.

For unto you is born this day in the city of David a Savior, which is Christ the Lord.

And this shall be a sign unto you; Ye shall find the babe wrapped in swaddling clothes, lying in a manger.

And suddenly there was with the angel a multitude of the heavenly host praising God, and saying,

Glory to God in the highest, and on earth peace, good will toward men. (Luke 2:8-14.)

No Peace in the Land

Over the centuries the doctrine has been promulgated in the churches that the Savior so born brought peace into the world, a peace which we will call "secular," as affecting peoples and bodies politic. This ignores the fact that while in the whole Roman Empire there was more peace in it than had been found, perhaps, for other long periods of time before, and while there is some record to justify, in recognition of this, the fact that the temple of Janus appears to have been closed at this time (the rule being that the temple of Janus in Rome should be closed in time of peace), yet the facts are that there was no peace in Palestine itself, but that the Savior was born in a period when there were disturbances, civilly and religiously, far more intense than was usual in this trouble-torn little piece of territory in the Near East.

Students note that here and there, there were instances where the mob sought to kill the Savior, but these are regarded generally as more or less isolated incidents in the life of the Messiah and are not correlated with the general condition in Palestine at that time. Such persons are usually unaware of the general conditions in Palestine at that time. They are not familiar with the fact that in Galilee there was a tremendous non-Israelitish population that was more or less constantly fomenting trouble, often bloody. They are unfamiliar with the fact that the Samaritans, a mongrel group, occupied an area that lay between the northern area of Palestine and the southern area. They are not familiar with the fact that there were more than a "baker's dozen" of Jewish sects, orders, and societies, some of them characterized as possessing religious distinctions, others professional distinctions, a third group political distinctions, and then the great secret society, the Assassins or Sicarii.

Jewish Sects and Orders

As among the Jews only, there were other classes: the Sanhedrin, Proselytes, Publicans, and Hellenists, all forming a conglomerate mass of Jewish sects and orders that made against a unified front that under other circumstances might have been formed inimical to and facing their religious and philosophical ideas. These have been classified as characteristic of both the Old and the New Testament. These various groups were neither merged with nor destroyed by the followers of Christ.

Thus we must seek to find some recognizable and sensible meaning to the "peace" of which the angels spoke in their annunciation to the shepherds.

Politically and civilly the whole history of Palestine as of this time proves that the peace that the angelic hosts spoke of was not the civil and political peace as usually understood among men and as operative in the

political life of peoples and nations. Palestine at this
time was passing through perhaps one of the bloodiest
times that ever occurred in its history, when it came
to the civil and political life. They were divided into
sects, into political parties, and civil tumult and strife
were the rule and not the exception.

A careful reading of the New Testament and ancillary reading of the secular history of Palestine negatives
the idea that the peace of which the hosts spoke was the
secular peace as among nations and peoples. Christ evidently understood this, for he said:

Think not that I am come to send peace on earth: I came not
to send peace, but a sword.

The words immediately following indicate that he
had no intention of applying this to the secular peace as
usually understood. His full statement was:

Think not that I am come to send peace on earth: I came not
to send peace, but a sword.

For I am come to set a man at variance against his father,
and the daughter against her mother, and the daughter in law
against her mother in law.

And a man's foes shall be they of his own household.

He that loveth father or mother more than me is not worthy
of me: and he that loveth son or daughter more than me is not
worthy of me.

And he that taketh not his cross, and followeth after me,
is not worthy of me.

He that findeth his life shall lose it: and he that loseth his
life for my sake shall find it. (Matt. 10:34-39.)

It seems quite clear that the Savior is here describing
the tremendous spiritual struggle that must ensue primarily in the religious thinking of many but also extend-
ing in many cases to the social and political struggle
which must be an incident to the change from the ritualistic worship of Moses to the highly abstract and spiritual concepts that were involved in the great dictum that

hereafter worship was to be with a broken heart and a
contrite spirit.

Revolution of Ritualistic Worship

It is difficult for us of today to realize the tremendous
revolution involved in altering the ritualism of the Law
of Moses into the humble and lowly concept of worship,
not with the sacrificial blood of animals, but with this
broken heart and contrite spirit of the worshiper.

It is an interesting reflection that up to the time
of Christ, apparently, the peoples of the world, not alone
Israel, but seemingly all pagan nations, worshiped with
the ritual which in reality, but usually unconsciously,
looked forward to the sacrifice of the Son by substituting
animal sacrifice as under the Mosaic Law and reaching
even to the sacrifice of human beings under the great pagan religions of the earth.

The sacrifice was always vicarious. Animals were,
with some, sacrificed, as under the Mosaic Law, for the
sins of the individual and for the sins of the people, and
among other and pagan religions, human sacrifice was
made for the same purpose, but it was always a vicarious
sacrifice, apparently with little actual sacrifice except for
the value of the animal sacrificed, by the individuals
themselves, to cancel the debit, so to speak, against their
lives and living in the eyes of the Almighty One. The
sinner seemingly, in general, took on no obligation and
considered himself under no obligation to abandon his
sins, but took on only the obligation to offer sacrifice
therefor.

But under the new covenant that came in with
Christ, the sinner must offer the sacrifice out of his
own life, not by offering the blood of some other creature;
he must give up his sins, he must repent, he himself
must make the sacrifice, and that sacrifice was calculated

to reach out into the life of the sinner in the future so that he would become a better and changed man.

This was a great evolutionary and revolutionary step in the development of righteousness among men. It moved from a vicarious offering for the sin of the past, with no obligation to abandon the sin in the future, to the personal obligation of the individual for his wrong-doing, including not only something for the past, but also the abandonment of the obligation of purchasing forgiveness in the future by a repetition of the same vicarious offering but with no accompanying resolution himself to abandon the sin in the future.

Forgiveness of Sins Based on Repentance

It is not to be wondered at that in establishing this great revolutionary principle there was to be the bitterest war in the minds and the consciences of the people, in moving from a life where forgiveness of wrongdoing by the individual might be purchased by the sinner through the vicarious offering of the lifeblood of some other creature, moving from that sacrifice to where the sinner had to acknowledge his sin and then abandon it and thereby make unnecessary any future vicarious sacrifice for the sin committed.

Clearly from the standpoint of the light that has come to us through modern revelation that began with the Divine Sacrifice of the Son for the sins of all men, to the present situation and condition of men where every sinner must answer for the sins which he has committed and not only answer for those of the past for which he makes answer, but have a true repentance by an absti-nence in the future of a repetition of the sins of the past, under the modern law, every sinner so repenting, every sinner so sorrowing for the past by an abandonment of the practices of the past, moves into a new world where, with proper covenants, he thrusts away out of his life the wrongs of the past and moves into this new world, following the teachings of the great Master who declared, "I am the way, the life, the light, and the truth" of the world.

"... Fear not: for, behold, I bring you good tidings of great joy, which shall be to all people."

Luke 2:10

Some Christmas Messages

MAY THE joy, the peace, the blessings of the Season be unto you!

They have joy who have righteousness; peace, who know no hatred; blessings, who covet not their neighbor's.

Out of the Passover chamber, as he prepares to sacrifice himself for the sins of the world, comes Christ's celestial voice, declaring his bequest to all men of all times:

Peace I leave with you, my peace I give unto you: not as the world giveth, give I unto you. Let not your heart be troubled, neither let it be afraid.

May this full blessing descend upon you and yours, now and in the days to come.

Out from the shut-in walls of the city, went the wise men, wished on their way by the deceit and cunning of the crafty Herod,—out they went into the way that led to the Christ Child in the manger in Bethlehem, out into the freedom of body and soul had by those who serve the Lord and keep his commandments.

Years later the Christ was to say to the multitudes that gathered around him on the Mount:

Enter ye in at the strait gate. . . .
Because strait is the gate, and narrow is the way, which leadeth unto life, and few there be that find it.

May the Lord help all of us to enter that strait gate and tread that narrow way.

Still the Christian sees, with the inner light of the spirit, the shepherds watching by night their flocks on the hillside, with the angel of the Lord, clothed in glory, proclaiming to them the good tidings. Still, his spirit listening, the Christian hears the angel's message and the divine blessing first carolled by the heavenly hosts:

Glory to God in the highest, and on earth peace, good will toward men.

Still the Christian glimpses the infant Christ lying in a manger, wrapped in swaddling clothes, and the mother, Mary, and the patient, trusting Joseph.

May the Lord grant to us the power so to live as never to lose this vision.

Again it is Christmas—remembrancer of Jesus, son of Mary, Son of God.

Jesus the Christ: In the beginning with God; himself God; author of our salvation and exaltation; creator of the world and all that in it is; the light and life of the world; our Savior dying on the cross for us; our intercessor with the Father, who time and again said: "This is my beloved Son; hear him"; bestower of infinite love and mercy; soul of compassion and forgiveness; healer of sick bodies and broken hearts; friend of the friendless; giver of divine peace, his peace.

God grant to each of us this knowledge, this testimony.

Greetings this Christmastide!

Nearly two millenniums ago, appeared in the heavens the Star of Bethlehem, God's blazing herald to his earthly children the world round, proclaiming that to earth had come the Only Begotten to carry out his great mission of the redemption of mankind. In the west, darkness fled the heavens for a day, a night, and another day. God's promise to his children through his prophets from the beginning was being fulfilled, heavenly choirs attended, singing praises and proclaiming peace.

The light of the world was come to it, shedding its life-giving rays into the souls of men, to their salvation. Death would be conquered, the grave become a couch to rest the weary body, waiting for the trump of the resurrection morn.

Peace had come to the troubled hearts of the poor, humility to the haughty pride of the rich.

Completed finally on the cross would be the plan of God's work and glory, to bring to pass the immortality and eternal life of man.

God grant this boon to all of us.

In the center of God's great plan of earth's creation, of human mortality and experience, of final redemption, in every part and place of man's divinely decreed destiny, stands Jesus the Christ in the eternal majesty of Godhood.

His coming was heralded by heavenly choirs, and witnessed by a guiding star of great magnitude in the firmament, yet was he cradled in a manger; the inn-keeper found in the inn no room for the birth of Divinity.

He grew to manhood as a lowly carpenter.

He lived and died to atone for the Fall, so redeeming us from eternal burial in the tomb, and so bringing within the grasp of every one of God's children born to earth, immortality and eternal life—the work and glory of God.

He is the way, the life, and the light of the world.

His is the only "name under heaven given among men, whereby we must be saved," for "as in Adam all die, even so in Christ shall all be made alive."

May the Holy Ghost increasingly bear record of this to each and all of us, to our salvation and exaltation.

Again nears the day of remembrance of when, forth
from the infinite glory and power of the throne of God
to be born to mortality in the manger-cradle in Bethlehem, came him thenceforth to be called son of Mary,
Son of man, Son of God, Jesus the Christ, the Only
Begotten of the Father.   God incarnate, he came not to
royal courts, not to the palace of the rich, not to the home
of earthly honor nor of vaunted learning of the wise and
powerful, but to the humility of a lowly cottage of a village carpenter, to the home of one of us common folk.

He descended below all things that he might rise to
take even captivity captive,—

O death, where is thy sting?   O grave, where is thy victory?

Manhood found him out with the poor, the down-
trodden, the oppressed, the sick, the afflicted of the earth
in body and spirit, teaching his truth to their peace, their
comfort, their eternal salvation and exaltation, their
everlasting happiness.

The fishermen and the common folk heard, loved,
and followed; the high and powerful turned their backs,
scorning, deriding, reviling; they walked not after him.

He chose the foolish things to confound the wise; the
weak to confound the mighty.   He blessed the poor in
spirit, promised comfort to them that mourn.   He blessed
them that hungered and thirsted for righteousness and
them that are merciful.   He declared the peacemakers
should be called the children of God; the pure in heart
should see God.   He blessed the persecuted for righteousness' sake, for theirs would be the kingdom of God.   He
blessed the meek to inherit the earth.

He speaks to all of us who suffer for his sake, bidding
us to come to him:

Come unto me, all ye that labour and are heavy laden, and I will give you rest.

Take my yoke upon you, and learn of me; for I am meek and lowly in heart: and ye shall find rest unto your souls.

For my yoke is easy, and my burden is light.

So, to now and hereafter while time flows on, the Author of our being and of our salvation speaks. His words are the assurance of the lowly and humble; the hope of the mighty and great.

God help us this Christmas time to know the divine virtue of the spiritual ointment which, to ease our wounded souls, his Son gave us as his mortality was speeding to its end. It was in the Upper Chamber the night before he poured out his life blood on the cross, so overcoming the world, an Atoning Sacrifice for the Fall of Adam and for your sins and for mine, that he bestowed this priceless heritage upon his disciples grouped around him, upon all men then and since living, and upon those hereafter to be born:

Peace I leave with you, my peace I give unto you: not as the world giveth, give I unto you. Let not your heart be troubled, neither let it be afraid.

God grant it may so be.

Almost two thousand years ago, the angel of the
Lord, enveloped in his glory, brought to the lowly, "sore
afraid" shepherds, night-watching their flocks on the
hills near Bethlehem, Judea, "good tidings of great joy"
for the peoples of the earth, and declared that on that day
was born "a Savior, which is Christ the Lord." And suddenly there was with the angel a multitude of the heavenly host praising God and saying: "Glory to God in the
highest, and on earth peace, good will toward men."
Isaiah's "Prince of Peace" had come.

In the temple precincts, during the last week of his
mortality, a lawyer questioned him,—"Which is the great
commandment in the law?" Jesus answered, quoting the
law from the days of Moses. The first commandment was
to love the Lord our God with one's whole soul; and the
second was like unto it, to love one's neighbor as one's
self, for on these two hang all the law and the prophets.

Israel, using the free agency God gave them, forgot
the commandment of Moses, and heeded not the words of
Jesus. For centuries they have been dispersed among the
peoples of the earth, driven and persecuted. Peace has
fled from them. Till now, equally unheeding, have been
the men and peoples of the earth, Christian and pagan
alike, vainly seeking the peace proclaimed by the heavenly
host, which has found no home among them.

Who can plumb the depths or climb the heights of
the soul-filling joy of his peace that will come with its
blessings and glory when we live the law, when every
knee shall bow and every tongue confess to God, that
Jesus Christ is Lord, to the glory of God the Father.

The peace, yet vainly sought by men, peoples, and
nations, patiently awaits our offering, on the altar of
sacrifice, our selfishness, greed, ambition, our thirst for

unrighteous power and dominion (still nourished in the minds of men), that peace eagerly, hopefully looks for the day of our living the great commandments,—our soul-filling love of God, our love of neighbor as ourselves.

There will be no permanent peace, till the sacrifice is made and the commandments lived.

God give us the faith and the power to plant Christ's promised peace in our hearts, that we may assure our own salvation and exaltation, and so stand guiltless before the Lord for the wickedness and warfare of the nations.

Once more the earth has circled her orbit back to the recurring day when the glory of the Lord shone round the shepherds on the hills and an angel brought to them good tidings of great joy to all people. For on that day Christ the Lord was born. Suddenly there was with the angel a multitude of the heavenly host praising God and saying:

Glory to God in the highest, and on earth peace, good will toward men.

On the last night of his mortality, Jesus, praying in the Garden to the Father, reminded the Father of their lives together in heaven before Jesus came to make the Atonement. He pleaded for help in his coming sacrifice:

O Father, glorify thou me with thine own self with the glory which I had with thee before the world was.

From that eternity through to the hour he now faced he had done the will, rendered the service to the Father; created worlds without number and peopled them; had guided the Father's children in their free agency; had sought to save them and lead them to exaltation; had prepared to give his own life for their redemption and exaltation; and now a final request at this critical, sacred hour:

Father, I will that they also, whom thou hast given me, be with me where I am; that they may behold my glory, which thou hast given me: for thou lovedst me before the foundation of the world.

As mortal death cast its shadow ahead and enshrouded him, there passed before him all he had done for our Father's children, then the final offering, even the

sacrifice of mortal life itself for their sakes. He gazed upon Jerusalem, the summation of his hopes, his struggles,
his admonitions, his pleadings, of all his services. There
came to him, in poignant grief, the knowledge that Jerusalem would continue to scourge and persecute the prophets and the wise men sent to them, to crucify and kill
them, that upon Jerusalem would "come all the righteous
blood shed upon the earth, from the blood of righteous
Abel unto the blood of Zacharias son of Barachias, whom
ye slew between the temple and the altar." Then he cried
out from the depths of his soul:

O Jerusalem, Jerusalem, thou that killest the prophets, and
stonest them which are sent unto thee, how often would I have
gathered thy children together, even as a hen gathereth her
chickens under her wings, and ye would not!
Behold, your house is left unto you desolate.

But God watches over all. Never did he let the
righteous all go to destruction. More than once his divine
love and mercy intervened to save an obedient remnant:

First, Noah and his family, saved by the hand of
God from the engulfing flood waters that drowned the
world so that the earth might be repeopled.

Next, Moses, prophet-leader, law-giver for all peoples since born, led Israel miraculously treading the
depths of the Red Sea dry-shod, then wandering for forty
years in the Wilderness of Sinai, till, tested and purified,
they entered the Promised Land, free and worshiping
the true God.

Then the righteous of Israel, led back to the Holy
Land from captivity, that worship of the true God might
still be found on his footstool.

Then, modern Israel, fleeing the oppressions and
persecutions of the emissaries of unrighteousness, out
from Nauvoo over the frozen waters and sloughs of the
mighty Mississippi, into the wilds of the trackless plains

of America, the abode of wild beasts and savage Indians, into and through the mountain fastnesses of the Rockies, out into the bleak and barren embraces of the Great American Desert. They came for conscience sake and for freedom. They trekked a thousand miles. The Lord was their companion.

They toiled; they knew privation and want, success and discouragement; they built factories and tamed the earth; they built villages, towns and cities, churches, temples, and schools; they worshiped.

Another righteous remnant had been saved. The Lord had again vindicated his plans and purposes.

May God bless the righteous and the sinners unto repentance. May he bless you always.

Simeon declared the Christ:

Then took he him up in his arms, and blessed God, and said,
Lord, now lettest thou thy servant depart in peace, accord-
ing to thy word:
For mine eyes have seen thy salvation,
Which thou hast prepared before the face of all people;
A light to lighten the Gentiles, and the glory of thy people
Israel.   (Luke 2:28-32.)

Once more our minds and hearts and spirits crowd
themselves together in reverent love and adoration for
the birth and life and work of our Lord and Savior, Jesus
Christ. Again we try to comprehend his divinity, his
mortal birth, his life, his mission, the final sacrifice, the
resurrection, that brought to each and all of us the
precious blessings of our destinies. Again we seek to
understand his going back to his eternal home, taking his
place in the Godhead.

God declared his work and his glory are to "bring
to pass the immortality and eternal life of man,"—a
resurrected being, each in the image of God himself, with
eternal progress before him, Jesus declared our destiny
to the multitude on the Mount:

Be ye therefore perfect, even as your Father which is in
heaven is perfect.

Blessed are we that in the earliest days of his ministry, Jesus taught Nicodemus:

For God so loved the world, that he gave his only begotten
Son, that whosoever believeth in him should not perish, but have
everlasting life.

Later he rebuked the disciples, angered because a

Samaritan village refused him lodging, and asking him
to call destructive fire, as did Elias of old, saying to them:

Ye know not what manner of spirit ye are of.
For the Son of man is not come to destroy men's lives, but
to save them.

How blessed we are for his words to the Samaritan
woman, herself a sinner, declaring that the water he had
to give to drink was living water springing up to eternal
life, and whosoever drank of it would never thirst again.

How blessed are we for the eternal words companion
to these, uttered to those who followed him across the
sea, after he had fed with five loaves and two fishes,
five thousand men and their women and children:

I am the bread of life: he that cometh to me shall never
hunger; and he that believeth on me shall never thirst.

The bread and water that Christ, our Lord gives,
are the spiritual food that can bring salvation and exaltation to every human soul.

How blessed are we for our own credo: "We believe
that through the Atonement of Christ, all mankind may
be saved, by obedience to the laws and ordinances of the
Gospel,"—all mankind may be saved, those that have
lived from the beginning, through our work for the dead,
those now living and those to be born in the future
through our spread of the Gospel, till God's plan is completely fulfilled.

How blessed are we to have this never dimming,
always glowing hope, and the eternal knowledge that
belongs to us, to comfort us and to urge us on through
life, that we may add to God's declared work and glory
by gaining for ourselves, and for all believers and doers,
the priceless destiny of immortality and eternal life.

May God grant us the power so to live is my prayer
for you.

Ever returning till time shall be no more and we live in eternity, shall yearly come back to us the anniversary of that glorious night when there came to earth our Savior to bring to us redemption and the resurrection.

As the wise men saw the glorious star in the heavens that led to the Infant Christ, so may his worshipers, as they look into the vaulted star-field, see there in spirit that same guiding star which leads to the eternal home of the Royal Son.

As heard the shepherds of old, so may his worshipers, in the humble spirit of silence, hear the heavenly multitude praising God and declaring Christ's message to all the Father's children:

Glory to God in the highest, and on earth peace, good will toward men.

As the shepherds keeping their flocks in the fields hearkened to the angel and hastened to Bethlehem, city of David, where wrapped in swaddling clothes, lying in a manger (the sign the angel promised) they saw the Infant Christ, the Lord, so in sacred contemplation, his worshipers may see the Infant Royal Babe, lying in a manger, King of all born to earth, yet eternally Royal, member of the Godhead, next to God himself.

As the shepherds came from their visit to the Christ, returning to their flocks, "glorifying and praising God for all the things that they had heard and seen, as it was told unto them," so his worshipers, so envisioned, come therefrom to their tasks of daily life, glorifying and praising God for their testimonies and knowledge that Jesus, so born, is the Son of God, his Father and our Father, Christ, the Only Begotten, proclaimed from the beginning.

His worshipers know that Christ is the way, the truth, the life, and the light.

That no one comes to the Father except through Christ.

That in his great prayer, Christ declared that life eternal was to know the Father the only true God, and Jesus Christ whom he had sent.

That Peter declared to the questioning Sanhedrin, that Christ was the only name under heaven given among men whereby they must be saved.

That in the Passover chamber, he said to the Apostles and to us all:

Peace I leave with you, my peace I give unto you: not as the world giveth, give I unto you. Let not your heart be troubled, neither let it be afraid.

To the humble housewife Martha, he declared:

I am the resurrection, and the life: he that believeth in me, though he were dead, yet shall he live:
And whosoever liveth and believeth in me shall never die.

To all which I bear my humble testimony, praying that God will bring to all his children, a sustaining, saving, burning testimony of the Christ and his peace and mission to God's children on this earth.

Again we near the day we celebrate as the anniversary of the birth of our Lord and Savior—Jesus Christ, the Son of God, the Atoning Sacrifice that none but an Infinite Being, the Son of God himself, could offer to redeem man from the Fall, and enable him to bring to pass the great declaration of the Father that "my work and my glory [is] to bring to pass the immortality and eternal life of man."

Born in a stable, cradled in a manger, yet his coming was heralded by a heavenly host, proclaiming to the shepherds, tending their flocks on the hillsides, "Glory to God in the highest, and on earth peace, good will toward men" in fulfillment of the foretelling of the angel to them that "unto you is born this day in the city of David a Savior, which is Christ the Lord."

"Peace on earth,"—not world peace, but the peace he promised in the Upper Chamber to all when he said:

Peace I leave with you, my peace I give unto you: not as the world giveth, give I unto you. Let not your heart be troubled, neither let it be afraid.

The peace that passeth human understanding.

The peace of a "pure heart and a contrite spirit."

The peace of the new sacrifice that replaced the sacrifice of the Law of Moses, where man sought forgiveness for his sins by offering the flesh and blood of animals. Under the new covenant man gained forgiveness by placing on the altar of sacrifice his own unrighteousness, offering to our Heavenly Father the pure heart and contrite spirit.

Each Christian is armed with a sword by which he is to divide the old law from the new covenant, the ritual of sacrifice for the simple righteousness of life; by which he cleaves from his soul all that is base and ignoble in him, and these being destroyed and cast out of his life, then comes the blessed peace from him who promised peace, his peace—not the peace of the world of ease, luxury, idleness, absence of turmoil and strife, but the peace born of the righteous life: the peace that lifts the soul; the peace that, day by day, brings us ever nearer to the home of Eternal Peace, the dwelling place of our Father.

God grant to all of us this peace, which the Lord gives to all who live "godly in Christ Jesus."

*Again we have reached the time in the circling of the years when we have come to the anniversary on which we recognize the birth of him who gave us the Divine Plan through which we may gain salvation and exaltation in the Kingdom of God.

As the years flow by, this earthly anniversary brings to us who love and honor him and recognize him for what he is, a new sense of obligation to him for the Atoning Sacrifice which, in the Meridian of Time, he made to redeem us from the Fall.

To those of us who are increasing in the years of our sojourn and experience here, there comes a deeper and fuller realization of that great Atoning Sacrifice.

Few there are who recognize and appreciate what it is.

Few ever receive the lightning-like flash of light that brings us to even an approximate understanding of the origin of man, the meaning of the Fall, the need for the Atonement, and the birth and mission of Jesus Christ.

Too few of us can appreciate the statement of God himself, when he said:

For behold, this is my work and my glory—to bring to pass the immortality and eternal life of man.

But to all of us there may come a knowledge of the redemption that brings the resurrection to every man born on earth, and the opportunity to grow in righteousness until it brings even the most sinful man unto repentance and within the purview of the Divine Plan of Salvation.

---

*Drafted by J. Reuben Clark, Jr., just prior to his death, to be his 1961 Christmas Message.

Fortunately, the plan is self-operative and does not need to be understood to be effective.

Fortunate they are who glimpse the great value of the redemption and the resurrection.

Fortunate they are who do not need to understand too much nor too clearly, indeed not at all, what the resurrection means and the great blessing it brings to every man and woman born on earth.

May the Lord be good to us and give us knowledge and inspiration and testimony that will enable the great bulk of us to live sufficiently near to that plan that we shall not only be heirs to the self-operative part of that plan, the universal resurrection, but that there may come to us in some measure at least and in sufficient measure so that we shall know of the meaning of the balance of that plan, so that we will be willing to serve him and keep his commandments.

All his purpose, all his aim is bound up in the exaltation of man, a purpose towards which he has worked in all the eternities that have gone before and will work in all those which are to follow after.

God grant that every person born on his footstool shall recognize his earthly responsibilities and shall strive to do his part to fulfill this great, Divine, eternal purpose.

"... Now his parents went to Jerusalem every year at the feast of the passover.
"And when he was twelve years old, they went up to Jerusalem after the custom of the feast. ..."
Luke 2:41-42

The Journey from Nazareth to Jerusalem

I T WAS a spring day at the end of March (near the middle of the seventh Hebrew month, Nisan), the fields were yellowing with the ripening crops, the hills and valleys were covered with wild flowers, all nature was rejoicing, as Joseph and Mary and Jesus, with their kinsfolk and neighbors, left Nazareth with its white rocks and cliffs, splotched with green, and started down through the foothills to the valley floor of the plain of Jezreel, one thousand feet below. They were going to Jerusalem to observe the Passover, as had been their wont over the years, in obedience to the Rabbinical law, commending (and in certain instances requiring) the observance of the feast in Jerusalem by the Levitically clean males of Israel. The women were not legally bound to attend. The feast was a jubilee of great rejoicing, for it marked the anniversary of Israel's delivery from a grievous bondage to the Egyptians, and also her birth as a nation.

This journey has particular significance because it is the first appearance of Jesus in the sacred record, following his return with Mary and Joseph, to Nazareth from Egypt. After this appearance in the temple, the record is silent about the next succeeding eighteen years, when Jesus, being about thirty years old, appears on the banks of the Jordan to be baptized of John.

While history is silent about those first twelve years, we may reasonably know what his life was like. Joseph was a carpenter, and Jesus was undoubtedly learning the trade, for years after, when friends and neighbors for the second time rejected him from Nazareth, they asked: "Is not this the carpenter, the son of Mary . . . ?" (Mark 6:3.)

A Son of the Law

But, "from the first days of its existence, a religious atmosphere surrounded the child of Jewish parents." (Alfred Edersheim, *The Life and Times of Jesus, the Messiah* (Longmans, Green and Co., New York, 1927, Courtesy of David McKay Company, Inc.), Vol I, p. 227 ff.) This would come first from the mother, but the father was under a sacred obligation to teach his son. At the age of five or six the child was sent to school, where he began a regular course, the Bible being the exclusive textbook until the boy was ten years of age. This Bible study began with Leviticus, then passed to the other parts of the Pentateuch, thence to the Prophets, and thence to the Hagiographa—that portion of the Bible not in the law and the prophets. From ages ten to fifteen, the child studied the Mishnah, or traditional law. When he reached the academies of the Rabbis he studied the Gemara or Talmud, but a boy might not enter these till he was fifteen. We have no means of knowing whether or not Jesus attended one of these schools, but the astonishment of the doctors in the temple over his learning would indicate he had received from somewhere, most unusual and profound wisdom and knowledge.

But at twelve years, a boy became a "son of the law," subject to the fasts and under obligation to attend the feasts.

So as these pilgrims wended downward over the foothills in the afternoon (in Palestine the first day of the journey was always a short one), they were a joyous group, chanting as they went, the "Psalms of Ascent" (Psalms 120-134), to the accompaniment of a flute.

As we think of them moving slowly down into the valley with their donkeys laden with necessary supplies, picking their way among the boulders that strewed the path, we cannot escape wondering what were the thoughts of Jesus. That he was exceeding wise, the experience in the temple shows. But was this wisdom earthborn from his studies, or did he have also a spiritual memory that brought to him a recollection of all that had before happened, and a vision to show what was thereafter to happen along this road to Jerusalem, a road richer in incidents of God's dealings with his children, than any other road on the face of the earth?

Memory of the Past and Vision of the Future

As to memory of the past, we do know that during his later Judean ministry, while speaking to the Jews in the treasury to the temple, he declared: "I do nothing of myself; but as my Father hath taught me, I speak these things. . . . I speak that which I have seen with my Father." (John 8:28, 38.) And out on the Mount of Olives, after they had left the Passover chamber, on the night before the crucifixion, Jesus said to his Apostles: "For all things that I have heard of my Father I have made known unto you." (*Ibid.*, 15:15.) Thus in his later ministry, his mind was filled with knowledge gained in his pre-existence.

We do not know the details of their journey to Jerusalem, but they may well have stopped the first night at Nain, where later he raised the son of the widow; or if the start were early enough they might have gone on to Jezreel, once the second capital of the northern kingdom. One wonders if, as he came to Nain, he saw a vision of his future miracle of kindness there. And here we may recall that in pre-vision he said to Peter in the Passover chamber, answering Peter's protestations of faithfulness: "I tell thee, Peter, the cock shall not crow this day, before that thou shalt thrice deny that thou knowest me." (Luke 22:34.) And later, after the resurrection, after they had eaten their early morning meal on the shores of Galilee—Jesus, and Peter, "and Thomas called Didymus, and Nathanael of Cana in Galilee, and the sons of Zebedee, and two other of his disciples," Jesus turning to Peter and signifying by what death Peter should glorify God, said: "Verily, verily, I say unto thee, When thou wast young, thou girdedst thyself, and walkedst whither thou wouldest: but when thou shalt be old, thou shalt stretch forth thy hands, and another shall gird thee, and carry thee whither thou wouldest not." (John 21:2, 18.) And in the great Olivet discourse of the third day of the Passion Week, Jesus vividly describes the terrible scenes of the destruction of Jerusalem by Titus.

When he came to the neighborhood of Jezreel, did he see in vision the disastrous defeat of Josiah on the plain of Esdraelon by Pharaoh Necho, at Megiddo, a defeat so terrible and worked so deeply into the Hebrew heart, that John speaks of the great last battle as Armageddon— "the Hill of Megiddo?" (Rev. 16:16.) Or did he see the earlier conflict in the time of the Judges, when Barak, Deborah the prophetess guiding, defeated Sisera, leading the forces of Jabin, on that same plain of Esdraelon, and did he see again the deed of Jael afterwards? And did there also come before him the iniquities and tragic fate of Ahab and Jezebel, and the Lord's vengeance worked through Elijah against the priests of Baal, and the flight of Elijah to Carmel, the passing of the Lord before Elijah in the "still small voice"? For Jesus was the Lord who spoke to and commanded his ancient prophets.

Journey of the Second Day

But wherever the first night was spent, the start the next morning was early. They now moved on Roman roads, as they passed on southwards toward the city of Samaria. Crossing the headwaters of the River Kishon (which both waters and drains the plains of Esdraelon), they would begin the ascent of the pass over the Carmelite range, the hill slopes probably covered with the yellow flowers of the broom. Villages dotted the high points along the way. They found rich orchards and vineyards on the summit and as they looked around them they could catch, here and there, glimpses of the Mediterranean (off to the west) and looking back to the north, they could see the snowy summit of Mount Hermon. Over to the left as they climbed up the pass, they had seen the rugged volcanic mountains of Gilboa, at the foot of which was fought the great battle between Saul and the Philistines, and where Saul killed himself. To the northeastward was Endor, the place where the witch lived whom Saul consulted, the Lord having failed to direct him, "neither by dreams, nor by Urim, nor by prophets." (1 Sam. 28:6.)

As they went forward over the undulating pass, they crossed a part of the plain of Dothan, where Joseph was sold to the Ishmaelites. Finally, passing the summit, they descended by easy grades to the city of Samaria, located on an isolated hill 300 feet above the surrounding country. Samaria was the next capital of the northern tribes after Shechem. It had been frequently destroyed but now, as Jesus came to it, it was a great city, rebuilt by Herod the Great, with magnificent palaces, temples, and a stadium. The plain surrounding the city was exceedingly fertile, covered with orchards of figs and olives. Its beauty and its future provoked Isaiah to speak of its "glorious beauty, which is on the head of the fat valley, shall be a fading flower, and as the hasty fruit before the summer." (Isa. 28:4.) But here in the years long gone, before this visit, there had been planted a grove of Astarte (Venus), and Jezebel had erected a great temple to that same heathen goddess. Elisha had lived at the foot of the hill on which the city rested; and to this house came Naaman, the Syrian leper, to be healed. Elisha dwelt here when he disclosed to Ahab the plans of the Syrian generals. Here, when Benhadad the Syrian besieged it, was the scene of the great famine, so sore it was that women ate their own sons.

What must have been the feelings of the young Jesus
as he looked at this present magnificence and then recalled
the past, and (it seems it must be) visioned the future!

As the pilgrims went forward they were joined by
others also going to the Passover in Jerusalem.   On
through the day, as newcomers flowed into the group,
they renewed, time and time again, the chant of the
"Psalms of the Ascent." They lived over again in thought
and story, how the Lord had blessed them and delivered
them from Egyptian bondage.   But of all the throng, no
one but he himself knew that that Lord traveled with
them, for we must believe there was with him a spiritual
recollection, a divine knowledge, of the past.

Whether they stopped at Samaria or went on two
hours further to Shechem, we do not know. But they were
traveling over historic ground that reached in incident
clear back to Abraham.   They may, because of the preju-
dice against the Samaritans, have so planned their journey as to pass through Samaria in one day.   But we cannot tell.

The Cradle of Israel

As they journeyed into the midst of Shechem itself,
they came to the very spot where the waters divided,
those flowing to the west into the Great Sea, those to the
east into the Jordan.

The city lies where the two mountains, Ebal and
Gerizim, falling away one from the other, leave a beautiful, fertile valley—the very cradle of Israel. To this valley, running out west and east from the city, came Abraham and Lot, forsaking at the Lord's command their own
country under a promise that this land should be theirs.
Here lived Jacob and his family; Jacob whose name was
here changed to Israel. Here Joshua gathered the people and had them repeat the curses and blessings declared
by Moses in the wilderness—Reuben, Gad, Asher, Zebu-

lun, Dan, and Naphtali to stand upon Mount Ebal for the curses, and Simeon, Levi, Judah, Issachar, Joseph, and Benjamin to stand on Mount Gerizim for the blessings, the Levites repeating the curses and the people shouting amen. Here was consummated the rebellion which divided Israel, after which Jeroboam built Shechem, and brought about the return of idolatry to Israel.

Here in the immediate area was Joseph's tomb; at the eastern foot of the valley is the traditional site of the oak of Abraham, beneath which he built an altar, "the first sanctuary to Jehovah in the Land of Promise," (Cunningham Geikie, *The Holy Land and the Bible*, (Hurst & Co., New York, c. 1883), p. 476), and afterward Joshua built there an altar "under an oak, that was by the sanctuary of the Lord." (Josh. 24:26.) Near to the site of this sanctuary is Jacob's Well.

On the top of Mount Ebal, Joshua placed the stones on which he had written the law. The Samaritans believed the stones were atop Mount Gerizim. On the top of this mountain the Samaritans held their Passover Feast, and the woman of Samaria, years later, said to Jesus at Jacob's Well near the foot of Gerizim: "Our fathers worshipped in this mountain"; to which Jesus replied: "Woman, believe me, the hour cometh, when ye shall neither in this mountain, nor yet at Jerusalem, worship the Father." (John 4:20-21.) The Samaritans claimed that to this mountain Abraham came to offer Isaac as a sacrifice.

As Jesus looked at all these, possibly for the first time with his mortal eyes (as some scholars would have us believe), there must have crowded in upon his consciousness the scenes of the actual events. The divinity that was in him must have reached back into the past even as, when later in his ministry, after the first Passover, he traveled northward through Samaria and stopped at the well to get a drink from the Samaritan woman drawing water from the well, he reached into the past of this sinful woman. As he taught her, and she understood not, he said: "Go, call thy husband, and come hither." "I have no husband," said she. "Thou hast well said, I have no husband," he replied, "for thou hast had five husbands; and he whom thou now hast is not thy husband." (*Ibid.*, 4:4 ff.) If the past was not hidden from him as to the woman, why should it be hidden as to Israel? And, as at twelve he now beheld the well, did he vision the future meeting with the woman and his sermon on the living water?

Journey of the Third Day

But whether the pilgrims stopped at Samaria or at Shechem, or whether before they reached there or after, yet as they went on towards Jerusalem along the Roman road, they passed constantly the places where other great happenings in Israel's history took place.

About halfway, going southward, between Shechem and Bethel lies Shiloh. It was here that Joshua came with the Tabernacle and Ark after he left Gilgal, and it was here that he cast lots for the division of the Promised Land among the tribes. It was from Shiloh that the Benjamites (following the terrible punishment inflicted upon them by Israel for the abuse of the concubine of the Levite), stole the dancing virgins for wives. Here lived Eli and here was trained Samuel; and to Shiloh came the Philistines, and defeated the sons of Eli and carried off the Ark.

As the group moved southward from Shiloh towards Bethel, there would likely join them, increasingly as they neared Jerusalem (for under the Rabbinical law every male Jew over twelve years living within fifteen miles of Jerusalem was obliged to attend the Passover), other pilgrims to the temple and the great feast. And ever as they marched forward over the Roman highway, they would be chanting the sacred Psalms.

On the right, to the westward, shortly after the group left Shiloh, lay the old Ephraimite Gilgal, whence went Elijah and Elisha on their way to the Jordan before Elijah was taken into heaven. From a hill at the side of a wild pass a little farther south, they could look back and still see Mount Hermon with its cap of snow. As they went down the other side of the pass, they traveled through great orchards of fig trees and olives. This was the rich territory of Ephraim.

Sanctuary of Bethel

And then came Bethel, a great sanctuary.

Abraham came to Bethel from Shechem, and again after his return from Egypt. On his first visit he built an altar, to which he returned after Egypt. It was here that Israel assembled when they determined to war on Benjamin for the violation of the concubine of the Levite. It was here also that, after the rebellion of the Ten Tribes, Jeroboam set up one of the two golden calves he made for them to worship, the other calf went to Dan. One can but wonder how shallow must have been Israel's conversion to the true God, to be so easily turned back to Egyptian idolatry. Jehu left the calf though he rooted out Baal, but Josiah broke down the altar and "stamped it small to powder." (2 Kings 23:15.)

To the east and slightly to the south of Bethel, was Ai, and still further south, Ramah and Gibeon. Between these two latter Joshua fought the great battle against the Amorites, when, the day waning, without time to finish his victory, that great warrior cried out, "in the sight of Israel, Sun, stand thou still upon Gibeon; and thou, Moon, in the valley of Ajalon. . . . So the sun stood still in the midst of heaven, and hasted not to go down about a whole day." (Josh. 10:6 ff.)

The growing group was also now near Michmash—
close to where Jonathan with only his armorbearer put
to rout the Philistines, for Jonathan had said: "It may be
that the Lord will work for us: for there is no restraint
to the Lord to save by many or by few." (1 Sam. 14:6 ff.)

Still nearer to Jerusalem was Gibeah, the site of the
shameful deed of Benjamin, and the home and head-
quarters of Saul while he was king.

Arrival in Environs of Jerusalem

The pilgrims were now in the environs of Jerusalem. If they reached there just before the Passover, they
found the roads choked with the tens of thousands who
were coming to the city of David to attend the feast,
bringing with them their burnt and peace offerings, for
none might appear empty. In Jesus' time as many as
256,000 lambs were slain for the Passover. The population of the city at Passover time varied from 2,500,000 to
3,000,000. Many who came camped outside the city;
others found quarters within the city walls with friends
or relatives who hospitably took them in, the guests leaving, as they took their departure, "the skins of the Passover lambs and the vessels which they had used in their
sacred services" (Alfred Edersheim, *The Temple*, (Flem-
ing H. Revell Co., New York, 1874), p. 184) ; still others
went to neighboring towns, Bethphage and Bethany being
mentioned in the Talmud as especially hospitable. The
shouts of greeting that passed between old friends again
meeting; the chanting of the sacred Psalms by the coming
worshipers keyed to a high pitch by their long journey
of anticipation, their outbursts of joy over their ap-
proaching presence in the city of the fathers and their
nearness to the Passover, and their reverent expressions
of gratitude for their ancient deliverance, mingled with
the lowing of the cattle brought for burnt offerings, the
bleating of the sacrificial lambs, the cooing of the doves

brought for peace offerings—all must have merged into a babel of sound never to be forgotten, and, heard from afar, must have been like the roar of a distant waterfall.

We must believe that Joseph and Mary, and the youth Jesus, of the royal lineage of David, had awaiting them somewhere a joyous welcome from friends honored in the chance to give them food and shelter. One cannot escape the question whether they went on to Bethany, eastward of Jerusalem, for their lodgings, to the home where in the years to come Jesus spent so many happy hours in a home that loved and honored him.

Did the youth Jesus know the youth Lazarus, and the maidens, Mary and Martha?

Or did they, in reverent commemoration, go back to Bethlehem, where twelve years before the Messiah was born in a manger?

"And it came to pass that after three days they found him in the temple, sitting in the midst of the doctors, both hearing them, and asking them questions."
Luke 2:46

Jesus in the Temple Courts with the Doctors

W E ARE now at the third day of the Passover—Unleavened Bread Feast, Nisan 16th.

As we have already noted, personal attendance was necessary on the first two days only of this seven-day-long feast. The first and the last of the feast days were "holy convocations"; the intermediate days were "half-holydays," or days of "minor festivals" or "Moed Katon." (Edersheim, Vol. I, p. 246; *The Temple*, pp. 215, 224 ff.)

On the first day, the Paschal lamb had been killed and eaten and the necessary burnt offering had been made; on the second day, Joseph had offered his peace offering or "festive sacrifice," and in the evening of that day (though strictly by Jewish reckoning, the beginning of the next day), the "first sheaf" had been garnered and threshed and the omer of flour waved and offered to the Lord. These were the full essentials for which personal presence was required.

Joseph and Mary and Jesus were now free to return home, for "they had fulfilled the days." Did they so return or did they stay in Jerusalem till the Feast of Unleavened Bread was ended?

Scholars are not agreed on this point, some believing they did remain, others that they did not. While the matter does not seem to be one of final consequence, yet it has an interest and bearing as to the place in the temple grounds where Jesus met the doctors, though this point is not of last importance, either, the one essential point being that he did meet the doctors and that he "astonished" them with both his "hearing them, and asking them questions."

Location of Incident in Temple Precincts

Those scholars who interpret the statement, "when they had fulfilled the days" as meaning that Joseph and Mary remained the full days of the feast, declare (some of them) that Jesus met the doctors in a synagogue that was on the temple grounds, or (as others affirm) that he met them in a theological academy (Beth ha-Midrash) that was within the temple precincts.

Edersheim critically examines these suggestions and concludes there is no historical evidence that a synagogue existed within the temple enclosure and that, if one did exist, the services therein held would not admit of the recorded incident of the interview between Jesus and the doctors. Edersheim also concludes there was no theological seminary in the enclosure and that, if there had been, Jesus would not have been admitted thereto. On the other hand, he points out that the Talmud affirms "the members of the Temple-Sanhedrin, who on ordinary days sat as a Court of Appeal, from the close of the Morning- to the time of the Evening-Sacrifice, were wont on Sabbaths and *feast-days* to come out upon 'the Terrace' of the Temple, and there to teach. In such popular instruction the utmost latitude of questioning would be given. It is in this audience, which sat on the ground, surrounding and mingling with the Doctors—and hence *during*, not *after* the Feast—that we must seek the Child Jesus." (Edersheim, I, pp. 246-247; II, p. 742, App. x.)

It is rather in the intimacy and informality of such a gathering as Edersheim describes, that we should expect to find the Youth. We shall work in accordance with Edersheim's conclusions.

Return Journey Begun

So we come to the third day of the feast, Nisan the 16th. We shall assume that Joseph and Mary began the return journey on this day. As we have already seen, in Palestine the first day of a journey was always a short one. The morning would doubtless be spent in preparation for the home-going, in paying good-bye visits and saying farewell to friends. The returning pilgrims would start in the late afternoon, to escape the heat of the sun; they would expect to travel only six or eight miles. While perhaps not so great as when coming to the Passover (for then they had with them large numbers of sacrificial animals) nevertheless the confusion of the many streams of returning worshipers, coming from various parts of the city and emptying into the few roads leading northward, the din from the shouts of the camel drivers and the muleteers, the screams of mothers whose children were in danger of being trodden underfoot, the shrieks of the children themselves, the loud greeting of village friends, now homeward-bound, meeting for the first time since they came to the Passover, the anxious calls of parents seeking to gather their families together, the braying of the donkeys, the laughter, the singing—all combined to make a tumult that would never be forgotten. As they went along the road, families would be constantly reunited as the older children, traveling for a time with friends, searched out their own parents and brothers and sisters. So the slow-moving multitude, unorganized and undirected, would creep steadily forward as the sun lowered and sank in the west, then on through the fast fading twilight, into the darkness, when flaring torches added to the picturesque weirdness of this plodding, on-marching mass—all winding like a giant, sluggish, flickering, dull-lighted glowworm over hills, down and out of ravines, around bluffs, until, the day's journey finished, camp was made, the evening meal eaten, and as the dying fires, casting huge, weird, shifting shadows, finally flickered out, quiet came and night and the stillness of the desert settled down over the weary mass.

Tradition gives Beer or El Bireh (a town some ten miles northward from Jerusalem) as the site of the first stop of the returning pilgrims. Edersheim, however, is quoted as saying the first stop was made at Sichem, "if the direct road north through Samaria was taken." (Samuel J. Andrews, *The Life of Our Lord* (Charles Scribner's Sons, New York, 1891), p. 109.)

Absence of Jesus Detected

Remembering that Jesus was now a "son of the law," entitled to wear, if not wearing, the Tephillin or phylacteries, we can realize that he would not be under such strict supervision as when younger; he would be given greater responsibility and allowed greater freedom. Furthermore, maturity comes earlier in the tropics and near-tropics than with us, and Jesus would probably be allowed many privileges that amongst us would come three or four years later. It is not strange, therefore, that his absence from the group was not detected until the evening camp was reached, when Joseph and Mary, not finding him "among their kinsfolk and acquaintance," returned to Jerusalem to find him.

Authorities are not a unit on the question of the period covered by the expression "after three days they found him in the temple." Was the day of departure from Jerusalem the first, the day of their return to Jerusalem the second, and the day of their finding him in the temple the third; or was the day of their return the first, a day of searching the second, and the day he was found the third? "Some, with much less probability, count three days from the day of their return." (Andrews, *op. cit.*) However, this point has no real apparent importance, save as giving ground for the show of impatience and the mild reproof of the mother, not Joseph, when the Youth was finally found.

There can be no doubt that Jesus had been deeply stirred by what he had seen and heard and done on this his first participation in the temple sacrifices and ceremonies of the Passover. We have, from time to time, raised the question as to how much Jesus was conscious of the past of which he was the directing power, and with what fulness did he foresee the future. The events we shall now recount leave little reasonable doubt that he remembered, in part at least, the past and foresaw at least some of the future. It can hardly be questioned that while his mortality put him under limitations (when they were not consciously thrown off), yet that mortality and its limitations did not dominate his divinity.

That Jesus deliberately planned to stay behind when the others went, can admit of little question. The record has no suggestion that his failure to go with Joseph and Mary was either a matter of chance or accident. Yet the episode given to us shows his remaining in Jerusalem was not from the wilful desire of the Youth for mere adventure. He may have wished to see the remainder of the feast, yet remembering his divinity and its attendant knowledge this could hardly have been a controlling reason. One cannot escape the feeling that, notwithstanding his attendance at the feast, he yet had work now to do in the temple, that he knew he must now begin to 'be about his Father's business.' He must make his beginning.

Lodgings of Jesus During Absence

We would be interested to know where he lodged during the days Joseph and Mary sought him. If he had lodged with friends or relatives of Jerusalem and its vicinity, they could have told the searchers at once where he could be found, and there would have been no need for the long seeking; so it seems unlikely he lodged with them.

It may be that, as he returned to the temple the first day without Joseph, Jesus may have met there friends who were remaining for the entire feast week—friends

either from home or friends whom he had made during
his attendance at the feast; these may have cared for
him, for as already pointed out, everyone made a point of
generous hospitality on the occasion of this great feast.
Or he may have gone at once on the first day to the doctors—he must have seen them holding their interviews
with visitors during the two days he was at the temple
with Joseph.   This thought certainly has some reason
behind it.   If he did so, the doctors, struck with his wisdom and intrigued with his intellectual powers, might
have wished to probe his mind, and so have arranged to
have him lodge with some of them.   Or did the priests at
the temple care for him, as a kind of youth—waif, left or
lost by his parents as they started homeward?   Or did the
angels care for him as in the after-days of the Temptation—"and, behold, angels came and ministered unto
him." (Matt. 4:11; Mark 1:13.)

Mary and Joseph Search for Jesus

"After three days they found him in the temple, sitting in the midst of the doctors, both hearing them, and
asking them questions."   There is no indication as to
where Joseph and Mary might have begun their search
for him.   But we may feel sure they would first go to the
place where they had lodged, and then to other relatives
or friends, and then, perhaps, to likely quarters in the
city itself.   At any rate, the temple was the last place they
searched.

But the search for him in the temple itself must have
been difficult.   And as the record is wholly silent in the
matter, we may indulge our fancy as to how and where
Joseph and Mary may have spent the third day seeking
for Jesus in the temple enclosure.

Always there were groups of people attending the
morning and evening sacrifices, and these now would be
greatly enlarged by the numbers of Passover pilgrims

who were remaining to finish out the full days of the
Feast of Unleavened Bread.

So as Joseph and Mary again crossed the Royal
Tyropœon Bridge and came through the great arch into
the temple precincts, they would again come into a seeth-
ing, jostling multitude of worshipers, of animals to be
sacrificed, and of money changers, dove vendors, and the
like—all congregated in the Court of the Gentiles.   To
find a youth in this milling mass would be an almost
hopeless task. So we may believe they would first walk
through the stately corridors of the Royal Porch along
the south wall of the temple enclosure, on the chance they
would find him in the cool shades of the porch. But they
would not find him there, so they might have gone on
looking for him in the cool shadows under the pillared
canopy of Solomon's Porch, along the east wall of the
temple.—It was here at a Feast of the Dedication, that,
years later, Jesus parried the demand of the Jews that
he tell them plainly whether he was the Christ.

But Jesus would not be here, and they might well
then have sought him in the Court of the Women, the
farthest point toward the temple to which Mary might
go except she were upon a sacrificial errand. For in this
court there was a simple colonnade, and galleries for the
women, which might give relief from the heat of the blazing sun.—It was in this court that years later Jesus saw
the widow cast her mite into the treasury of the temple
and declared: "This poor widow hath cast more in, than
all they which have cast into the treasury: for all they
did cast in of their abundance; but she of her want did
cast in all that she had, even all her living." (Mark 12:41
ff.; Luke 21:1-4.)

As indicated above, since Mary was with Joseph
when they found Jesus, and since Mary could not, on this
nonsacrificial errand, go nearer the temple than into this
court, it is clear Jesus was not in the Court of Israel, nor

in the Court of the Priests holding his discussions with
the doctors, and of course he was not actually in the temple itself to which only priests were admitted and they
only for ceremonial purposes.

Not finding Jesus in the Court of the Women, Mary
and Joseph would have no place to resume their search
except in the Court of the Gentiles.

So, it may have been that, as a last resort, they
would begin to move about among the crowds in the Court
of the Gentiles.—It was from this court that Jesus twice
drove the money changers, and here it probably was that
he confounded the scribes and Pharisees who, tempting
and baiting him, brought to him the woman taken in
adultery.

They Search the "Chel" of the Temple

Tired as Joseph and Mary were, after a long day in
the heat and confusion of the temple crowds, one can see
them involuntarily moving into the less crowded areas of
the court. So they would come to the ornamental marble
balustrade with its Greek and Latin inscriptions warning
gentiles not to go within it toward the temple on pain of
death. Inside the balustrade were eight separate flights
of fourteen steps, each nine inches high (four flights on
the north side of the temple and four on the south side),
each flight leading upwards to a gate in the inner temple
wall, through which admission was gained into the Court
of the Priests. These steps seemingly led to a terrace,
some fifteen feet broad, that entirely encircled the inner
temple wall, and from this terrace there was immediate
entry through the gates into the Court of the Priests. This
is the "Chel" of the temple. It was here, so Edersheim
says, that the members of the Temple-Sanhedrin came to
teach on Sabbaths and feast days. We do not know whether
these teachers met at a particular place every day, or
whether they met at different places on different days, or

whether their place of meeting varied during each day with the position of the sun—the teachers, in the hot afternoons, seeking the "Chel" on the north side where the shadow of the temple would give a welcome relief from the direct rays of the sun.

It would be reasonable to assume that, at least part of the time, they would meet on the "Chel" just outside the "Gazith," or "Hall of Polished Stones," which was a chamber within the inner wall and just east of the third gate, counting from the west, on the south side of the temple. This was the room in which the Sanhedrin sat.— According to some authorities it was to this chamber that Jesus was brought on the morning of the crucifixion, for the final and only legal hearing which Christ had at the hands of the Jews; but other authorities affirm that it was not held in the "Gazith."

Those coming to the temple entered at the southwest corner of the temple enclosure, having passed over the Royal Tyropœon Bridge, and through the great arch. They then went east, thence northward around the Court of the Women, and thence westward and out through the gate at the northwest corner of the temple enclosure.

So it might be that Joseph and Mary would decide, as a last hope, to go back to the west end of the "Chel" and going eastward follow it around to the exit on the northwest.

The record says they found Jesus "after three days." It must now have been near the end of this third day. Joseph and Mary were weary, anxious, almost despairing, after hours of straining eyes and vain enquiries. They must often, in these three long days, have spoken of the thoughtlessness of the Youth. They may have censured him, for almost irritation would have come to each of them—the patient, righteous Joseph, and Mary the mother, as they walked and walked and watched, hour after hour, for the lost Youth.

Jesus Found in the Midst of the Doctors

As Joseph and Mary would walk eastward, then northward, in front of the Beautiful Gate, the entrance to the Court of the Women, and to the temple proper, then westward, along the "Chel," around the outside of the inner temple wall, they would scan carefully the crowd below them in the Court of the Gentiles for some glimpse of the missing Boy. They would go forward slowly, probably paying little attention to those who might be in front of them on the "Chel" itself. So, we may think, Joseph and Mary would pass on till they came to the shadow of the temple falling across the terrace on the north side of the building, where, suddenly, they would come upon a quiet group, craning forward with intense interest, absorbed in their eager listening to a youthful voice, speaking in terms of authority and of deep learning and wisdom; and as they came to the group, the searchers were "amazed," for there in the midst of the doctors was Jesus whom they had sought for three long, anxious days— "amazed" at finding him in this place, in this company, in this relationship to the learned and mighty ones of the nation.

The Sacred Record does not tell us of the subjects the doctors discussed with Jesus; it merely says: "And all that heard him were astonished at his understanding and answers." But in the Apocryphal New Testament it is recorded that Jesus taught the "doctors and elders, and learned men of Israel" concerning his Messiahship, "the books of the law, and precepts and statutes: and the mysteries which are contained in the books of the prophets; things which the mind of no creature could reach"; also concerning astronomy, physics, and natural philosophy, and metaphysics. But all this is tradition. (1 Infancy 2:1 ff.)

But Joseph and Mary, coming thus suddenly upon him, and seeing him safe and well, had uppermost in their

minds only a sense of overwhelming relief and gratitude,
whetted by a resentment of their needless poignant anx-
iety and sorrow at his long absence, and so his mother,
not Joseph, broke forth in such reproof as she could offer
to the hitherto perfect Son: "Son, why hast thou thus
dealt with us? behold, thy father and I have sought thee
sorrowing."

"I Must Be About My Father's Business"

And the Son, unabashed, unchastised, unafraid, with
the calm dignity of the divinity that was his, replied to
this reproof with a question—in the after years of his
ministry, this answering a question by a question, was
to be a favorite shield against his scheming, hypocritical
inquisitors. To Mary the mother he said: "How is it that
ye sought me? wist ye not that I must be about my
Father's business?"

Then says the record: "And they understood not the
saying which he spake unto them."

But we of today, with the history of the earthly ministry of Christ before us, in Palestine, and on this hemisphere, with the knowledge of his premortal existence,
and his postmortal resurrected place and work, we may
perceive, in part at least, the truths that lay in and behind these sayings.

From Mary's statement "thy father and I have
sought thee sorrowing," we may glimpse that in the inti-
macies of the family circle at Nazareth, Jesus gave to
Joseph the love and respect of a son, and called him father. But Jesus knew that Mary knew and that Joseph
knew better than this, and so came the saying, "wist ye
not that I must be about *my* Father's business?"

Some have judged these words as if falling from the
lips of a wholly mortal child, and so have found in them
a rebuke from the Son to his mother. But this could not
be, for the Christ Child could not be unkind. With divine

knowledge and wisdom he thus brought in simple language to Joseph and to Mary the recollection that he was the Son of God, a fact that, for the moment at least, seems to have passed from their minds.

Recollection of Divine Mission

But there was more in the saying than was known to Joseph and Mary. There was the consciousness in Jesus not alone of who he was but of his mission here on earth. He knew that centuries before God had declared to Moses: "For behold, this is my work and my glory—to bring to pass the immortality and eternal life of man." (Moses 1:39.) This was his "Father's business," and he must be about it.

Thus there must have been before him the whole divine design, framed in the Great Council in Heaven before the world was formed. He must have remembered when the hosts, gathered together in heaven, determined: "We will go down, for there is space there, and we will take of these materials, and we will make an earth whereon these may dwell,"—these children of God who were to take on mortality and "prove" themselves to see "if they will do all things whatsoever the Lord their God shall command them." (Abraham 3:24 ff.)

And if that recollection came, another would come also—that of the rival plans offered by himself and by Lucifer, a Son of the Morning, and of the choice of his own plan. And then would surge up in his mind the recollection of the rebellion in heaven, the casting out of Lucifer and his followers—a third of the hosts of heaven, and the creation of the earth by himself—for "In the beginning was the Word, and the Word was with God, and the Word was God. The same was in the beginning with God. All things were made by him; and without him was not any thing made that was made. . . . And the Word was made flesh, and dwelt among us. . . ."

(John 1:1-3, 14.) He would remember the peopling of the earth, beginning with Adam; he would recall Adam's Fall, and the need for an Atonement and a Redeemer of men from the mortal death of the Fall, and his own choice as this Redeemer, "the Lamb is slain from the foundation of the world." (Moses 7:47.) He must have recollected the long course of God's dealings with his children, their waywardness, and proneness to evil, so that they came "to be carnal, sensual, and devilish." (*Ibid.*, 5:13.) He knew how the Father, through himself, had sought to bring them to lives of righteousness, how he had, through all the dispensations, proclaimed the Gospel to men, how he had given them the law under which Judah and Joseph then lived. No wonder he astounded the doctors with his knowledge of the law! He knew, too, the work he was to do, he saw its problems, its hardships, its persecutions, and it must be his ultimate sacrifice.

He seems to have been deeply touched by his visit to the temple and his witnessing of the rites and ceremonies typifying his own mission and destiny, by his observance of the hyprocrisy and corruption of the priesthood, by his consciousness of how the people were misled to their condemnation, by his appreciation of how much there was to do and how little the time to do it. Yet with all these things before him, as it would seem they must have been, how careful and considerate, how dutiful he was, when to the trivial complaint (for trivial it was in view of all this) of his mother, he uttered the single sentence that proclaimed his divinity and his task—"wist ye not that I must be about my Father's business?"

Return to Nazareth

But the divinity that was in him, told him also, under the spur of the mother's mild rebuke, that his time had not yet come, that there was mortal preparation for himself yet to make, that the minds of men must be further ripened, both in sympathy for truth and in hatred for him and love for the works of Satan, that the work of John the great forerunner must yet be done that the hearts of men might be fallowed for the real beginning of his ministry. So "he went down with them, and came to Nazareth, and was subject unto them."

Again he became the dutiful Child obeying the behests of Joseph the carpenter, until he, himself, was also known as the Carpenter.

But while Joseph and Mary "understood not the saying which he spake unto them," yet "his mother kept all these sayings in her heart." Years after, at the marriage feast in Cana, she showed she had come more to realize who he was, and his divine powers, for when they wanted wine she said unto the servants, after telling Jesus about it, "whatsoever he saith unto you, do it." (John 2:1-11.)

So to Nazareth where the grain fields were now yellowed with ripened crops, the hills and valleys still covered with wild flowers; to Nazareth among the white rocks and cliffs splotched with green, with goats and sheep lazily grazing on the warm hillsides; to Nazareth with the houses climbing row on row up and out from the little valley floor, to the brink of the cliff from which his neighbors would one day seek to cast him down; to Nazareth, quiet, unperturbed, with its slender cypresses and fig trees, and the evenness, frugality, and wholesomeness of a village life dominated by the presence of divinity—to this Nazareth came Joseph and Mary and Jesus who "increased in wisdom and stature, and in favour with God and man" against the day and hour of his destiny.

"... Whom do men say that I am?
"... And they answered, John the Baptist: but some say,
Elias; and others, One of the prophets.
"... And he saith unto them, But whom say ye that I am?
And Peter answereth and saith unto him, Thou art the Christ."
Mark 8:27-29

The Personality of God

M Y REMARKS will deal with one phase only of this great subject, the Personality of God, and that phase will be in a sense the least important one because it deals with a negative—what God is not instead of what God is. But no adequate understanding of the whole subject can be had from the viewpoint of the Latter-day Saint, except this phase be first disposed of.

Of the fundamental differences between the beliefs of the Latter-day Saints and other Christian sects, none is more important, none reaches deeper along the roots of their faiths than their respective conceptions of God and his relationship to man.

The character and attributes of God, the nature and descent of the Holy Priesthood after the Order of the Son of God, the universality of the salvation of man, including work looking to the exaltation of those who died without the law, or without yielding obedience to it, the eternity of the relationship between the righteous husband and the righteous wife, when sealed by the power of the Priesthood, and the doctrine of continuous revelation, are matters upon which the Latter-day Saints have no compromise to offer to any sect or denomination in the world. If the Latter-day Saints are wrong in these fundamental concepts, their religious faith is a tragic delusion and a fateful snare; if they are right in these, then all men must accept and live them or abide the penalty, a failure of the blessings which God has planned for those who are obedient to his laws.

It is the humble, devout faith, it is a knowledge by and of the spirit, of hundreds of thousands of Latter-day Saints, living and dead, that the Gospel of Christ as taught and practiced by them, is the very truth of which

Christ spoke when he said, "Ye shall know the truth, and the truth shall make you free." (John 8:32.)

The great Christian sects of the world declare a belief in a God "without body, parts, or passions," "one only, eternal, incomprehensible, spiritual essence," who is omniscient (that is, all-knowing), omnipotent (that is, all-powerful), and omnipresent (that is "He is in all parts of the universe and with every individual"); "God is everywhere" (everywhere present at the same time, and in and a part of God's creations).

Since the Beginning of Time

But this is not the God of the Latter-day Saints; nor are these the attributes of him they worship. The belief and contention of the Latter-day Saints is that neither the Holy Scriptures of old nor those composed of modern revelation reveal any such God as has been described. The Latter-day Saints declare that such a being is not the God of Adam, Noah, and Enoch, nor of Abraham, Isaac, and Jacob; that it is not the God that made Israel his covenant people, nor that led Israel dryshod through the Red Sea; that it is not he who guided the wanderings in the wilderness, nor that traced upon stone, amidst the thunders of Sinai, the great moral law of the world.

The Latter-day Saints further declare that the scriptures fully attest that Israel and her mighty ones conceived God as a deified being of their own order, with a body, parts, and passions, omniscient, omnipotent, and omnipresent in the sense that operating by and through his influence, power, and authority he brings all men into his presence, but that God himself is not otherwise "in all parts of the universe and with every individual" nor is he "everywhere" at the same time. The Latter-day Saints affirm that this was the one-God concept to which Israel was brought back when they were delivered from bondage, and to which they held while living in the midst of and mingling with the idolatrous paganism of surrounding peoples in Palestine; that this was the concept which either came to them because they were the chosen people of God under the covenant or the concept on account of which the covenant was made to them, and they became the chosen people of God. Any other concept of God than this belies all his recorded dealings with his people, and with the peoples of the world since the beginning of time.

The Latter-day Saints believe in the same God that declared Israel to be his chosen people.

It seems clear on reflection that the fundamental error in the sectarian concept of a God "without body, parts, or passions" composed of an "incomprehensible, spiritual essence," is to be found in the alleged attribute of "omnipresence" which is defined to be "the quality of being everywhere present at the same time . . . in theology universal presence of the divine essence."

The Keystone of the Arch

Being thus the keystone of the arch, it is worth-while to consider the scripture passages which are usually cited to sustain this sectarian doctrine.

I will take first (merely because it appears earliest in the Bible text) the passage from Solomon's prayer at the dedication of the temple he had built. He said:

> But will God indeed dwell on the earth? behold, the heaven and heaven of heavens cannot contain thee; how much less this house that I have builded? (1 Kings 8:27.)

Behind this prayer of Solomon lay these facts: David, having peace from his enemies, said to Nathan, the prophet of God, "Lo, I dwell in an house of cedars, but the ark of the covenant of the Lord remaineth under curtains." Nathan, the man, said to David, "Do all that

is in thine heart; for God is with thee." But on the same
night, the word of God came to Nathan saying:

> Go and tell David my servant, Thus saith the Lord, Thou
> shalt not build me an house to dwell in:
> For I have not dwelt in an house since the day that I
> brought up Israel unto this day; but have gone from tent to
> tent, and from one tabernacle to another. . . .
> . . . I will raise up thy seed after thee, which shall be of thy
> sons; and I will establish his kingdom.
> He shall build me an house . . . (1 Chron. 17:1-5, 11-12.)

When David in solemn assembly gave counsel to
Israel and Solomon prior to his death, he recounted this
command in these words:

> And he said unto me, Solomon thy son, he shall build my
> house and my courts: for I have chosen him to be my son, and I
> will be his father. . . .
> And thou, Solomon my son . . .
> Take heed now; for the Lord hath chosen thee to build an
> house for the sanctuary: be strong, and do it. (1 Chron. 28:6,
> 9-10.)

Obedient to Instructions

Obedient to these instructions, Solomon built a house
to the Lord, and now, dedicating it, he seems to have
recalled that the word that came to his father, David,
was that God had not need for a house to dwell in, and
that he had been content to dwell in tents; and Solomon,
apprehensive that the house built might not be acceptable
to God, skeptical perhaps that he could be lured from
heaven to earth, exclaims:

> But will God in very deed dwell with men on the earth?
> behold, heaven and the heaven of heavens cannot contain thee;
> how much less this house which I have built! (2 Chron. 6:18.)

Solomon had not in mind that God could not dwell

in his house because he was an omnipresent, formless, spiritual essence.

Indeed, if God were everywhere, he would be already in the temple, and Solomon would be doing a vain thing to importune his presence there. That Solomon prayed for his presence, is proof that Solomon did not believe he was already there. The plain import of these simple words is that Solomon believed God dwelt elsewhere than in this temple, or on this earth and there came to him the conviction that he could not bring him to earth and confine him to the house he had built, nor indeed to any dwelling upon this earth, because he could not be confined even in heaven or in the heaven of heavens. God moves as and where and when he wills.

Another passage cited to show God's omnipresence in the sectarian sense, is taken from Job's answer to Eliphaz's third discourse:

Behold, I go forward, but he is not there; and backward, but I cannot perceive him:
On the left hand, where he doth work, but I cannot behold him: he hideth himself on the right hand, that I cannot see him. (Job 23:8-9.)

Poetic Outpouring

This beautiful lament seems so obviously the poetic outpouring of an almost despairing soul, seeking from his God a love and consolation which seemed constantly to elude him, that it is almost sacrilege to attempt to wrench it into an announcement of a scientific fact. Moreover as the announcement of such a fact, its effect is to affirm not that God is everywhere and in everything, and therefore then present with Job, but that he is nowhere to be found.

A third passage uniformly cited as sustaining the omnipresence of God, is from the 139th Psalm, where David exclaims:

Whither shall I go from thy spirit? or whither shall I flee from thy presence.

If I ascend up into heaven, thou art there: if I make my bed in hell, behold, thou art there.

If I take the wings of the morning, and dwell in the uttermost parts of the sea;

Even there shall thy hand lead me, and thy right hand shall hold me. (Psa. 139:7-10.)

If this is to be taken as the outcry of the conscience-stricken, self-condemned defiler of Bathsheba and the murderer of Uriah, it does but show how the consciousness of guilt remains with the sinner to whom God has vouchsafed the spirit of repentance. If it be a figurative allusion to the sins and punishments of Israel, it teaches the same lesson. That David was not here consciously declaring the omnipresence of a formless, spiritual essence, and that he did not so conceive his God, is clear from his contemplation of the infinite goodness of God and his exclamation, "in the uttermost parts of the sea; even there shall thy hand lead me, and thy right hand shall hold me."

But these passages admirably illustrate the omnipresence in which the Latter-day Saints believe—an omnipresence that operates by and through God's influence, power, and authority, an omnipresence of men before God, not of God in men.

All in His Presence

A man standing on the mountain peak has within his presence all that lies within his horizon—every cliff, canyon, mountain stream, brook, and river; every hill and valley; every hamlet, town, and city. He sees the lightning play here, the rain fall there; he sees the clouds and the whirlwind; the sunshine and the shadow; the tiny beetle at his feet, the bird that soars overhead, the beasts of the field; men come and go in the distances;

the life of his world is before him. All are in his presence. But how manifestly error to say that since all are in his presence, that he is in and a part of each and every of them.

So God, enthroned upon the pinnacle of his omniscience and omnipotence has the universe, with all his creations, in his presence, and this is his omnipresence; but that does not put him in his creations, does not make them a part of himself. With the instruments of God's influence, power, and authority, with the instrumentalities by and through which he performs his works, and governs and controls the multiplicity of his creations, we are not now concerned.

Still another passage cited to sustain the concept of an omnipresent, formless, spiritual essence is the Proverb: "The eyes of the Lord are in every place, beholding the evil and the good." (Prov. 15:3.)

This is quite obviously a figurative expression however considered. But if to be taken literally it indicates a God with parts, not a formless spiritual essence. From any view it shows rather that God is omniscient—all-knowing—than that he is omnipresent.

Some commentators quote two passages from Isaiah as showing the omnipresence of a God of a formless, spiritual essence. The first reads:—

For thus saith the high and lofty One that inhabiteth eternity, whose name is Holy; I dwell in the high and holy place, with him also that is of a contrite and humble spirit, to revive the spirit of the humble, and to revive the heart of the contrite ones. (Isa. 57:15.)

Definite Abiding Place

But Isaiah here fixes a definite abiding place for God where dwell also the spirits of the humble. If by this passage God is declared to be omnipresent in the sectarian concept, so also must it be considered that the spirit of the humble is likewise so omnipresent, for God and this spirit dwell together, but this would prove too much.

The other passage reads:

Thus saith the Lord, The heaven is my throne, and the earth is my footstool: where is the house that ye build unto me? and where is the place of my rest?

But the verse immediately following, begins:

"For all those things hath mine hand made. . . ." (Isa. 66:1-2.)

Surely there is here again no suggestion other than that of definite location for God, highly figurative as the first part of the declaration is; while the final sentence expressly declares he possesses bodily parts,—"For all those things hath mine hand made."

The Prophet Jeremiah is also invoked to support the sectarian omnipresence of a God of a formless, spiritual essence:

Am I a God at hand, saith the Lord, and not a God afar off? Can any hide himself in secret places that I shall not see him? saith the Lord. Do not I fill heaven and earth? saith the Lord. (Jer. 23:23-24.)

Jeremiah, abiding with "the poorest sort of the people of the land" which Nebuchadnezzar had left at Jerusalem when he carried away to Babylon the first great contingent (2 Kings 24:14), is here engaged in reproving captive Israel, even including the prophets for their iniquities. God seemingly wished to correct the error into which Israel appears occasionally to have fallen —that he was the God of a particular place, the Promised Land. Hence he declared, "Am I not a God at hand, saith the Lord, and not . . . afar off?" He, the all-knowing, the all-powerful, could reach the false prophet in Babylon as well as in Jerusalem. They could not hide their iniquities from his omniscience, they could not escape his omnipotence, which filled heaven and earth.

One Final Passage

One final passage cited by the commentators, may be noted. Paul speaking to the Athenians on the text, "To the unknown God," declared:

> God that made the world and all things therein, seeing that he is Lord of heaven and earth, dwelleth not in temples made with hands. (Acts 17:24.)

Murphy's note to this sentence reads, "God is not contained in temples; so as to need them for his dwelling, or any other uses, as the heathens imagined. Yet by his omnipresence, he is both there and every where." (Douay Version, *Murphy Red Letter Edition* (John Murphy Company, Baltimore & New York), *ad loc.*)

Truly God could not in the time of Paul, and cannot now, any more than he could in the days of Jeremiah, be led captive and confined in any particular place. Omnipotent, he moves as he wills; omniscient, he sojourns where wisdom requires. Paul speaking to the Athenians was challenging the fundamentals of their paganism, that God dwelt and must be worshiped in temples, and that the service he required was worship only with men's hands. Paul, the trained Pharisee, the metaphysician, the mystic, would, had he wished to announce the sectarian omnipresence of a God of a formless, spiritual essence, have used other and far different language than this. A prophet who believed in such a God would hardly write to the Ephesians concerning the "God of our Lord Jesus Christ, the Father of glory," and say:

> And what is the exceeding greatness of his power to us-ward who believe, according to the working of his mighty power,
> Which he wrought in Christ, when he raised him from the dead, and set him at his own right hand in the heavenly places,

Far above all principality, and power, and might, and dominion, and every name that is named, not only in this world,
but also in that which is to come. (Eph. 1:19-21.)

Nor could a prophet believing in the sectarian God
have written to the Colossians that Christ "is the image
of the invisible God" (Col. 1:15), nor to the Philippians
that Christ is "in the form of God." (Phil. 2:6.)

Appreciating Difficulties

But commentators, appreciating the difficulties into which this sectarian concept of omnipresence drives
them, admit that "He is not everywhere in the same
sense, but he is in some places in a way that he is not
in others," and in support of this they cite the words of
Christ spoken in the Passover chamber just before he
left for the Garden of Gethsemane:

Ye have heard how I said unto you, I go away, and come
again unto you. If ye loved me, ye would rejoice, because I said,
I go unto the Father: for my Father is greater than I. (John
14:28.)

They cite also the words spoken to Mary Magdalene
who, discerning the Christ and not the gardener, evidently rushed toward him when "Jesus saith unto her, Touch
me not; for I am not yet ascended to my Father: but go to
my brethren, and say unto them, I ascend unto my Father,
and your Father; and to my God, and your God." (*Ibid.*,
20:17.)

Surely it must be that if God were everywhere, how
unnecessary for Christ, the Only Begotten, the Firstborn,
of the Godhead, to ascend to his Father and his God.

The Gospels, too, clearly show Christ's intimate com-
munion with the Father during his whole mission on
earth, to justify a contention that he must go from where
he was to the Father if the Father, being everywhere

present, were then actually with him. The forced admission of the learned commentators itself shows the error of their concept. Had God been actually present with Christ, no matter where Christ was (as God must be if everywhere present) then how unnecessary, how deceptive Christ's message to Mary and the Apostles that he must go elsewhere to join his Father and God. Here was one moment for the Christ to make plain the truth. If God was then with him, about him, and part of him, this was the time for the declaration. Another moment was when having gone for a last walk with the Apostles, he reached Bethany and raising his hand in a blessing, he ascended into heaven. Why the deceptive going to God, if God was there with him?

Nor does the sectarian concept of omnipresence stop, nor can it stop with God. The words of Christ regarding himself require the commentators to attribute sectarian omnipresence to him also, to him of body, parts, and passions, and to attribute to Christ such omnipresence, such a formless, spiritless essence, while he, Christ, still lived and moved among men and ministered unto them.

"In the Midst of Them"

Christ, teaching the troubled, vacillating, faint-hearted Nicodemus declared, "And no man hath ascended up to heaven, but he that came down from heaven, even the Son of man which is in heaven." (John 3:13.)

Interpreted as the commentators interpret analogous passages referring to God, this must mean that though Christ was there present in the flesh with Nicodemus, he was also and at the same time then present in heaven.

When the Apostles came to Christ at Capernaum disputing who should be greatest in the kingdom of heaven, Christ, after declaring to them that "Whatsoever ye shall bind on earth shall be bound in heaven: and whatsoever ye shall loose on earth shall be loosed in

heaven," further declared: "For where two or three are
gathered together in my name, there am I in the midst
of them." (Matt. 18:18, 20.)

Interpreted as the sectarian concept of omnipresence
requires, this passage would mean that if two worshiping groups met in Christ's name at different places at
the same time, then Christ, the being of flesh and blood
and bone must be actually with both groups at the same
time. If it shall be said that not his physical body but his
influence or "spirit" would be present, that his presence
would be with them as was the presence of the man on
the mountain peak with his world, then there is destroyed
the omnipresence for which the sectarian contends, and
there is declared and revealed the God of ancient Israel
and of the Latter-day Saints who is become omnipresent
in the true sense.

Again, just before his ascension into heaven, and
while giving to the Apostles their final commission for
their ministry, Christ said, "lo, I am with you alway,
even unto the end of the world." (Matt. 28:20.)

Here also if Christ were to be with each and every
of his Apostles always as he says, then he, the being of
flesh and bone, he, the physical individual (both before
and after the resurrection), must be in two or more places
at the same time, a conception quite beyond the powers
of the human mind.

Attributes of the Father

With the actual omnipresence here predicted of the
Christ, the Latter-day Saints have no dispute. They believe and maintain that Christ, being in the image of
the Father, has the attributes of the Father. They have
no difficulty with the concept that the influence, the
wisdom, the power, the authority of God and of Christ
can be exercised at any point at any time.

Reflection raises the question as to what difference

there is between the sectarian concept of the omnipresence of God, that he is everywhere, which necessarily puts him in and makes him a part of everything, and the old pagan philosophy which gave to every hill, and grove, and brook its own particular deity. Is there a difference in essence between these beliefs, or is sectarian omnipresence a mere spiritualization of the earlier pagan concept?

The foregoing passages present the full case for the concept of the omnipresence of God. Treated as evidence, each and every one of them, and all of them together, fail when tested by the ordinary rules applicable to matters of evidence (either in law or in logic), to establish the fact for which they are cited. Evidence of the probative value of this would be rejected as a ground for action in any of the material affairs of life.

God has given to all his creations upon the earth, to the very earth itself, a due and proper individual form. Every plant, every animal has its own shape that lasts through life; and to the successor of each comes that same shape. The minerals of the earth have each their due and proper form when left to obey the law and order of their creation. Lastly, man has his form to him given, and his offspring after him. The laws of God, as shadowed in his works, know only order and form; these they inexorably demand. When God gave to his children his greatest gift, without which they were lost to him, he gave the gift in due and proper form and figure,—a man, the Christ who was in the image of the Father—our Father, Christ's Father.

Who shall say that God has made a law and given an order for his creations which violate the principles of his own existence?

No. God is not a formless, spiritual essence, not a being without body, parts, or passions. All his works cry out in protest at the thought. God is an exalted, omniscient, omnipotent, deified being of the same divine order as the children of his creation and of his own First-born and Only Begotten.

"And God said, Let us make man in our image, after our likeness. . . .

"So God created man in his own image, in the image of God created he him; male and female created he them."

Genesis 1:26-27

The Personality of God from a Biblical Standpoint

T HE VERY beginning of the record of God's dealings with man announces his creation in the image of God.

> And God said, Let us make man in our image, after our likeness. . . .
> So God created man in his own image, in the image of God created he him; male and female created he them. (Gen. 1:26-27.)

Thus was man created and put upon the earth. The Latter-day Saints accept this statement in its plainest and simplest import, they do not believe the language is figurative; their conception of God does not permit them to believe it is either deceptive or equivocal. They believe that Elohim standing at the pinnacle of the work of creation of this world and its peopling life, declared in simple language and straightforward statement the great eternal truth that man is the offspring of God, in form and figure the same as God, of the same order of being with God, with an eternal intelligence implanted within him, which shall forever grow in grace, wisdom, knowledge, and understanding, even finally unto perfection.

In Very Deed and Fact

We are not unacquainted with the doctrine that "This *image* of God in man, is not in the body, but in the soul; which is a *spiritual* substance, endued with understanding and free will"; nor with the statements of other commentators that the likeness here is a "spiritual, intellectual and moral likeness." (See Douay Version, *Murphy Red Letter Edition*, and *The New Indexed Bible* (John A. Dickson Publishing Co., Chicago, 1901), *ad loc.*)

But with these doctrines as applied to this text, we are not in accord.

That man is spiritual and temporal, that, as Paul declares, "There is a natural body, and there is a spiritual body" (1 Cor. 15:44), is one of the fundamental beliefs of the Latter-day Saints; but they affirm that the creation here recorded is the creation of man's natural or temporal body, which is in very deed and fact in the image and likeness of God, its Creator, for as he said later when giving to Noah the law governing murder, "in the image of God made he man." (Gen. 9:6.)

That such is the true meaning of creation in an image or likeness, as those words are used in the Bible text, appears to be put beyond controversy by the record of the birth of Seth. The scriptural record reads:

> . . . In the day that God created man, in the likeness of God made he him;
> Male and female created he them. . . .
> And Adam lived an hundred and thirty years, and begat a son in his own likeness, after his image; and called his name Seth. (Gen. 5:1-3.)

It is the belief of the Latter-day Saints that there is the same image and likeness between God the Creator and man, that there is between Adam the father and his posterity; they firmly believe that these words, image and likeness, are used with identical meaning and signification in both texts.

It is worthy of reflection that God thus declared his act and his purpose in the beginning of the record of his dealings with his children, and leaves man with this one account thereof, as if by this means to prevent, by avoiding multiplicity of statement, even the possibility of misinterpretation and misunderstanding.

God Appears to Man as Personage

But that God has a body, of which man is an image and likeness, is shown by an abundance of other direct evidence. Time and again God has shown himself to men as a man, from the time of Adam even until the present.

To Abram on the plain of Moreh the Lord appeared and first announced and made with him the great covenant, later repeatedly confirmed, that his seed should possess the land. (Gen. 12:7.)

Later, "when Abram was ninety years old and nine, the Lord appeared to Abram, and said unto him, I am the Almighty God; walk before me, and be thou perfect. . . . And Abram fell on his face: and God talked with him. . . ." (Gen. 17:1-3.) It was on this occasion that God changed his servant's name from Abram (a higher father) to Abraham (a father of many nations). (*Ibid.*, v. 5.)

A little later, Abraham sat at his tent door on the plains of Mamre, in the heat of the day, and the Lord, with other personages, again appeared unto him, and Sarah prepared a meal and they ate. Later the personages "turned their faces from thence, and went toward Sodom: but Abraham stood yet before the Lord." Then occurred that wonderful discussion between God and Abraham as to the destruction of Sodom and Gomorrah, where, upon Abraham's persistent intercession, God finally promised, "I will not destroy it for tens' sake. And the Lord went his way, as soon as he had left communing with Abraham: and Abraham returned unto his place." (*Ibid.*, 18:1-8, 22, 32-33.)

Nothing appears in this text to justify the interpretation (made in Murphy's note, Douay Version) that the three personages were angels and that two went away immediately "whilst the third, who represented the Lord, remained with Abraham," for the record says the Lord talked with Abraham; the record shows that Abraham believed he was talking with the Lord after the other

personages had left. It is not conceivable that the Lord
and his angels would have practiced deception not only
upon Abraham but upon mankind since born.

After Abraham died, Isaac, to escape a famine,
journeyed to the land of Gerar, apparently on his way to
Egypt.

And the Lord appeared unto him, and said, Go not down
into Egypt; dwell in the land which I shall tell thee of. (*Ibid.*,
26:2.)

A little later when Isaac, now the well-digger, had,
at the behest of Abimelech, gone to the valley of Gerar
and dwelt there, "the Lord appeared unto him . . . and
said, I am the God of Abraham thy father: fear not, for
I am with thee, and will bless thee, and multiply thy seed
for my servant Abraham's sake." (*Ibid.*, 26:16, 24.)

To Jacob there came visitations also.

And God appeared unto Jacob again, when he came out of
Padanaram, and blessed him. . . .
And God said unto him, I am God Almighty. . . .
And God went up from him in the place where he talked
with him. (*Ibid.*, 35:9-13.)

Commentators are of the opinion that the description in Ezekiel refers to God where that prophet said,

. . . and, behold, there was a man, whose appearance was
like the appearance of brass, with a line of flax in his hand, and
a measuring reed; and he stood in the gate. (Ezek. 40:3.)

A Man's Voice

So of the vision recorded in the eighth chapter of
Daniel, where that prophet declares—

. . . behold, there stood before me as the appearance of a man.
And I heard a man's voice between the banks of Ulai, which

called, and said, Gabriel, make this man to understand the vision. . . .

Now as he was speaking with me, I was in a deep sleep on my face toward the ground: but he touched me, and set me upright. (Dan. 8:15-18.)

So also the subsequent vision of the glory of God by Daniel:

. . . I was by the side of the great river, which is Hiddekel;

Then I lifted up mine eyes, and looked, and behold a certain man clothed in linen, whose loins were girded with fine gold of Uphaz:

His body also was like the beryl, and his face as the appearance of lightning, and his eyes as lamps of fire, and his arms and his feet like in color to polished brass, and the voice of his words like the voice of a multitude. . . .

Therefore I was left alone, and saw this great vision, and there remained no strength in me. . . .

Yet heard I the voice of his words: and when I heard the voice of his words, then was I in a deep sleep on my face, and my face toward the ground.

And, behold, an hand touched me, which set me upon my knees and upon the palms of my hands. (*Ibid.*, 10:4-10.)

John's Vision

While the vision of John on the Isle of Patmos, as recorded in the first chapter of Revelation, is by some commentators regarded as a theophany (Scofield), yet the Latter-day Saints believe that the Being so appearing to John was the Son and not the Father (Rev. 1:10-19, D & C 19:1); yet John did in vision see God the Father and his Son, the Lamb, for he bears witness:—

. . . I beheld, and, lo, a great multitude, which no man could number, of all nations, and kindreds, and people, and tongues, stood before the throne, and before the Lamb, clothed with white robes, and palms in their hands;

And cried with a loud voice, saying, Salvation to our God which sitteth upon the throne, and unto the Lamb. (Rev. 7:9-10.)

Thus to Abraham, Isaac, Jacob, Ezekiel, Daniel, and John, there came the glorious vision of God the person. In two of them the record expressly affirms he came as a man and each of these holy men talked with God.

Like unto their testimony, is the record that "Noah was a just man and perfect in his generations, and Noah walked with God." (Gen. 6:9.)

And so of the great Enoch, "translated that he should not see death" (Heb. 11:5), Enoch, the only prophet of God who, as the Latter-day Saints believe was ever able to lead his people completely to righteousness (Moses 7:69), of whom the record says, "And Enoch walked with God: and he was not; for God took him." (Gen. 5:24.)

Surely it cannot be that God has vouchsafed such a record so simple and plain in the natural meaning of its text to his children, as declaring something which is not. God would not sport with us over the prize of eternal life, which comes through a knowledge of him. Who shall face his God at the judgment day, having in the flesh denied his personage.

References to Physical Attributes

The scriptures are filled with reference to the parts of God's body. While Israel was camped at the foot of Sinai,

. . . he said unto Moses, Come up unto the Lord, thou, and Aaron, Nadab, and Abihu, and seventy of the elders of Israel; and worship ye afar off.

And Moses alone shall come near the Lord: but they shall not come nigh; neither shall the people go up with him. . . .

Then went up Moses, and Aaron, Nadab, and Abihu, and seventy of the elders of Israel:

And they saw the God of Israel: and there was under his feet as it were a paved work of a sapphire stone, and as it were the body of heaven in his clearness.

And upon the nobles of the children of Israel he laid not

his hand: also they saw God, and did eat and drink. (Ex.
24:1-2, 9-11.)

Written with God's Finger

Later at the Mount, when God gave unto Israel the
law, it is recorded:

And he gave unto Moses, when he had made an end of communing with him upon mount Sinai, two tables of testimony,
tables of stone, written with the finger of God. (*Ibid.*, 31:18.)

The Lord had already said unto Moses:

. . . Come up to me into the mount, and be there: and I will
give thee tables of stone, and a law, and commandments which
I have written; that thou mayest teach them. (*Ibid.*, 24:12.)

Moses later repeated the account to Israel:

And the Lord delivered unto me two tables of stone written
with the finger of God; and on them was written according to all
the words, which the Lord spake with you in the mount out of
the midst of the fire in the day of the assembly. (Deut. 9:10;
for obvious figurative uses of the phrase "finger of God," see
Ex. 8:19; Luke 11:20.)

The New Testament again and again asserts that
Christ sits in heaven on the right hand of God. Mark
records that "after the Lord had spoken unto them, he
was received up into heaven, and sat on the right hand
of God." (Mark 16:19.) Paul so affirmed to the Romans
(Rom. 8:34), to the Ephesians (Eph. 1:20), to the
Colossians (Col. 3:1), and to the Hebrews (Heb. 10:12).
Peter likewise declared it in the first of his Epistles (1
Pet. 3:22) and again at Pentecost (Acts 2:33).

But of all the testimony to this point, none reaches so
far and explains so clearly as that of Stephen, the first
martyr, who, having arraigned Israel for its unbelief, and
the council maddened, having "gnashed on him with their

teeth," cried out, when he "looked up stedfastly into heaven, and saw the glory of God, and Jesus standing on the right hand of God. And said, Behold, I see the heavens opened, and the Son of man standing on the right hand of God." (Acts 7:55-56). Surely Stephen, his body racked with the agony of a barbarous death, did not falsify a record concerning his Maker whom he was about to meet.

God Talks with His Children

From the first day when "God said, Let there be light" (Gen. 1:3), until Malachi closed his record with God's promise to send Elijah, "before the coming of the great and dreadful day of the Lord" (Mal. 4:5-6), from generation to generation during this full time of recorded history, at each of the glorious theophanies, God is declared to have talked with men, his children. He commanded Adam not to eat of the tree of knowledge; after the Fall, Adam and Eve heard "the voice of the Lord God" who "called unto Adam" and "said unto the woman," and "said unto the serpent." (Gen. 3.) "Noah walked with God. . . . and God said unto Noah. . . ." (*Ibid.*, 6:9-13). The Lord talked with Abraham (*ibid.*, 12:1; 13:14; 22:1 *et seq.*), and the Lord spoke unto Isaac (*ibid.*, 26:2) and unto Jacob (*ibid.*, 31:3; 35:1).

So in the great covenants which God has given to his children, from the time when after blessing them he gave to Adam and Eve the great elemental command, "Be fruitful, and multiply, and replenish the earth, and subdue it" (*ibid.*, 1:28), down through the covenants with Adam, after the Fall (*ibid.*, 3:14-19), with Noah, after the Flood (*ibid.*, 8:20-22; 9:1-27), with Abraham (*ibid.*, 12:1-3; 13:14-18; 15:1-18; 17:6-8; 22:15-18), with Isaac (*ibid.*, 26:1-5), and with Jacob (*ibid.*, 28:13-15), covenants which God remembered (Ex. 2:24), down through the covenant he made with the whole people of Israel through the great law of Sinai (Ex. 20), and the covenant for the gathering again to Palestine (Deut. 30:3), until God said to Nathan in the Davidic covenant, "Go and tell my servant David, Thus saith the Lord" (2 Sam. 7:4-17; 1 Chron. 17:7-15)—in each and every of these the divine record is that God verily spake the words by which he and his children were to be bound, and be judged and be blessed throughout the ages.

To Moses, at the very beginning of his mission "God called . . . out of the midst of the bush" (Ex. 3:4), proclaiming who he was and that Moses was to deliver Israel. But Moses, demurring, said unto God, "Behold, when I come unto the children of Israel, and shall say unto them, The God of your fathers hath sent me unto you; and they shall say to me, What is his name? what shall I say unto them? And God said unto Moses, I AM THAT I AM: and he said, Thus shalt thou say unto the children of Israel, I AM hath sent me unto you." (*Ibid.*, 3:13-14.) And from that time until Moses finished his work, God talked with, commanded, pleaded with, and instructed Moses, until, as the record goes, "the Lord spake unto Moses face to face, as a man speaketh unto his friend." (*Ibid.*, 33:11.) In chapter after chapter, on page after page, the holy record bears witness that God spake with Moses "whom the Lord knew face to face." (Deut. 34:10.)

As to all of these the language is that God said, or spoke, and the text either expressly states, or leaves room for no reasonable doubt that the speaking was by voice as man to man. When some means of communication other than this is used, the scriptures clearly so state, as when the record declares that he "came unto Abram in a vision" (Gen. 15:1), or when he communicated through angels (*ibid.*, 22:11 *et seq.*).

God Has Passions

The scriptures are likewise filled with testimony that God possesses and exercises the same great elemental

feelings that are possessed by man. He himself declared
at Sinai, "for I the Lord thy God am a jealous God, visiting the iniquity of the fathers upon the children unto the
third and fourth generation of them that hate me; and
shewing mercy unto thousands of them that love me, and
keep my commandments" (Ex. 20:5-6); and when the
second tables of stone were given to Moses, the Lord
passed before him and proclaimed, "for the Lord, whose
name is Jealous, is a jealous God." (*Ibid.*, 34:14.)

Nahum declared "God is jealous, and the Lord re-
vengeth . . . and is furious; the Lord will take vengeance
on his adversaries, and he reserveth wrath for his enemies. The Lord is slow to anger . . . and will not at all
acquit the wicked." (Nah. 1:2-3.)

Moses sang of God, "To me belongeth vengeance, and
recompence." (Deut. 32:35.) Paul exclaimed, "Vengeance is mine; I will repay, saith the Lord" (Rom.
12:19); and David cried out, "O God, to whom vengeance
belongeth, shew thyself." (Psa. 94:1; see also Psa. 99:8;
Isa. 34:8; 35:4; Jer. 50:15; 2 Thess. 1:8; Heb. 10:30;
Jude 7.)

And when Moses and Israel sang their song unto
God, they declared, "The Lord is a man of war" (Ex.
15:3); not, suggest the commentators, as the Vulgate has
it, the "Lord is as a man of war." (Bishop A. J. Maclean in
Hastings' Dictionary of the Bible, sub voce "God.")

"Who," said Nahum, "can stand before his indigna-
tion? and who can abide in the fierceness of his anger?
his fury is poured out like fire." (Nah. 1:6.) Paul declared to the Romans, "For the wrath of God is revealed
from heaven against all ungodliness and unrighteousness
of men, who hold the truth in unrighteousness" (Rom.
1:18), and he exhorted the Colossians to abandon evil
things "For which things' sake the wrath of God cometh
on the children of disobedience" (Col. 3:6); God speaking
to Moses of the Children of Israel worshiping the golden

calf, said, "Now therefore let me alone, that my wrath
may wax hot against them, and that I may consume them"
(Ex. 32:10), and to Eliphaz, the Temanite, he said, "My
wrath is kindled against thee, and against thy two
friends." (Job 42:7.)

But God is not wholly a being of wrath and vengeance, not wholly a God of war. He declared to Moses,
as he gave the second tables: "The Lord, The Lord God
merciful and gracious, longsuffering, and abundant in
goodness and truth, keeping mercy for thousands, forgiv-
ing iniquity and transgression and sin." (Ex. 34:6-7.)

Paul writing to the Romans in reproof of their sins,
said, "And thinkest thou this, O man, that judgest them
which do such things, and doest the same, that thou shalt
escape the judgment of God? Or despisest thou the riches
of his goodness and forbearance and longsuffering; not
knowing that the goodness of God leadeth thee to repentance?" (Rom. 2:3-4.)

A God of Love

He is a God of love, for Christ himself declared to
Nicodemus that "God so loved the world, that he gave his
only begotten Son"; later Jesus said that "he it is that
loveth me"; that "the Father himself loveth you"; and in
the intercessory prayer he declared to the Father, thou
"hast loved them, as thou hast loved me. . . . for thou
lovedst me before the foundation of the world." (John
3:16; 14:21; 16:27; 17:23-24.)

Paul repeatedly affirmed the love of God (Rom.
5:8; Eph. 2:4-5), and John declared "God is love"
(1 John 4:8-16); and so through almost endless expressions with which the Old and the New Testaments are
filled, bearing record of God's infinite love.

Thus the Holy Writ is filled with the testimony of
God's holy men from Adam to the Apostles of the Master,
that God is a Personage, having a body, having parts, and

possessed of the great elemental passions; that man is in the image and likeness of God. The Latter-day Saints affirm that taken all together these evidences leave no reasonable doubt that God is a Being of the same order as man; and that in his recorded appearances to man he was not "veiled in angelic form," but that he appeared to them in his own proper person, in form of a man. (See *The Scofield Reference Bible*, C. I. Scofield, ed., (Oxford University Press, New York, 1917), p. 1115.)

But all the evidence thus far adduced falls short of that given by the work, the life, the being of Christ, "the only begotten of the Father." (John 1:14.)

Paul's Testimony

That Christ was in the image and likeness of God, Paul time and time again declared. To the Corinthians he said Christ "is the image of God." (2 Cor. 4:4.) To the Colossians he exclaimed in exaltation of Christ, he "is the image of the invisible God." (Col. 1:15.) To the Hebrews he affirmed that Christ is "the express image of his person" (Heb. 1:3; in A.S.V., "the very image of his substance," and in the Douay Version, "figure of his substance"); to the Philippians he bore testimony that Christ was "in the form of God" (Phil. 2:6), and commentators have declared that the word "form" here used means "the form by which a person or thing strikes the vision, the external appearance." (*Scofield, ad loc.*)

Christ himself speaking in Solomon's Porch at the Feast of the Dedication, declared, "I and my Father are one." (John 10:30; and see *ibid.*, 14:11.) Prior to this time while attending the Feast of the Tabernacles, he had said, "Ye neither know me, nor my Father: if ye had known me, ye should have known my Father also. . . . I speak to the world those things which I have heard of him. . . . I do nothing of myself; but as my Father hath taught me. . . . I speak that which I have seen with my Father." (*Ibid.*, 8:19, 26, 28, 38.)

In the last hour in the Passover chamber when, in reply to the question of Thomas, "How can we know the way?" Christ had said, "If ye had known me, ye should have known my Father," but Philip, doubting as much as did Thomas later and almost demanding a sign, begged, "Lord, shew us the Father, and it sufficeth us," and "Jesus saith unto him, Have I been so long time with you, and yet hast thou not known me, Philip? he that hath seen me hath seen the Father; and how sayest thou then, Shew us the Father?" (*Ibid.*, 14:5-9.)

The Same Figure and Form

Christ here spoke of himself while still in mortality, as he lived and moved among men, while he still ate and drank with them, while he still blessed and rebuked them, suffered with them, healed them of their infirmities, physical and spiritual; he was here Christ, the man, with form and figure, that could cleanse the temple of those who had made of the house of God "a den of thieves"; and it was the same Christ, the same man, the same figure and form, with the same hands and feet, and body, who still spoke as he had always spoken, face to face, man to man, and who said to his Apostles after his resurrection: "Behold my hands and my feet, that it is I myself: handle me, and see; for a spirit hath not flesh and bones, as ye see me have" (Luke 24:39); and later to Thomas, "Reach hither thy finger, and behold my hands; and reach hither thy hand, and thrust it into my side: and be not faithless, but believing." (John 20:27.) Christ, "the image of the invisible God," and resurrected to immortality, still looked and acted as a man, still mingled with men as a man, still taught them with the voice of a man, still ate and drank with them as a man. (Luke 24:42-43.)

Who in the face of all this can doubt that God is in

the form of man, of the same order of being as man, for Christ "the only begotten of the Father" who "is the image of the invisible God," so stood both as mortal man and as man resurrected to immortality.

To know this, is to know God, and to know God is life eternal. Christ in the most beautiful of all prayers, petitioned, just before he entered the Garden, "Father, the hour is come; glorify thy Son, that thy Son also may glorify thee: as thou hast given him power over all flesh, that he should give eternal life to as many as thou hast given him. And this is life eternal, that they might know thee the only true God, and Jesus Christ, whom thou hast sent." (John 17:1-3.)

Which may God grant to all of us.

"And now, after the many testimonies which have been giv-
en of him, this is the testimony, last of all, which we give of him:
That he lives!
"For we saw him, even on the right hand of God. . . ."
Doctrine and Covenants 76:22-23

Modern Revelation on the Personality of God

W E HAVE discussed the belief of the Latter-day Saints that God is not a formless, omnipresent, spiritual essence, and that on the contrary the declarations of the prophets of God and the records of his dealings with his children, as recorded in the Bible, clearly establish that God is a Being of the same order as men, with body, parts, and passions. Now we are to discuss the personality of God from the standpoint of modern revelation. This will lead us to the ancient records revealed in these last days, the revelations given to the prophets of this dispensation, the inspired utterance of these same prophets, and the theophanies granted to him who, by and through the grace, power, and authority of God, opened this, the greatest and last dispensation.

Pearl of Great Price Testimony

The account of the creation recorded in the Pearl of Great Price puts beyond doubt that man is in the actual image and form of God. To Moses, who declared to Satan, "For behold, I am a son of God, in the similitude of his Only Begotten," God said, "I am the Beginning and the End, the Almighty God. . . . And I, God, said unto mine Only Begotten, which was with me from the beginning: Let us make man in our image, after our likeness; and it was so. . . . And I, God, created man in mine own image, in the image of mine Only Begotten created I him; male and female created I them." Adam, prophesying after the birth of Seth, said, "In the day that God created man, in the likeness of God made he him; in the image of his own body, male and female, created he them, and blessed them, and called their name Adam, in the day when they were created and became living souls in the land upon the footstool of God." (Moses 1:13; 2:1, 26-27; 6:8-9.)

Book of Mormon

The Book of Mormon bears an equal testimony. King Limhi speaking to his people declared "that man was created after the image of God." (Mosiah 7:27.) Ammon, instructing King Lamoni, said, "I am a man; and man in the beginning was created after the image of God . . ." (Alma 18:34); later Aaron preaching to the father of King Lamoni, affirmed, "God created man after his own image" (Alma 22:12); and in the revelation given to Joseph Smith in April, 1830, on church organization, it is declared that God "created man, male and female, after his own image and in his own likeness, created he them." (D & C 20:18.)

Repeated references are made to the parts of God's body. Alma, the son of Alma, declared, after his conversion, ". . . then shall they confess, who live without God in the world, that the judgment of an everlasting punishment is just upon them; and they shall quake, and tremble, and shrink beneath the glance of his all-searching eye" (Mosiah 27:31); and Jacob instructing the people of Nephi, after the death of Nephi, declared he must speak unto them "under the glance of the piercing eye of the Almighty God." (Jacob 2:10.)

Lehi, blessing Joseph, his lastborn in the wilderness, and repeating a prophecy of Joseph who was sold into Egypt and who foresaw the deliverance under Moses, declared that the Lord had said, "But I will write unto him my law, by the finger of mine own hand." (2 Nephi 3:17.)

Amulek, recounting his ancestry unto the people who were in the land of Ammonihah, declared he was a descendant of Aminadi; the "same Aminadi who interpreted the writing which was upon the wall of the temple, which was written by the finger of God." (Alma 10:2.)

A Voice out of Heaven

When, after his resurrection, the Savior appeared to the people of Nephi, in the land Bountiful, his approach was heralded by "a voice as if it came out of heaven"; and they understood it not, either at the first or second call, but on the third, "they did understand the voice which they heard; and it said unto them: Behold my beloved Son, in whom I am well pleased, in whom I have glorified my name—hear ye him." (3 Nephi 11:3, 6-7.)

So in the writings of Moses regarding the Fall, Adam and Eve "heard the voice of the Lord God, as they were walking in the garden, in the cool of the day; and Adam and his wife went to hide themselves from the presence of the Lord God amongst the trees of the garden. And I, the Lord God, called unto Adam, and said unto him: Where goest thou? And he said: I heard thy voice in the garden, and I was afraid. . . ." (Moses 4:14-16.)

The glorious theophanies of Moses recorded in the same writings place the matter beyond any possible doubt.

Moses, says the record, "saw God face to face, and he talked with him, and the glory of God was upon Moses; therefore Moses could endure his presence. And God spake unto Moses, saying: Behold, I am the Lord God Almighty, and Endless is my name; for I am without beginning of days or end of years; and is not this endless? And, behold, thou art my son. . . thou art in the similitude of mine Only Begotten." (*Ibid.*, 1:2-6.)

When this vision closed, Moses exclaimed in an ecstasy of joy: "But now mine own eyes have beheld God; but not my natural, but my spiritual eyes, for my natural eyes could not have beheld; for I should have withered and died in his presence; but his glory was upon me; and I beheld his face, for I was transfigured before him." (*Ibid.*, 1:11.)

Another Visitation

To Moses there came another visitation from God, after Satan had tempted him. Calling upon the name of God, he, Moses, "beheld his glory again, for it was upon him; and he heard a voice, saying: Blessed art thou, Moses, for I, the Almighty, have chosen thee.... Moses called upon God, saying: Tell me, I pray thee, why these things are so, and by what thou madest them? And behold, the glory of the Lord was upon Moses, so that Moses stood in the presence of God, and talked with him face to face." (Moses 1:25, 30-31.)

But God has revealed further knowledge as to his personality. It will be remembered that Paul repeatedly declared that Christ was in the image and form of God. (2 Cor. 4:4; Col. 1:15; Heb. 1:3; Phil. 2:6.) We have just seen that God declared he made man in the image of himself and the Only Begotten. (Moses 2:26-27.) I recall to your minds also that Paul declared, "There is a natural body, and there is a spiritual body," though Paul seems not to have understood the exact relationship between the two. (1 Cor. 15:44-46.) But the writings of Moses made known through Joseph Smith make the matter clear. Moses records that God, after reciting that, "Thus the heaven and the earth were finished, and all the host of them," and after declaring that "I, God, created man in mine own image, in the image of mine Only Begotten created I him; male and female created I them," further declared: "For I, the Lord God, created all things, of which I have spoken, spiritually, before they were naturally upon the face of the earth. ... And I, the Lord God, had created all the children of men; and not yet a man to till the ground; for in heaven created I them; and there was not yet flesh upon the earth. ..." (Moses 2:27; 3:1, 5.) Thus man was created "spiritually" in the image of God and of the Only Begotten.

Became a Living Soul

The record then continues:

> And I, the Lord God, formed man from the dust of the ground, and breathed into his nostrils the breath of life; and man became a living soul . . . nevertheless, all things were before created; but spiritually were they created. . . . (Moses 3:7.)

As to this "natural" body or body of flesh and bones, Adam declared, in a prophecy already quoted:

> In the day that God created man, in the likeness of God made he him;
> In the image of his own body, male and female, created he them . . . in the day when they were created and became living souls in the land upon the footstool of God. (Moses 6:8-9.)

Thus man was created "naturally" in the image of God.

That the natural body of man is in the image of the spiritual body of man, that the two bodies of man, natural and spiritual, are very counterparts, is put beyond question by the record of the glorious manifestation of Christ to the brother of Jared, millenniums before Christ took upon himself a body,—for Christ himself has declared, "I was in the beginning with the Father." (D & C 93:21; and see Moses 2:26.)

The brother of Jared, having built the vessels by which he and his people were to "cross this great deep" was importuning the Lord to touch the stones which he "did molten out of a rock," so that, being touched, they would light the vessels on the voyage. So great was the faith of this mighty man that "the Lord stretched forth his hand and touched the stones one by one with his finger. And the veil was taken from off the eyes of the brother of Jared, and he saw the finger of the Lord; and it was as the finger of a man, like unto flesh and blood. . . ." (Ether 2:25; 3:1, 6.)

But the vision did not end here, for after declaring to the brother of Jared, "never have I showed myself unto man whom I have created, for never has man believed in me as thou hast. Seest thou that ye are created after mine own image? Yea, even all men were created in the beginning after mine own image," the Lord proclaimed, "Behold, this body, which ye now behold, is the body of my spirit; and man have I created after the body of my spirit; and even as I appear unto thee to be in the spirit will I appear unto my people in the flesh." (Ether 3:15-16.)

By His Own Testimony

Thus by his own testimony Christ had a spirit, a spiritual body, and was to have, and did have, a body of flesh and bone. It is the belief of the Latter-day Saints that since, as Paul says, Christ "is the image of the invisible God" (Col. 1:15), that God also has a spirit, a spiritual body, and a body of flesh and bone. Nor may we pass on without observing that since man is "in the similitude of his Only Begotten" (Moses 1:13), man also has a spirit, a spiritual body, and a body of flesh and bone.

And this the scriptures declare, for the Lord showing Abraham the creation in vision, said, "I came down in the beginning in the midst of all the intelligences thou hast seen . . . and he stood in the midst of them, and he said: These I will make my rulers; for he stood among those that were spirits . . . and he said unto me: Abraham, thou art one of them; thou wast chosen before thou wast born." (Abraham 3:21, 23.)

The Latter-day Saints believe that these intelligences were co-eternal with God. As the Lord said to the Prophet in a revelation given at Kirtland in 1833, "I was in the beginning with the Father, and am the Firstborn. . . . Ye were also in the beginning with the Father. . . . Man was also in the beginning with God. Intelligence, or the light of truth, was not created or made, neither

indeed can be. . . . Behold, here is the agency of man.
. . . For man is spirit." (D & C 93:21, 23, 29, 31, 33.)

That man has a spiritual body is evidenced by the
account already given in the writings of Moses that man
was created spiritually in heaven before he was given a
natural body. That man has a natural body, we are, ourselves, the final evidence. Thus man is indeed "in the
similitude of his Only Begotten" (Moses 1:13), who "is
the image of the invisible God" (Col. 1:15), with a spirit
or intelligence, a spiritual body, and a temporal body,
which latter are the counterparts, one of the other. Evidence could not be stronger that man and God are of the
same order of being.

Like a Man in Form

It was these facts which lay behind the declaration
of the Prophet Joseph when he announced at King Fol-
lett's funeral the principle that made havoc of the er-
roneous doctrines of Christendom:

> God himself was once as we are now, and is an exalted man,
> and sits enthroned in yonder heavens! That is the great secret.
> If the veil were rent today, and the great God who holds this
> world in its orbit, and who upholds all worlds and all things by
> his power, was to make himself visible,—I say, if you were to
> see him today, you would see him like a man in form—like your-
> selves in all the person, image, and very form as a man; for
> Adam was created in the very fashion, image and likeness of
> God, and received instruction from, and walked, talked, and con-
> versed with him, as one man talks and communes with another.
> (*Teachings of the Prophet Joseph Smith*, compiled by Joseph
> Fielding Smith, (2nd ed., Deseret News Press, 1940), p. 345.)

Here is the language of very assurance, of actual
knowledge. By what right did the Prophet so speak?

Dispensations of the Gospel

From the earliest beginning of recorded time until

now, man has traveled spiritually in identic, recurring cycles. Through this full stretch of history God has, time after time, striven with the co-eternal spirits which he tabernacled with spiritual and material bodies, seeking to lead them not only to salvation but to exaltation, and the great body of these same spirits, so embodied, have as each renewed effort was made, exercised their free agency and wandered into forbidden paths.

In this effort of God to bring these spirits to exaltation, the first dispensation came to Adam, Michael, the prince, the archangel. (D & C 107:54; 128:21; 88:111-116; Rev. 12:7.) He possessed the power and authority of God through the Melchizedek Priesthood, or the Holy Priesthood, after the Order of the Son of God (D & C 107:2-3, 41), he having received this Priesthood "in the Creation, before the world was formed." (The Prophet on Priesthood, July 1839, *History of the Church*, Vol. 3, pp. 385-386.)

Adam walked and talked with God who taught and led him; Adam had the Gospel to save men, for Moses declared, "And thus the Gospel began to be preached, from the beginning, being declared by holy angels sent forth from the presence of God, and by his own voice, and by the gift of the Holy Ghost." But while Enoch was able so to lead his people that he "and all his people walked with God," yet Cain brought murder and corruption and the spirit of disobedience into the human heart, and the peoples of the earth waxed in wickedness and corruption until "God said unto Noah: The end of all flesh is come before me, for the earth is filled with violence, and behold I will destroy all flesh from off the earth." (Moses 5:58; 7:69; 8:30.)

Then came the Flood.

The next dispensation came to Noah after the Flood, who was commanded to multiply and replenish the earth (Gen. 9:1); he also possessed the Melchizedek Priesthood,

received at the hands of Methuselah (D & C 107:52);
he also had the Gospel, received before the Flood, in a
truth and purity which had sanctified Enoch and his
people; he also "was a just man and perfect in his generations, and Noah walked with God." (Gen. 6:9.) Yet
the people dwindled in unbelief and wickedness and the
peoples of the world were lost to God. The second cycle
of God's power and authority, of a Gospel plan, of belief, of unbelief, of disbelief, and of wickedness to destruction had run its course.

The Almighty was forced to call Abraham from a
heathen worship and an idolatrous family to usher in
the next dispensation, by and under the authority of the
Priesthood and to restore the Gospel. (Abraham 1; D & C
84:14.) And God came to Abraham and talked with and
blessed him. (Gen. 12:7; 17:1-5; 18:1-8; 18:22, 32-33;
26:2.) So was ushered in the Abrahamic dispensation.
But after Isaac and Jacob, to whom God also appeared,
and whom he instructed and blessed, there came the bondage in Egypt and then even the chosen people forgot their
God and departed from his ways. Thus again there was
a falling away from the true path; for a third time the
cycle was complete.

Face to Face

Then God came to Moses, first in the burning bush,
afterwards in the glory of the appearance of Sinai (Ex.
3:4; ch. 19, 20; 24:1-11; 31:18), and Moses opened his
dispensation endowed with the Melchizedek Priesthood
(D & C 84:6), having talked with God "face to face, as
a man speaketh unto his friend." (Ex. 33:11.) Moses
"sought diligently to sanctify his people that they might
behold the face of God; but they hardened their hearts
and could not endure his presence. . . . Therefore, he
took Moses out of their midst, and the Holy Priesthood

also; and the lesser priesthood continued. . . ." (D & C
84:23-26.) The fourth cycle had run its course.

Then came the Meridian of Time, the Atonement
of the Only Begotten; the establishment of the Apostolic
Church; the falling away and final apostasy; the loss
of the Priesthood. Man was again wandering in the
spiritual wilderness. Once more the cycle had been completed.

And now was the time come, predicted at Patmos,
when God decreed that again his Priesthood should be
restored to earth, his Church again established, in this
the last dispensation, that man should again have opportunity to exercise his free agency until salvation or
condemnation. "And I saw another angel," said John,
in words familiar to the ear of every Latter-day Saint
and dear to his heart, "fly in the midst of heaven, having
the everlasting gospel to preach unto them that dwell
on the earth, and to every nation, and kindred, and
tongue, and people, saying with a loud voice, Fear God,
and give glory to him; for the hour of his judgment is
come: and worship him that made heaven, and earth,
and the sea, and the fountains of waters." (Rev. 14:6-7.)

In Mighty Prayer

Troubled in spirit, devoutly and honestly humble,
and moved by a faith which might have removed mountains, a lad, for "the word of the Lord was precious in
those days; there was no open vision" (1 Sam. 3:1),
having read that, "If any of you lack wisdom, let him ask
of God, that giveth to all men liberally, and upbraideth
not; and it shall be given him" (James 1:5), went to
his God in mighty prayer, just as Adam and Noah and
Abraham and Isaac and Jacob and Moses had done before
him, and God, answering that prayer dealt with this lad
just as he had dealt with them of old. Uncertain as to
which of all the ways followed by the various Christian

sects was the right way, the lad appealed to God. Let him tell his own story:

At length I came to the conclusion that I must either remain in darkness and confusion, or else I must do as James directs, that is, ask of God. I at length came to the determination to "ask of God," concluding that if he gave wisdom to them that lacked wisdom, and would give liberally, and not upbraid, I might venture.

So, in accordance with this, my determination to ask of God, I retired to the woods to make the attempt. It was on the morning of a beautiful, clear day, early in the spring of eighteen hundred and twenty. It was the first time in my life that I had made such an attempt, for amidst all my anxieties I had never as yet made the attempt to pray vocally.

After I had retired to the place where I had previously designed to go, having looked around me, and finding myself alone, I kneeled down and began to offer up the desire of my heart to God. I had scarcely done so, when immediately I was seized upon by some power which entirely overcame me, and had such an astonishing influence over me as to bind my tongue so that I could not speak. Thick darkness gathered around me, and it seemed to me for a time as if I were doomed to sudden destruction.

But, exerting all my powers to call upon God to deliver me out of the power of this enemy which had seized upon me, and at the very moment when I was ready to sink into despair and abandon myself to destruction—not to an imaginary ruin, but to the power of some actual being from the unseen world, who had such marvelous power as I had never before felt in any being— just at this moment of great alarm, I saw a pillar of light exactly over my head, above the brightness of the sun, which descended gradually until it fell upon me.

Two Personages

It no sooner appeared than I found myself delivered from the enemy which held me bound. When the light rested upon me I saw two Personages, whose brightness and glory defy all description, standing above me in the air. One of them spake unto me, calling me by name and said, pointing to the other—*This is My Beloved Son. Hear Him!*

My object in going to inquire of the Lord was to know which

of all the sects was right, that I might know which to join. No sooner, therefore, did I get possession of myself, so as to be able to speak, than I asked the Personages who stood above me in the light, which of all the sects was right—and which I should join.

I was answered that I must join none of them, for they were all wrong; and the Personage who addressed me said that all their creeds were an abomination in his sight; that those professors were all corrupt; that: "they draw near to me with their lips, but their hearts are far from me, they teach for doctrines the commandments of men, having a form of godliness, but they deny the power thereof."

He again forbade me to join with any of them; and many other things did he say unto me, which I cannot write at this time. When I came to myself again, I found myself lying on my back, looking up into heaven. (P. of G.P., Joseph Smith, 2:13-20.)

Let me ask who doubts or disbelieves this simply told, matter-of-fact story of this the most glorious vision of all recorded time—for here for the first time, has the Father and the Son appeared together as glorified Personages—if God appeared to Adam, to Enoch, to Noah, to Abraham, to Isaac, to Jacob, to Moses, and to the prophets of Israel then following, if God appeared to the lad Samuel in the temple, why not to the lad Joseph in the woods? Who shall deny God's power to appear when his divine purpose sanctions or requires? And while the personalities of those mighty ones of ancient days are so obscured by the mists of time that the faith-needing critics of today even deny their existence, we know that Joseph lived, that he gave the testimony we have read, and that he sealed that testimony with his life, for no one can doubt but that to live in peace he had only to retract. Men do not willingly die for a lie.

As in All Dispensations

Following this vision, God moved his work forward as in all the preceding dispensations. The Priesthood was restored; the Gospel, "the everlasting gospel" of John, was revealed in its ancient purity; the Church was organized in the exact similitude of that established by the Son and his Apostles. Man had again his free agency, coupled once again with full opportunity, and woe to him, declare the scriptures, who chooses the way of darkness. The last cycle for man has begun.

Once again the Father and the Son appeared together in this dispensation, this time to Joseph and Sidney Rigdon, appeared to them just as he appeared to Moses and Aaron, to Nadab, Abihu, and the seventy elders of Israel (Ex. 24:9-11), just as certainly, just as actually; and of this further vision the two declare:

And now, after the many testimonies which have been given of him, this is the testimony, last of all, which we give of him: That he lives!

For we saw him, even on the right hand of God; and we heard the voice bearing record that he is the Only Begotten of the Father—

That by him, and through him, and of him, the worlds are and were created, and the inhabitants thereof are begotten sons and daughters unto God. (D & C 76:22-24.)

Thus does modern revelation and vision and teaching (I have scanned but a few of them) declare that God is a personal Being, of the same order as man, with body, parts, and passions. Well might the Prophet declare at Ramus, "The Father has a body of flesh and bones as tangible as man's; the Son also; but the Holy Ghost has not a body of flesh and bones, but is a personage of Spirit." (*Church History*, Vol. 5, p. 325.)

This is the faith and belief of the Latter-day Saints; it is the doctrine upon which they are prepared to rise to eternal glory or fall to eternal condemnation. On this faith they hazard eternal life, nothing doubting.

Circumscribed by Law

To those who deny to God a body and who make of him a spiritual essence—a mere force, god-force if you will, I beg to suggest this thought—but without entering the field of metaphysical philosophy: The postulated god-force must, from its manifestation, be not only intelligent, but also all-intelligent and hence all-powerful. The Latter-day Saints believe that "the glory of God is intelligence." (D & C 93:36.) The great forces of which man knows—heat, light, electricity, are each and all bound and circumscribed by law; they move and operate in an appointed and prescribed way; they are not masters, but slaves, slaves of intelligence, even that of the finite mind. Man knows no intelligent force. Intelligence is manifest to man only through material entities as if intelligence itself were entitative, as indeed the infinity of human intelligence is proof, and as the Latter-day Saints believe. All human experience, all human knowledge protest the concept of a god-force; they sanction an intelligence functioning through a material entity.

To those who look for and await a scientific demonstration of God, that shall lead to a knowledge devoid of any "if," I offer this thought: A knowledge of the scientifically knowable comes only by and through a demonstration to the senses of man: science repudiates any allegation of knowledge which is not demonstrable to the senses. To that which science cannot hear, see, feel, taste, or smell, or the effect of which it cannot experimentally demonstrate to the senses, it denies existence. But as these senses are exercised by finite man, they have the imperfection of finitude. No two men hear, see, feel, taste, or smell in precisely the same way. Thus, sense-knowledge must always be imperfect, not because the knowable is imperfect, but because the means of knowing are imperfect.

Nothing Doubting

And because of this and because finite mind cannot know when it has the infinite truth, man cannot know when he has reached the ultimate truth; there is and must always be—it is of the very essence of the true scientific spirit—an "if" in sense-knowledge. So when man seeks to find God by sense-knowledge, when he looks for scientific demonstration of God's existence and attributes, he shall never escape that "if" which his very method of knowing postulates. You who seek and expect thus to escape the "if" in your God, will perish in despair. The grief of the doomed shall be your portion. And in this we see how unstable the belief of those who depend for their testimony of God upon signs, for signs are but sense-knowledge which tempt unbelief.

If you shall escape the "if," if you would know God, you must go to God in faith and prayer, nothing doubting, and to you shall come the knowledge of the Spirit, which, beyond compare, exceeds the knowledge of the senses. And remember faith is the gift of God. (Eph. 2:8.)

Paul declared to the Corinthians:

> For what man knoweth the things of a man, save the spirit of man which is in him? even so the things of God knoweth no man, but the Spirit of God.
> Now we have received, not the spirit of the world, but the spirit which is of God; that we might know the things that are freely given to us of God. . . .
> But the natural man receiveth not the things of the Spirit of God: for they are foolishness unto him: neither can he know them, because they are spiritually discerned. (1 Cor. 2:11-12, 14.)

Again I come to the elemental thought of the wonderful prayer of intercession, the preamble to the final act of the atoning mission of the Only Begotten:

> Father, the hour is come; glorify thy Son, that thy Son also may glorify thee:
> As thou hast given him power over all flesh, that he should give eternal life to as many as thou hast given him.
> And this is life eternal, that they might know thee the only true God, and Jesus Christ, whom thou hast sent. (John 17:1-3.)

"The foxes have holes, and the birds of the air have nests; but the Son of man hath not where to lay his head."

Matthew 8:20

My Kingdom Is Not of This World

IT IS A trite expression that we live in an age of materialism, a materialism which has enthroned worldly things and in a materialism that has cast a shadow even over our spirituality. As I see it, one of the great reasons for this is the shadow which we have cast over Jesus as the Christ. Even some of our great sectarian churches, like ourselves sons of our Heavenly Father, are forsaking him. They are making of Christ, as I have often said, a great teacher, a great philosopher, a great character, they do not question that, but they deny to him that he was and is the Christ.

Of all of the innumerable testimonies regarding his personality, I should like to call your attention only to two or three. The first is the great prayer which he offered on the night before his crucifixion, after they had left the chamber and gone out to the Mount of Olives, that great prayer: "And this is life eternal, that they might know thee the only true God, and Jesus Christ, whom thou hast sent." (John 17:3.) And the testimony of Peter before the Sanhedrin, when challenged as to the name by which he had performed the miracle at the Gate Beautiful of the temple, he replied: ". . . the name of Jesus Christ of Nazareth . . . for there is none other name under heaven given among men, whereby we must be saved." (Acts 4:10, 12.)

And that testimony embodied in that great declaration of the Father himself to Moses, because it is the epitome, the summary of the Gospel of Jesus Christ: "For behold, this is my work and my glory—to bring to pass the immortality and eternal life of man." (Moses 1:39.)

Born in Lowly Home

There has been an apostasy from that knowledge
of the Christ. You know, the more I contemplate the life
of the Savior, the more I am impressed, the more I come
to value his lowliness, born in the home of a lowly carpenter, not in the halls of the great, not in the palaces
of national rulers, but with royal blood in his mortal
veins. I am impressed with the observation which he
made to a man who came seeking to follow him, to go
with him, and he said to the man, "The foxes have holes,
and the birds of the air have nests; but the Son of man
hath not where to lay his head." (Matt. 8:20.)

He was indifferent, so indifferent to the worldly
things. His mind was fixed quite otherwise. The very
temptation that came to him from Satan, when Satan
offered him all the kingdoms of the world if he would
merely bow down and worship him, offered him all the
power that could be bestowed through human hands; but
he cast that aside.

I recall how after he fed the multitude of five thousand, they would have taken him and made him king,
but he thrust that aside also. Worldly power had no
allurement. Worldly power was not for him.

I recall that as he stood before Pilate, Pilate's first
question was political: "Art thou the King of the
Jews? ..." (Matt. 27:11.) And finally he said to Pilate,
who six times tried to get the Jews to release Jesus—he
finally said to Pilate, "My kingdom is not of this world,"
and that his mission was to establish truth, and then
that poor, perplexed Pilate queried, "What is truth?"
(See John 18:36-38.)

Furnishes Food and Money

I have in mind the things which he did, the miracles
which he performed. There were only three occasions,

I believe, when he undertook specifically to provide food for the multitude or for anyone. The first was the feeding of the five thousand on the mount, the second was the feeding of the four thousand on the plain, and the third was that beautiful incident on the Lake of Galilee after he was resurrected when, as the fishermen, the Apostles who had turned again to fishing, drew near the shore with their nets empty, he, the resurrected Christ, stood on the shore with coals of fire and fish and bread prepared for eating.

I recall but one instance where in fact he furnished money, and I am not sure of another incident somewhat similar to it. I refer to the time when he lacked money for taxes, and he sent Peter down to secure it from the mouth of a fish. He was not providing money to those with whom he worked. The other incident where money was involved directly for him, was when he was asked if taxes should be paid to Caesar, and he, taking a coin and showing the image thereon, said, "Render therefore unto Caesar the things which are Caesar's; and unto God the things that are God's." (Matt. 22:21.)

As to Wealth

As to wealth: You will remember how the rich young ruler came to him and asked what he should do. The Savior told him to obey the commandments. He said, "Master, all these have I observed from my youth." Then said the Master, "Sell that thou hast, and give to the poor . . . and follow me." And the rich young man turned away. (Matt. 19:16-22; Mark 10:17-31.) He wanted all of the spiritual blessings which God could bestow, but at the same time he wanted to retain his wealth.

John's disciples came questioning:

Now when John had heard in the prison the works of Christ, he sent two of his disciples,

And said unto him, Art thou he that should come, or do we look for another?

Jesus answered and said unto them, Go and shew John again those things which ye do hear and see:

The blind receive their sight, and the lame walk, the lepers are cleansed, and the deaf hear, the dead are raised up, and the poor have the gospel preached to them. (Matt. 11:2-5.)

That is the work of the Savior.

On another occasion, he said unto another, "Follow me," but the other said:

Lord, suffer me first to go and bury my father.

Jesus said unto him, Let the dead bury their dead: but go thou and preach the kingdom of God.

And another also said, Lord, I will follow thee; but let me first go bid them farewell, which are at home at my house.

And Jesus said unto him, No man, having put his hand to the plough, and looking back, is fit for the kingdom of God. (Luke 9:59-62.)

Worldly Position Not Necessary

Much more along this line might be said, but I want to call your attention to his formula, the principle which guided him, and how beautiful it is, and how it lets all of us who are poor come to him, and how it promises to us his spirit. He said in the closing of the incident that was connected with the coming of the disciples:

Come unto me, all ye that labour and are heavy laden, and I will give you rest.

Take my yoke upon you, and learn of me; for I am meek and lowly in heart: and ye shall find rest unto your souls.

For my yoke is easy, and my burden is light. (Matt. 11:28-30.)

His Gospel can be lived, can be enjoyed by the poorest of us; the poorest of us may enjoy the blessings of the Gospel, the blessings of the Priesthood which accompany it. We need neither worldly position nor wealth in order to enjoy all that he has to give. His is the salvation and exaltation, if we follow him, of all of us. There is nothing requiring more than a broken heart and a contrite spirit, and all that flows therefrom.

May the Lord give us the power so to live that we may have the blessings which he has promised; may he give us, to each of us, the broken heart and the contrite spirit; may we turn to Jesus the Christ, the Author of our salvation, our Elder Brother; may we worship him in spirit and in truth; may we approach our Heavenly Father through him, that his blessings may be ours.

"Behold the Lamb of God, which taketh away the sin of the world."
John 1:29

Testimonies of the Divinity of the Savior

J ESUS, returning from his forty days in the wilderness, came into the midst of the multitude gathered together at Bethabara to hear John and receive of his baptism, whereupon John proclaimed: "Behold the Lamb of God, which taketh away the sin of the world." The next day Jesus came again, and John bore further witness, this time regarding the manifestation of the Holy Ghost at the baptism of Jesus, saying: "And I saw, and bare record that this is the Son of God." (John 1:29, 34.)

So solemnly testified John to the Jewish world and to all men born on earth in whatever time; and in this testimony is bound up the basic truths of Christian faith and knowledge—the identity of Jesus as the Messiah, the Fall of Adam, and the Atonement for Adam's Fall by Jesus the Christ, the Only Begotten of the Father.

But John was not alone in this exact testimony of Christ as the Lamb of God, the Redeemer.—And I shall tell my story today mostly in the recorded language of God the Father, of Jesus the Christ, and of God's servants and prophets.

Years after the baptism, John the Revelator was to speak, under divine inspiration, of the "Lamb slain from the foundation of the world"; and Peter declared we are redeemed "with the precious blood of Christ, as of a lamb without blemish and without spot: who verily was foreordained before the foundation of the world." While Job cried out to his heckling friends in an ecstasy of joy and triumph: "I know that my redeemer liveth, and that he shall stand at the latter day upon the earth: and though after my skin worms destroy this body, yet in my flesh shall I see God," Paul, addressing the Corinthians in that great sermon on the resurrection, declared:

"For since by man came death, by man came also the resurrection of the dead. For as in Adam all die, even so in Christ shall all be made alive." (Rev. 13:8; 1 Pet. 1:19-20; Job 19:25-26; 1 Cor. 15:21-22.)

These testimonies all hold but one language,—that Jesus Christ is the Redeemer of the world, and that testimony must come to every child of God, for it is written that 'every knee shall bow, and every tongue confess that Jesus is the Christ.' (Isa. 45:23; Rom. 14:11; Phil. 2:10-11; Mosiah 27:31; D & C 88:104.)

Birth Foretold by Prophets

The birth of the Atoning Sacrifice, the Lamb of God, had also been foretold by the ancient prophets of Israel. Isaiah declared: "Behold, a virgin shall conceive, and bear a son, and shall call his name Immanuel," "which being interpreted," says Matthew, "is, God with us." The Psalmist sang of him as begotten of the Father, and spoke also of his goodness and mercy and righteousness, of his care for the poor and the needy whose souls he would save; the Psalmist boasted of the Messiah's strength and power, of his justice and judgment, and declared that through him the throne of David should endure forever; he repeated a supplication of the Lord to the Father and proclaimed the Lord a priest of Melchizedek who should judge among the heathen; he told in graphic detail of the agony on the cross even to Christ's almost despairing outcry, when all had forsaken him: "My God, my God, why hast thou forsaken me?" (Isa. 7:14; Matt. 1:23; Psa. 2, 72, 89, 102, 110, 22.)

Chronicled and Witnessed

When the hour was near for Jesus to come to earth and take a mortal body, an angel told Mary she should bear a son; and to Joseph the husband of Mary he re-

vealed that the son should save his people from their
sins. The unborn John bore witness to the presence
of Deity when Mary visited Elisabeth. On this hemisphere Jesus himself foretold his birth as of the next day.
In Palestine, an angel announced the birth to the shepherds tending their flocks on the hills, while a multitude
of heavenly voices caroled, "Glory to God in the highest,
and on earth peace, good will toward men." His star
appeared in the heavens. (Luke 1:26-56; 2:8-20; Matt.
1:18-25; 2:1-12; 3 Nephi 1:4-14; 21-22.)

Then was fulfilled the great prophecy of Isaiah:

For unto us a child is born, unto us a son is given: and the
government shall be upon his shoulder: and his name shall be
called Wonderful, Counsellor, The mighty God, The everlasting
Father, The Prince of Peace. (Isa. 9:6-7.)

So was the birth of the Lamb of God foretold long
before and chronicled and witnessed at the time.

Heralded by John

Who this person is who came to earth thus heralded
by the heavens, is told to us by John in the mighty preface
to his Gospel:

In the beginning was the Word, and the Word was with
God, and the Word was God.

The same was in the beginning with God.

All things were made by him; and without him was not any
thing made that was made. . . .

He was in the world, and the world was made by him, and
the world knew him not. . . .

And the Word was made flesh, and dwelt among us, (and we
beheld his glory, the glory as of the only begotten of the Father,)
full of grace and truth. (John 1:1-3, 10, 14.)

And in the prayer of the Great High Priest, Jesus
himself besought the Father: "And now, O Father, glori-

fy thou me with thine own self with the glory which I had with thee before the world was." (*Ibid.*, 17:5.)

Thus Jesus is the Christ, the Only Begotten of the Father, the Creator of the world and all it contains, the Redeemer of its people, the children of God, all of them, the Word that is God.

Nor do we who rejoice in these witnesses and their testimonies and who are blessed with a pure testimony of the truth of the Gospel of Christ, give up one hairsbreadth of that full divine stature given to Jesus, the Carpenter of Nazareth, by the scriptures; we accept it without cavil or reservation.

We cherish in our hearts the witness which God himself has borne of his Son.

We recall that when Jesus came up out of the water, after John had baptized him "to fulfil all righteousness," the Holy Ghost descended upon him, and God the Father's voice came from the heavens, declaring: "This is my beloved Son, in whom I am well pleased." (Matt. 3:17; Mark 1:11; Luke 3:22.) We acknowledge that the same voice and the same message came to Peter, James, and John as Jesus communed with Moses and Elias at the time of the Transfiguration. (Matt. 17:5; Mark 9:7; Luke 9:35.) We declare that the same voice and same message came, in our dispensation, to the boy Prophet Joseph praying in the woods.

Testimonies of Jesus

With equal fervor we keep ever present in our minds the testimonies of Jesus himself about himself.

We remember that when in the temple at twelve, he said to his mother and Joseph, who had sought for him three days: "How is it that ye sought me? wist ye not that I must be about my Father's business?" (Luke 2:49.)

We do not forget that when he first cleansed the

temple of the money changers and those selling therein oxen and sheep and doves he drove them out, saying: "Take these things hence: make not my Father's house an house of merchandise." (John 2:16.)

We rejoice in the contemplation of the words of Christ's great sermon to Nicodemus, a "ruler of the Jews" who came to him timidly by nightfall: "For God so loved the world, that he gave his only begotten Son, that whosoever believeth in him should not perish, but have everlasting life. For God sent not his Son into the world to condemn the world; but that the world through him might be saved"; and likewise we have joy and see salvation in his great declaration to the woman of Samaria: "I that speak unto thee am" the Christ. (*Ibid.*, 3:16-17; 4:26.)

We do not forget that while at the Feast of Tabernacles, he solemnly testified to those about him in the temple: "Ye are from beneath; I am from above: ye are of this world; I am not of this world. . . . I speak to the world those things which I have heard of him. . . . When ye have lifted up the Son of man, then shall ye know that I am he, and that I do nothing of myself; but as my Father hath taught me, I speak these things" (*ibid.*, 8:23, 26, 28); nor do we forget that later in Jerusalem as he taught the parable of the Good Shepherd, he again testified: "Therefore doth my Father love me, because I lay down my life, that I might take it again. No man taketh it from me, but I lay it down of myself. I have power to lay it down, and I have power to take it again. This commandment have I received of my Father." (*Ibid.*, 10:17-18.)

Likewise it is in our memories that at the time of his arrest, as he bade Peter, who would have used force, to put up his sword, Jesus said: "Thinkest thou that I cannot now pray to my Father, and he shall presently give me more than twelve legions of angels"; we remember that in the last discourse in the Chamber of the Last

Supper, he declared, answering Philip's question, the
oneness of the Father and himself; and that to the disciples disputing among themselves who should be greatest, he declared: "For the Son of man is come to save that
which was lost." (Matt. 18:11; 26:53; John 14:8 ff.)

So do we ever hold clear in our memories the words
between Jesus and Peter in the coasts of Caesarea Philippi: "But whom say ye that I am? And Simon Peter
answered and said, Thou art the Christ, the Son of the
living God. And Jesus answered and said unto him,
Blessed art thou, Simon Barjona: for flesh and blood
hath not revealed it unto thee, but my Father which is
in heaven." Also do we ever remember that rarely beautiful scene between Martha and Jesus, returned to Bethany
to raise Lazarus from the dead: "I am the resurrection,
and the life: he that believeth in me, though he were
dead, yet shall he live: and whosoever liveth and believeth in me shall never die. Believest thou this? She
saith unto him, Yea, Lord: I believe that thou art the
Christ, the Son of God, which should come into the world."
(Matt. 16:15 ff.; John 11:25 ff.)

We Cherish These Testimonies

We cherish up all these mighty things in our hearts,
these witnesses and these testimonies. They are the light
that guides our feet through these dark days that afflict
us; they are our cheer and our comfort in our sleepless
nights filled with anxieties over our loved ones on the
battle fronts; they give us the hope and the faith to go
daily to our tasks, never despairing amidst all this woe,
misery, and death; they spell our happiness and salvation in the life to come.

Every Christian remembers that as Christ and his
disciples left the temple for the last time and went and
sat on the Mount of Olives in the evening of the third
day of the week, his disciples, recalling his lament over
Jerusalem, and his teachings that he should come again,

asked him privately, "Tell us, when shall these things be? and what shall be the sign of thy coming, and of the end of the world?"

Jesus, answering, broke forth in a mighty prophecy that visioned in a few bold phrases, the signs of his coming at a later day. He spoke of plagues and earthquakes, of wars among the nations and of disturbances in the heavens, of persecutions of the saints, of false prophets, of betrayers, of false Christs, of deceivers, those of whom John later declared "confess not that Jesus Christ is come in the flesh," and that such a one "is a deceiver and an antichrist." (Matt. 24; Mark 13; Luke 21; 1 John 2:18 ff.; 4:3; 2 John 7.)

Speaking of this same time an ancient prophet of this hemisphere said the day would come when men "lifted up in the pride of their eyes" would "put down the power and miracles of God, and preach up unto themselves their own wisdom and their own learning," —iniquities of which Satan was the foundation. (2 Nephi 26:20 ff.)

Duty of Those Who Accept Christ

In these days when antichrists are abroad, just as Jesus foretold nearly two thousand years ago, denying Jesus, his Sonship and Messiahship, belittling things of the Spirit and magnifying all the pleasures of the flesh, it is fitting that we who accept the Gospel of Christ should declare our testimonies of the truth, for as he said: ". . . ye shall know the truth, and the truth shall make you free." (John 8:32.) We should fail in our duty, be recreant to our trust, did we do less than this.

We do not deny the Christ, we accept and proclaim him as the Son of God, the Redeemer of the world, the First Fruits of the Resurrection.

We do not deny the miraculous conception; we accept the virgin birth with all that this fact connotes and implies.

We do not deny his divinity; we accept it. He is the Only Begotten of the Father. He is the Word; he was with God "in the beginning," having the glory of the Father.

We do not deny he was the "Lamb of God, which taketh away the sin of the world," "slain from the foundation of the world," foreordained to his mission before the world was. We declare in all soberness, first, that the Fall of Adam brought the separation of man from the presence of God, a spiritual death; and next that it brought both mortality and mortal death. We declare that man may in himself overcome the spiritual death by so living and observing the commandments of God that he may ultimately again stand and live in the presence of God. This is given to man to do, through the exercise of his free agency, also a gift of God. Our Heavenly Father has from the first given man sufficient truth to enable him to do this. But to overcome the effects of mortality and mortal death, it was necessary that an Atonement should be made for the failure of Adam, exercising his free agency, to observe the commandment that God gave. So Christ came to earth. But "Adam fell that men might be; and men are, that they might have joy." Thus the Only Begotten of the Father came to earth, to make Atonement for Adam. For again, as Paul declared, "As in Adam all die, even so in Christ shall all be made alive." (John 1:29; Rev. 13:8; D & C 29:41-50; 2 Nephi 2:22-25; 9:5 ff.; Alma 12:16, 32; 40:26; Helaman 14:18; Moses 5:11; 1 Cor. 15:22.)

We do not deny his resurrection; we proclaim it, in its most literal sense. We declare that Christ took up the very body he laid down. And that through his death and resurrection, he opened the graves of all God's children, who in due time will all be resurrected,—the good and the bad, who thereafter will stand before the final judgment seat to receive whatever reward is due them for the lives they have led.

We do not deny the miraculous in Christ's life; we accept it as the most natural manifestation of the power and authority of the Son of God, whether the miracles be of healings or those sometimes called "nature miracles," which to us testify directly of his creative power.

We do not deny, we accept each and every of the doctrines and teachings of Christ, as they were pronounced by him. We declare they contain a full and complete plan of life and salvation and that exaltation in God's presence will come to all those who shape their lives thereby.

In that eventful third day of Christ's final week, in the temple certain Greeks came to Philip, saying, "Sir, we would see Jesus." But Jesus, finishing his discourse, went and hid himself. (John 12:21-26.)

Not To Be Seen from Casual Desire

Many today seek, just as did the Greeks, to see Jesus, as if the view of him would come for the mere asking. But he is not to be seen from the casual, curious, or doubting desire.

To the millions of the humble and honest in heart who are discouraged, weary, grief-stricken, despairing, and who would see Jesus, and who, seeing him, would know him, we repeat the words spoken by Jesus to this generation: ". . . every soul who forsaketh his sins and cometh unto me, and calleth on my name, and obeyeth my voice, and keepeth my commandments, shall see my face and know that I am." (D & C 93:1.)

"His will" is easy to know. The Gospel of Christ is simple. It is the "way of holiness" that is so plain that "wayfaring men, though fools, shall not err therein." (Isa. 35:8.)

To you who seek truth, we say leave off, sweep out of your path, the false reasonings, the rationalizing, the spirit-destroying questioning of men, who without faith themselves would kill the faith of others; leave off trying to make your finite mind reach into and comprehend the knowledge and wisdom of the infinite; read the Good Book yourselves in humility and faith; pray while you read; live the doctrines Jesus taught,—and God will not leave your soul barren, for it is written, "If any of you lack wisdom, let him ask of God, that giveth to all men liberally, and upbraideth not; and it shall be given him." (James 1:5.)

"Come Unto Me"

Then shall you see Jesus; you will walk and talk with him in spirit; and into your lives will come a joy that will fill your being to the brim: "And this is life eternal, that they might know thee the only true God, and Jesus Christ, whom thou hast sent." (John 17:3.) And Jesus himself bade us come to him. For he has said to all men of all times: "Come unto me, all ye that labour and are heavy laden, and I will give you rest." (Matt. 11:28.) For "Peace I leave with you, my peace I give unto you: not as the world giveth, give I unto you. Let not your heart be troubled, neither let it be afraid." (John 14:27.)

I leave with you my witness that Jesus is the Christ, the very Messiah that was to come, the Redeemer of the world, the First Fruits of the Resurrection, the Savior of us all.

May God add to and perfect the testimonies of all of us.

"And Jesus, walking by the sea of Galilee, saw two brethren, Simon called Peter, and Andrew his brother, casting a net into the sea: for they were fishers.

"And he saith unto them, Follow me, and I will make you fishers of men."

Matthew 4:18-19

The Perfect Missionary

IN THINKING a bit about missions and missionary work, I find myself running back in my mind to the great service and the activity of the Perfect Missionary, of the Missionary who was taught by his Father and our Father. Over and over again in the course of his ministry, he said he did only that which he had seen his Father do, and taught the things which his Father had taught.

As I ran back over some of his early experiences, I was struck with the incident that records the first words recorded in the scriptures of what he said. You will recall that on the occasion of his visiting Jerusalem to attend the Passover when he was twelve, he remained behind and his father and mother went on. Missing him, they came back and searched for him for three days. At the end of that time they found him in the temple precincts, talking, discussing with the learned ones of the Jewry, things concerning which the official record says little, but of which the Apocrypha tells us more.

Recognition of Christ's Divine Authority

You will recall that after their long searching, they finally found him, Joseph and Mary, so discoursing with these learned ones, and Mary, reproving him, said, "Thy father [meaning Joseph] and I have sought thee sorrowing." I have always thought that that indicated the kind of intimacy there was in the Nazareth home of the carpenter, where Joseph was called "father." To that reproof from the mother, Jesus answered, "Wist ye not that I must be about *my Father's* business?" (Luke 2:48-49.) I think that was a recognition of his divine authority, of his personality, an authority which is held by every missionary who goes out, one divinely commissioned, a mission to do, and authority to do it. You may call it a testimony if you will. It seems to me that that was the first thing that the Savior made clear,—his divinity and his authority.

The Lesson of Obedience

The second words, as recorded, had two elements in them, relating to missionaries. That was when he came to John to be baptized. John protested, saying, "I have need to be baptized of thee, and comest thou to me?" Jesus replied: "Suffer it to be so now: for thus it becometh us to fulfil all righteousness." (Matt. 3:14-15.)

The great lesson that I get there, more particularly as affecting the missionaries, is that of obedience, obedience to the law and the commandments. Then this was the due and the proper order of conversion and membership. You know the great revelation that came there,— the testimony of the Father himself, "This is my beloved Son, in whom I am well pleased," and the descent upon Jesus of the Holy Ghost. (*Ibid.*, 3:16-17.) The baptism is the first ordinance of the Gospel.

The Bestowal of the Holy Ghost

Then my mind turned on to the first recorded sermon of Jesus, which was preached to the timorous Nicodemus, who came to him at nighttime, too fearful to come under the broad light of day—the great sermon, "Except a man be born of water and of the Spirit, he cannot enter into the kingdom of God." (John 3:5.) He spoke of the necessity for the Holy Ghost and its bestowal. It descended upon Jesus as he came up out of the water on the river bank.

Gospel Fundamentals

The great fundamentals of the Gospel were the ones

Jesus thus taught. They came in due and regular order and to me it seems that those great essentials, and I am sure no one could disagree, are the great things which should be in the minds of all those who seek to teach, to instruct, to persuade, to convert members to the truth, that they may join The Church of Jesus Christ of Latter-day Saints.

May I wish for all of you and pray for you the very fullest measure of all the blessings that it is needful for you to have in the spread of the Gospel,—a burning testimony, patience, forbearance, charity, love, and all the rest of the great Christian virtues, that you may find through your words entrance to the minds and hearts of every soul who is seeking the truth, that you may bring to that soul the greatest blessing that he can receive, putting him on the way to immortality and eternal life.

"Enter ye in at the strait gate: for wide is the gate, and broad is the way, that leadeth to destruction, and many there be which go in thereat:
"Because strait is the gate, and narrow is the way, which leadeth unto life, and few there be that find it."
Matthew 7:13-14

The Straight and Narrow Way

I HAVE thought how much the fundamental idea in the dictum, "All roads lead to Rome," has come to mean among us. I do not know whether we are in the beginning, in the middle, or near the end of a time when we shall see what historians of the future may call a revolution. And may I say here, and it applies frequently to all of us in principle, we of the present make history, our successors away from us write; and out of it they get things which we do not now presently see. I fear, as I have talked and heard others talk, that there may be a feeling, in fact, I know there is among some, that it does not make very much difference to what church we belong, what creed we may have, and not too much difference, within very broad limitations, what we do. We seem to be, in a way, in the presence of a trend of thought that is national, indeed world-wide, that would have us to believe that all this does not make very much difference, for we will all go to heaven anyhow, do what we will, think what we will, believe what we will, have faith as we may.

I find great fault with that, great fault, and I came across, in connection with this thought, some passages of scripture upon which I thought I might say a few words. They are taken from the Sermon on the Mount and were repeated by the Savior in that great appearance which he made on this continent after his resurrection. They are identical in words. Remember that he said when he came to this continent that he had come to teach them the things that he taught in Palestine. And these are the words:

Enter ye in at the strait gate: for wide is the gate, and broad is the way, that leadeth to destruction, and many there be which go in thereat:

Because strait is the gate, and narrow is the way, which leadeth unto life, and few there be that find it. (Matt. 7:13-14; 3 Nephi 14:13-14.)

I was reminded, as I read that, of the dream of Lehi recorded in the Book of Mormon, dreamed in the early days of the life of migration of Lehi, where the latter part of that—"few there be" that get into the straight and narrow way, was really prophetic. For his people found application of this principle in Lehi's own descendants, for there developed in the life of his descendants on this continent, the bloody conflict of the Nephites and Lamanites that brought about the utter destruction of the one by the other.

The Way and the Law

That led me to these thoughts about Christ. To Nicodemus he said that he came not to condemn the world, but to save it. (John 3:17.) In the great prayer in the Garden, he uttered the great principle, "And this is life eternal, that they might know thee the only true God, and Jesus Christ, whom thou hast sent." (John 17:3.)

And then I remembered also what Peter said to the Sanhedrin, called before them as a judicial body in connection with the first miracle, it is said, performed in the early Christian Church by the Apostles. Being asked by what name he did the miracle, Peter answered: ". . . by the name of Jesus Christ . . . for there is none other name under heaven given among men, whereby we must be saved." (Acts 4:10-12.)

Then I remembered also, that Christ himself said, "I am the way, the truth, the light, and the life." And to those on this continent, he added, "I am the law." (3 Nephi 15:9.)

This, of course, as we believe, indicates what we must believe and think and do, in what we must have faith.

You know, the Savior came in the Meridian of Time to fulfil the law of Moses, and he said on more than one occasion, 'I want nothing to do with sacrifice and burnt offerings, I want mercy.' And then you will remember, he added at various times, as to the sacrifice he wished: ". . . a broken heart and a contrite spirit."

Sermons in Third Nephi

As I reflected on this, I reflected a bit on where might I go to find the real words of the Savior. I knew I could not go to the Bible. We do not believe the Bible is absolutely correct. Students tell us there are four thousand five hundred different manuscripts of the Bible, and a few years ago it was estimated that there were one hundred twenty thousand variations. Then it came to me almost as a revelation: Why do you not go to the Book of Mormon? So I took Third Nephi. I went over it with great care. I parallel-columned it with the parts of the New Testament concerning the Sermon on the Mount and the Sermon on the Plain. In the Old Testament I noted the instructions to Malachi as they were repeated by the Savior, because they had no record of Malachi, who lived after they left Jerusalem.

I found some differences, some omissions from the word that he was recorded as having spoken in Palestine. But I resorted to the Book of Mormon and to Third Nephi with the feeling that I was getting really what the Savior said. I commend an equal study by you of those great books of the Book of Mormon and so far as the Savior's immediate mission was concerned, of Third Nephi. There we may believe we have the true teachings, for the record was made by inspired men, abridged by another inspired man, and translated through the inspiration and revelation of the Lord himself. I commend that to you. Study it. If you never have done so, you will find great joy in the doing.

... strait is the gate, and narrow is the way ... and few
there be that find it. (Matt. 7:14.)

I repeat, the Savior said, "I am the light, the life,
the way, and the truth," and on this continent, "I am
the law." If you will go through Third Nephi with care,
and the earlier works, you will find a very complete discussion of how he fulfilled the law of Moses.

Only One Road to Heaven

So, my brethren and sisters, I come to you with this
simple message: There are not many roads that lead to
heaven. There is one and one only, and that is the road
that we profess to travel and should be traveled. It is
the road that is restored to us by the restoration of the
Gospel and the restoration of the Priesthood. Do not be
misled by the professions of men.

And to those verses that I have already read, I want
to add another which comes near the end of that part
of the Sermon on the Mount and to the people of the Land
of Bountiful, which says:

Not every one that saith unto me, Lord, Lord, shall enter
into the kingdom of heaven; but he that doeth the will of my
Father which is in heaven.

Many will say to me in that day, Lord, Lord, have we not
prophesied in thy name? and in thy name have cast out devils?
and in thy name done many wonderful works?

And then will I profess unto them, I never knew you: depart from me, ye that work iniquity. (Matt. 7:21-23; 3 Nephi
14:21-23.)

The earlier parts of the Sermon on the Mount do
not contain teachings that are too specific with reference
to this last, "depart from me" and that those who had
professed, and so performed, were not his. But you will
find rather a complete discussion of what that probably
means in the book of Alma, the thirty-fourth chapter,

where Amulek tells the things which are characteristic of those who worship our Lord and Savior and our Heavenly Father. Read them. It is worth your while.

Professors of religion, pretenders of being the offspring of our Heavenly Father's Gospel and principles, pretending to have the truth, beware of them. Beware of the idea that you do not have to live the Gospel in order to obtain the salvation and exaltation that are promised—not because God has imposed a penalty for your failure, but because, as I have already expressed to you at one time or another, I believe that the spirit grows or shrinks, as it is here in this mortal body, as it was intended that it should. I believe that bad acts, bad thoughts, inaccurate beliefs do not develop the spirit; but on the contrary, they may retard or dwarf it. I believe that all that we do that is good, builds us up, and helps us to "prove" ourselves, that we really are living our second estate.

Do Not Be Misled

Brethren and sisters, do not be misled, do not stray, do not imbibe the tendency of the age that it does not make any difference what you do. It makes all the difference in this world and in the hereafter. It makes the difference between salvation and exaltation and damnation. I examined the books to find out, if I could, whether the Savior had made any change in speaking on this continent and on the other side in fundamental sayings and doctrines. As I have said to you, there are some omissions, there are some changes, some of the changes are most important. Make the comparison I have made and find them out. But I found nothing whatsoever that changed the fundamental principle announced by the Savior in Palestine and here: "He that believeth and is baptized shall be saved; but he that believeth not shall be damned." (Mark 16:16.)

Brethren and sisters, do not stray, do not be misled, do not cuddle to yourselves the thought that you can do this or that or the other forbidden thing, that after all these things make no difference. I bear you my witness again that all your thoughts, all your acts, all your doings of any kind, have an effect, beneficial or otherwise, on your souls, and you cannot afford so to jeopardize the hereafter.

"... they draw near to me with their lips, but their hearts are far from me, they teach for doctrines the commandments of men, having a form of godliness, but they deny the power thereof."

Joseph Smith 2:19

Be Not Deceived

I WOULD like to begin what I have to say with a quotation of some scriptures. One scripture has already been frequently quoted that came from the great intercessory prayer which the Savior delivered the night before the day he was crucified: "And this is life eternal, that they might know thee the only true God, and Jesus Christ, whom thou hast sent." (John 17:3.)

Then I would like to quote the first three verses and the fourteenth of the first chapter of John:

In the beginning was the Word, and the Word was with God, and the Word was God.

The same was in the beginning with God.

All things were made by him; and without him was not any thing made that was made. . . .

And the Word was made flesh, and dwelt among us, (and we beheld his glory, the glory as of the only begotten of the Father,) full of grace and truth.

And finally, I will quote the passage from First Corinthians, where Paul, speaking to the backsliding Corinthians, among whom already began to appear what finally became the great apostasy, and complaining about them and their thoughts, he said, "For I determined not to know any thing among you, save Jesus Christ, and him crucified." (1 Cor. 2:2.)

Moral Teachings and Eschatology

There are all sorts of cults, all sorts of shadings of what we have called Christianity. There is one group of scholars that work insidiously sometimes, pretending Christianity and a belief in Christ, but nevertheless who subtly teach us things that do not come within what we understand as Christianity. The position of these has been stated by one scholar thus: "Christ . . . cannot have been both the same unclouded thinker of the moral sayings and the apocalyptic fanatic of the eschatological passages." (Willoughby C. Allen, "Criticism (New Testament)," *Encyclopedia of Religion and Ethics*, James Hastings, ed. (Charles Scribner's Sons, New York, 1928), Vol. IV, p. 320.)

And eschatology is defined as: "The doctrine of the last or final things, death, resurrection, immortality, the end of the world, final judgment, and the future state; the doctrine of last things."

These teachers who announce this difference as to the life of the Savior and his teachings, some of them, find place amongst us.

These critics say one of these two, the moral teachings or the eschatology, must be given up as historical and the one chosen to be got rid of is the eschatological. Anything beyond the moral teachings is put in the realm of myth, legend, popular exaggeration, symbolism, allegory, or transference of the miraculous from other departments of tradition into the life of Jesus.

Their standard of elimination is that any "event which lies outside the range of the known laws of Nature," must be disregarded. This destroys the divine origin of Jesus, his miracles, his resurrection, and much of his doctrine.

Warning of False Prophets

I want to read now just a few verses from the Olivet Discourse, the discourse which the Savior delivered on the Mount of Olives at the near conclusion, or conclusion of the third day of the Passion Week which he had spent in the temple or the temple precincts. I am going to read from all three Synoptists, because each says essentially the same thing, but in somewhat different language.

They had gone out to the Mount of Olives, Jesus and

his disciples; they asked if he would like them to tell him about the temple, and so on, and it was then that he predicted that the temple would be destroyed, and thereafter in this discourse he touched upon not only the destruction of the temple but the second coming. Not always can you be clear as to which he was referring, but the passages that I shall read have reference as to what should finally take place.

Tell us, when shall these things be? and what shall be the sign of thy coming, and of the end of the world?

And Jesus answered and said unto them, Take heed that no man deceive you.

For many shall come in my name, saying, I am Christ; and shall deceive many. . . .

Then if any man shall say unto you, Lo, here is Christ, or there; believe it not.

For there shall arise false Christs, and false prophets and shall shew great signs and wonders; insomuch that, if it were possible, they shall deceive the very elect.

Behold, I have told you before.

Wherefore if they shall say unto you, Behold, he is in the desert; go not forth: behold, he is in the secret chambers; believe it not.   (Matt. 24:3-5, 23-26.)

Mark said:

And Jesus answering them began to say, Take heed lest any man deceive you:

For many shall come in my name, saying, I am Christ; and shall deceive many. . . .

And then if any man shall say to you, Lo, here is Christ; or, lo, he is there; believe him not:

For false Christs and false prophets shall rise, and shall shew signs and wonders, to seduce, if it were possible, even the elect.

But take ye heed: behold, I have foretold you all things. (Mark 13:5-6, 21-23.)

And Luke says, more shortly than is recorded by the others:

And he said, Take heed that ye be not deceived: for many shall come in my name, saying, I am Christ; and the time draweth near: go ye not therefore after them. (Luke 21:8.)

I think perhaps when we first read these extracts we may think that the Savior is talking primarily of a person, somebody to come to impersonate the Christ and claim to be the Christ. It seems to me, however, from the way in which these records are made and what they say, that the Savior also had in mind anyone who would come and say to you, "This is Christ that I teach; that is Christ that I teach; that is the Christian doctrine." In that sense I think that these scholars about whom I have already read, who would discard everything that they could not account for by the known laws of nature, they are in effect false Christs, for they are telling us that the things that we believe in Christ are myths, tradition, symbolism, allegory; they did not exist.

Not Myth, Symbolism, Allegory

Now, that kind of a religion, that kind of Christianity would require that we discard all that we know about the Great Council in Heaven and what was determined there, because these things lie outside the known laws of nature, as those scholars understand them.

We would have to discard the Fall as being a myth, an allegory, symbolism.

We would have to discard the virgin birth, the divine conception, the very foundation of our religion; that would have to go.

We would have to discard the witness of the Father at the time of the baptism of the Savior; that would go as myth, symbolism, allegory.

We would have to discard practically all of the miracles as not taking place and those that might be accepted would be spoken of as signs. A sign can be a miracle, but not necessarily so. A miracle is a sign, but more than that.

We would have to discard the testimony of the
Father, at the time of the Transfiguration, that Jesus
was his Son.

We would have to discard that great occasion, the
raising of Lazarus and the incidents thereof, the reply
of the Savior to Martha:

I am the resurrection, and the life: he that believeth in me,
though he were dead, yet shall he live:
And whosoever liveth and believeth in me shall never die.
(John 11:25-26.)

That would have to go into the discard as myth,
allegory, symbolism, tradition.

Finally, we would have to discard all that we know
about the resurrection and its effect; all of that is gone.

As to these, and almost countless other matters:
be not deceived, believe them not, follow not after the
false Christs.

I would like you to appreciate that without the eschatology of the records of the Savior's life, we should have
nothing left but husks, moral teachings, and ethics which,
if lived, would make us a great people, a humane people,
a peaceful people, but would not carry us back into the
presence of our Heavenly Father.

Reversion to Paganism

In my view, that doctrine is not only sacrilegious,
but to me it is also blasphemy, something to be utterly
cast away. We have less left after they get through
with their discards than the old paganism, for that paganism, the old Greek mythology, did acknowledge and
have a kind of worship of divine beings which they conceived; they did believe in them and worship them.

My whole soul rebels against this emasculation of
Christianity. Jesus did live. First, there was the great
plan in heaven; that did actually occur. All that we know

about it took place there. There was the plan; the earth
was formed; Adam came; the human family followed.
We came here to prove ourselves. Finally, Christ was
born in the Meridian of Time. He lived. He taught.
He gave instructions. He was crucified. Then on the
morning of the third day, he was resurrected, thus bringing to each and every one of us the blessings of the resurrection. We all shall be resurrected. All of that has gone
for these people to whom I refer. It is myth, tradition,
allegory. Be not deceived by them; believe them not;
follow not after them.

Then we would have to discard all that transpired
in the restoration of the Gospel, the vision of the Father
and the Son, the coming forth of the Book of Mormon,
the giving of the great commandments which compose
our Doctrine and Covenants. We would have to discard
the Pearl of Great Price and all that it says.

Now, brothers and sisters, let us be aware of this
false Christ, false Christianity, which is taking root
among some of our intellectuals. Be not deceived, believe
it not, follow not after it, as the Lord said in those various records.

I bear my testimony as I have already indicated, to
the truthfulness of the Gospel, to the restoration of its
great principles, to the restoration of the Priesthood, to
the conferring of all of these things upon the Prophet
Joseph, to the passing down from the Prophet Joseph
through the Presidents of the Church until the present,
that our President of the Church, President David O.
McKay, has all of the rights and the prerogatives and
the powers and authorities that were conferred upon
the Prophet Joseph.

I bear you this testimony in soberness. I repeat, my
soul cries out against this heresy that is taught by this
group of so-called Christians.

God be with us and help us always.

"And it came to pass, when Jesus had ended these sayings,
the people were astonished at his doctrine:
"For he taught them as one having authority, and not as
the scribes."
Matthew 7:28-29

Divine Authority and the Latter-day Saints

IF THE present widespread and growing tendency among the Protestant laity, and clergy, too, to deny to Christ his Messiahship, his divine origin, and his resurrection, shall continue, it is not difficult to foresee a time when the Christian world will be divided into two great camps—those who will regard Christ merely as a great teacher and philosopher, the framer of a great ethical code, but without a divine parentage or resurrection, and those who, being the true followers of the lowly Jesus will hold to the Christ of the Gospels, the Epistles, and the Apocalypse, the Christ who has dominated and controlled the growth and development of the civilized world for nearly two thousand years, the Christ who with a love divine gave his life that man might be saved from that death to which the Fall of Adam subjected him, and provided for the children of God a salvation and exaltation in the worlds to come.

Among those churches which shall thus stand for Jesus as our Elder Brother and Savior, none will face the crisis more unflinchingly than The Church of Jesus Christ of Latter-day Saints. This is its duty and its privilege, declared from before the foundations of the world; and when that time shall come to the world, this Church as a Church must stand or fall upon the truthfulness of certain great principles which are fundamental to its philosophy.

The All-Important Question

Christ, at the very beginning of his ministry, convinced the people of the synagogue at Capernaum, of the deep and fundamental truth which underlay his ministry amongst the people,—the truth that he "taught them as

one having authority, and not as the scribes." (Matt.
7:29.) From this day at Capernaum to the day of his
ascension into heaven, the all-important question which
ever confronted those he taught, was the question, "Who
is Jesus,"—a question of authority.

When later Christ healed a demoniac in the synagogue, the people, with intensified feeling, cried out,—
"What a word is this! for with authority and power he
commandeth the unclean spirits, and they come out."
(Luke 4:36.) Nor, as his ministry grew, did this feeling
among the people lessen, for later at the conclusion of
that greatest of all his discourses—the Sermon on the
Mount—where he declared he came to fulfil, not to destroy, the law, and laid down the great elements of the
new commandments, the people again were astonished
at his doctrine, and again proclaimed that he taught as
one having authority and not as the scribes.

The belief in his authority found one of its most
perfect expressions in that beautiful, implicit faith of the
centurion, who, with an apparent comprehensive understanding of the Christ, besought him to heal the servant,
saying:

> Lord, I am not worthy that thou shouldst come under my
> roof: but speak the word only, and my servant shall be healed.
> For I am a man under authority, having soldiers under me:
> and I say to this man, Go, and he goeth; and to another, Come,
> and he cometh; and to my servant, Do this, and he doeth it.
> (Matt. 8:8-9.)

By What Authority—?

Again, in the final week of Christ's ministry, on
the day following his second cleansing of the temple, and
his cursing of the barren fig tree, the scribes and chief
priests, frightened at the effect of his doctrines upon the
people, fiercely, secretly plotting his death, and fearful
lest after all they might be rejecting the Messiah, de-

manded of Christ, teaching in the temple, "By what authority doest thou these things? and who gave thee this authority?" (*Ibid.*, 21:23.)

Thus with them the great problem was authority, for he had already told them that Satan also performed miracles, and, in their desperation, they thrust their enquiry at the very root of his mission.

When the final contest shall take place between good and evil, and there shall be again enacted that creation-old battle typified in the contest between Moses and the Egyptian magicians, then shall it be vital to man to know by what authority the members of The Church of Jesus Christ of Latter-day Saints perform their works.

What was this power and what was this authority which Christ exercised in his ministry among men? On this point the Gospels speak with the utmost clearness. Not only did the Savior again and again deny any credit or virtue in himself for the power he possessed and the authority he exercised, but he repeatedly affirmed that all he had was the Father's.

In that great sermon which he preached in the synagogue at Capernaum after he returned from the desert place belonging to Bethsaida, Christ said, "For I came down from heaven, not to do mine own will, but the will of him that sent me." (John 6:38.)

Later, speaking in the temple while in Jerusalem attending the Feast of the Tabernacles, Jesus declared: "My doctrine is not mine, but his that sent me." (*Ibid.*, 7:16.)

Then Shall Ye Know

Speaking again in the temple during the same feast and responding to the imperious inquiry of the Jews, "Who art thou?" the Savior said: ". . . he that sent me is true; and I speak to the world those things which I have heard of him. . . . When ye have lifted up the Son

of man, then shall ye know that I am he, and that I do
nothing of myself; but as my Father hath taught me,
I speak these things. . . . I proceeded forth and came
from God; neither came I of myself, but he sent me."
(*Ibid.*, 8:26, 28, 42.)

When the seventy returned from the missions upon
which he had sent them, Christ, in a hymn of praise to
God, declared: "All things are delivered to me of my
Father." (Luke 10:22.)

At the Feast of the Dedication at Jerusalem while
walking in Solomon's Porch of the temple, he again asserted, ". . . the works that I do in my Father's name,
they bear witness of me." And a little later, on this same
occasion, when the Jews took up stones to stone him, he
said: "Many good works have I shewed you from my
Father; for which of those works do ye stone me? . . . If
I do not the works of my Father, believe me not." (John
10:25, 32, 37.)

In the temple on the third day of the last week of
his ministry, while the scribes and Pharisees were drawing more closely about him their fatal net, Christ, declaring his Messiahship, said:

> For I have not spoken of myself; but the Father which
> sent me, he gave me a commandment, what I should say, and
> what I should speak.
> And I know that his commandment is life everlasting: what-
> soever I speak therefore, even as the Father said unto me, so I
> speak. (*Ibid.*, 12:49-50.)

Finally in his last address to his Apostles prior
to his crucifixion, delivered as he and they were on the
way to the agony and the betrayal of the Garden of
Gethsemane, Christ responding to Philip's request that
Jesus show them the Father, said to the Apostles: ". . . the
words that I speak unto you I speak not of myself: but the
Father that dwelleth in me, he doeth the works." (*Ibid.*,
14:10.)

Attributes of the Priesthood

Thus Jesus, during the whole of his ministry, from the first to the last, and always with a perfect understanding of the source of his powers and authority, gave to God the Father the full credit and honor for all the powers, authority, and strength which he ever possessed.

That these powers and authorities were the attributes of the Priesthood of God, seems clear from the words of Paul, who, in his Epistle to the Hebrews, asserted that Jesus was "made an high priest for ever after the order of Melchisedec," and continued:

> But this man, because he continueth ever, hath an unchangeable priesthood.
> Wherefore he is able also to save them to the uttermost that come unto God by him. . . . (Heb. 7:24-25.)

But the marvelous, Christlike works of many mighty men, ancient and modern, show that the powers and authority which Christ held and exercised and by which he performed his works, were on the earth before the time of Christ and have been restored since; and that these other workers also have been high priests after the order of Melchizedek.

What is this Priesthood of which Paul spoke? President Joseph F. Smith, speaking at the October conference of the Church in 1901, declared: ". . . the Holy Priesthood is that authority which God has delegated to man, by which he may speak the will of God as if the angels were here to speak it themselves; by which men are empowered to bind on earth and it shall be bound in heaven, and to loose on earth and it shall be loosed in heaven; by which the words of man, spoken in the exercise of that power, become the word of the Lord, and the law of God unto the people, scripture, and divine commands. . . . It is the authority by which the Lord Almighty governs his people, and by which, in time to come, he will govern the nations of the world. It is sacred, and it must be held sacred by the people." (Joseph F. Smith, *Gospel Doctrine*, 5th ed. (Deseret Book Co., Salt Lake City, 1939), p. 140.)

". . . which priesthood continueth in the church of God in all generations, and is without beginning of days or end of years."
Doctrine and Covenants 84:17

The Priesthood, an Everlasting Principle

ANCIENT and modern Apostles have declared that, "The Priesthood is an everlasting principle, and existed with God from eternity, and will to eternity, without beginning of days or end of years." (*Church History*, Vol. 3, p. 386; and see Ex. 40:15; Heb. 7:3.)

The Prophet Joseph Smith announced, "The Priesthood was first given to Adam; he obtained the First Presidency, and held the keys of it from generation to generation. He obtained it in the Creation, before the world was formed" (*ibid.*, pp. 385-386) ; and in the Book of Abraham, it is declared that the Priesthood "came down from the fathers, from the beginning of time, yea, even from the beginning, or before the foundations of the earth to the present time." (Abraham 1:3.)

The Lord has revealed in modern times that after and from Adam this Priesthood, the power and authority which God on occasion delegates to his servants, passed in regular succession down through the patriarchs of old, in an order which was instituted in the days of Adam (D & C 107) ; that it bridged the Flood through Noah, from whom it passed by due lineage to Abraham, who received it from Melchizedek, from whom the higher Priesthood takes its name. From Abraham the Priesthood passed by proper descent to Moses, who received it from the hands of Jethro. Moses attempted to lead Israel according to its precepts, but they would not follow, and then God "took Moses out of their midst, and the Holy Priesthood also," but left the lesser or Aaronic Priesthood, which "holdeth the key of the ministering of angels and the preparatory gospel; which gospel is the gospel of repentance and of baptism, and the remission of sins, and the law of carnal commandments." This lesser Priesthood, God "caused to continue with the house of Aaron among the children of Israel until John," who "was ordained by the angel of God at the time he was eight days old unto this power, to overthrow the kingdom of the Jews, and to make straight the way of the Lord before the face of his people, to prepare them for the coming of the Lord, in whose hand is given all power." (*Ibid.*, 84:25-28.)

This briefly is the account of the Holy Priesthood from Adam to the Lord, in whose hand was all power.

To Preach the Gospel

Did Christ leave any of this power and authority on the earth when he ascended to the Father?

Mark tells us that after Christ returned from the Second Passover he left the Sea of Galilee where he had been laboring and went into a mountain where he called unto himself "whom he would: and they came unto him. And he ordained twelve, that they should be with him, and that he might send them forth to preach." (Mark 3:13-14.)

Thus Jesus began to bestow upon his disciples, and first upon the Twelve, a part of the powers which he himself possessed "to preach the Gospel and administer in the ordinances thereof." (Articles of Faith.)

From the record in the Gospel it appears that Christ from this time forward to the end of his ministry, added authority upon authority to those of his chosen followers who were to carry on the work of God after he should go.

Shortly after his tragic visit to Nazareth, the home of his early life, where he was rejected by the people of Nazareth and apparently by his own family—his brethren and sisters, and they had attempted to destroy him, Christ went through Galilee teaching and healing. In the course of this ministry he sent on their first mission the Quorum of the Twelve. As they went he commissioned them with "power and authority over all devils, and to cure diseases"; they were to preach the kingdom of God, and to heal the sick; to take nothing for their journey, neither staves, nor scrip, neither bread, neither money; neither have two coats apiece; and they were to shake off the dust from their feet for a testimony against those who would not receive them. (Luke 4:29; 9:1-6.)

Messiahship Declared

Shortly after the visit of the Savior to Jerusalem to attend the Third Passover of his ministry, Jesus, returning to Galilee, went from thence to the regions of Caesarea Philippi. At this place occurred that wonderful discourse with his disciples in the course of which Peter for the first recorded time declared Christ's Messiahship, and was promised certain keys of the Priesthood. This great discourse began with the Savior's question: "Whom do men say that I the Son of man am?" The record continues:

> And they said, Some say that thou art John the Baptist: some, Elias; and others, Jeremias, or one of the prophets.
> He saith unto them, But whom say ye that I am?
> And Simon Peter answered and said, Thou art the Christ, the Son of the living God.
> And Jesus answered and said unto him, Blessed art thou, Simon Barjona: for flesh and blood hath not revealed it unto thee, but my Father which is in heaven.
> And I say also unto thee, That thou art Peter, and upon this rock I will build my church; and the gates of hell shall not prevail against it.
> And I will give unto thee the keys of the kingdom of heaven: and whatsoever thou shalt bind on earth shall be bound in heaven: and whatsoever thou shalt loose on earth shall be loosed in heaven. (Matt. 16:14-19.)

The promise to give thereafter unto Peter "the keys of the kingdom" seems clearly to show that up till this time, certain keys of the Melchizedek Priesthood had not been conferred upon the Apostles. What are these "keys"

of which the Savior spoke? President Joseph F. Smith
has declared that these "keys" are "the right or privilege
which belongs to and comes with the Priesthood, to have
communication with God. . . . It is the right to enjoy the
blessing of communication with the heavens, and the
privilege and authority to administer in the ordinances
of the gospel of Jesus Christ, to preach the gospel of
repentance, and of baptism by immersion for the remission of sins" (*Gospel Doctrine*, p. 142) ; and the Prophet
Joseph declared that these "keys have to be brought from
heaven whenever the Gospel is sent. When they are revealed from heaven, it is by Adam's authority." (*Church
History*, Vol. 3, p. 386.)

The Transfiguration

It was but six days after the great testimony of
Peter, and Christ's promise to him, that the Savior took
Peter, James, and John into a high mountain apart "and
was transfigured before them: and his face did shine as
the sun, and his raiment was white as the light. And,
behold, there appeared unto them Moses and Elias talking
with him," and a cloud "overshadowed them: and a voice
came out of the cloud, saying, This is my beloved Son:
hear him." (Matt. 17:1-2; Mark 9:7.)

Modern inspiration tells us that it was at this time
that the keys of the Melchizedek Priesthood were given
to Peter, James, and John under the administration of
the Savior, Moses, and Elias. (*Church History*, Vol. 3,
p. 337.)

Is it to be wondered at that now possessed of these
keys, Peter, in a burst of that emotion of which he of
all the Apostles possessed most, should exclaim: "Master,
it is good for us to be here: and let us make three tabernacles; one for thee, and one for Moses, and one for
Elias." (Mark 9:5.)

But the Twelve were not the only ones whom Christ

sent out to preach his Gospel and administer in its ordinances, and therefore, upon whom he conferred the Priesthood in whole or in part. Just after the Transfiguration, Jesus "appointed other seventy also, and sent them two and two before his face into every city and place, whither he himself would come." (Luke 10:1.)

These seventy were given power and authority similar to that given to the Twelve when they were sent out; they were to carry neither purse, nor scrip, nor shoes; they were to bestow peace upon whatsoever house they entered; they were to heal the sick, and to preach the kingdom of God; they were empowered to wipe off from their feet the dust of any city which did not receive them as a witness against it. When these seventy returned to Christ, they themselves were filled with wonderment and joy over their work, for, said they to the Lord, "even the devils are subject unto us through thy name." Then the Savior "rejoiced in spirit" at the power which the Father had vouchsafed unto them, and said, "I beheld Satan as lightning fall from heaven. Behold, I give unto you power to tread on serpents and scorpions, and over all the power of the enemy: and nothing shall by any means hurt you." (*Ibid.*, 10:2-21.)

Divine Patience

But not yet had Christ conferred upon the Twelve the full powers and authority which he was to bestow. More was to come. It was on the evening of the day of Christ's resurrection from the dead. The Apostles, fearful of the Jews, had assembled together behind locked doors. Suddenly Christ appeared in their midst with the greeting: "Peace be unto you." They sat terrified, believing they beheld a spirit, for in spite of all the instructions they had received, not yet did they understand his death and resurrection, nor did they believe therein. Christ, knowing the unbelief of their very hearts, said unto them: "Behold my hands and my feet, that it is I myself: handle me, and see; for a spirit hath not flesh and bones, as ye see me have." And when they had seen his hands and feet "they yet believed not." Then with a patience and charity that was divine, Christ asked for food and with them ate their broiled fish and honeycomb, that they might know it was indeed he. (Luke 24:36-43.)

The meal finished, Jesus said again unto the whole eleven present there: "Peace be unto you: as my Father hath sent me, even so send I you. And when he had said this, he breathed on them, and saith unto them, Receive ye the Holy Ghost: whose soever sins ye remit, they are remitted unto them; and whose soever sins ye retain, they are retained." (John 20:21-23.)

Signs Shall Follow

Finally, Christ again instructed the Apostles and again gave power and authority unto them just before his ascension. He was leading them from Jerusalem out towards Bethany, the home of Lazarus, Martha, and Mary—the place which seems to have held for him the most of peace, the most of sympathy, understanding, and love, the most of home, the home to which, in the hours of his sorest trials he turned, after his neighbors and kin, unbelieving and cruel, had rejected him at Nazareth. Whether as they walked on with him towards Bethany and that home, the Apostles knew of his impending leave-taking or not, and of the further commission he was to give them, the Gospels do not declare; but Christ knew, and we can imagine with what infinite tenderness and love, and perhaps sorrow and yet with what consciousness of divine power and authority he declared unto them:

All power is given unto me in heaven and in earth.
Go ye therefore, and teach all nations, baptizing them in the name of the Father, and of the Son, and of the Holy Ghost:

Teaching them to observe all things whatsoever I have commanded you. (Matt. 28:18-20.)

And these signs shall follow them that believe; In my name
shall they cast out devils; they shall speak with new tongues;

They shall take up serpents; and if they drink any deadly
thing, it shall not hurt them; they shall lay hands on the sick,
and they shall recover. (Mark 16:17-18.)

. . . and, lo, I am with you alway, even unto the end of the
world. (Matt. 28:20.)

Thus were the Apostles endowed with powers and
authority of the Holy Priesthood to establish the Apostolic
Church among the nations of the earth.

The promises made by the Savior as to the signs
which should follow believers were literally fulfilled. Beginning with Pentecost they did speak with new tongues
(Acts 2); beginning with the healing of the lame man
at the gate of the temple by Peter, they did heal the sick
(Acts 3); they did cast out demons (Acts 16:16; 19:12);
and Paul was bitten by a serpent and did feel no harm
(Acts 28:5).

For a time the Apostolic Church grew with vigor;
but soon errors in doctrine crept in; fundamental principles were abandoned; and a falling off began. One
cannot read the various Epistles of Paul, of Peter, of
James, and of John, nor the great visions of the Apocalypse, without perceiving how rapidly there came into
the Church that condition of which the Savior spoke when
leaving the temple and, awearied with the tumult, the
caviling, the abuse and insult of his murderers, he went
out toward Bethany and reaching the Mount of Olives,
sat down and told them the signs which should precede
his coming.

Evils Did Come

It is the faith of the Latter-day Saints that the evils
and the iniquities which Christ in that sermon predicted,
did come; that the false prophets and the false Christs

spoken of by him, did appear; and that the wickedness of
the peoples of the earth became so great that God took
from them those powers and authority appertaining to
the Holy Priesthood which Christ had bestowed upon the
early Apostles, and left man for generations in his wickedness without the directive and saving power of that
Priesthood.

It is the faith of the Latter-day Saints that finally
there came upon the earth that condition which is so
wondrously described by John when he tells of the woman
upon whose forehead was written, "Mystery, Babylon
the Great, the Mother of Harlots and Abominations of
the Earth"; the woman who was arrayed in purple and
scarlet color, and decked with gold and precious stones
and pearls, having a golden cup in her hand full of abominations and filthiness of her fornication, the woman
drunken with the blood of the martyrs of Jesus; the
woman about which the angel said, "I will tell thee the
mystery of the woman, and of the beast that carrieth
her, which hath the seven heads and ten horns. . . . These
shall make war with the Lamb, and the Lamb shall overcome them: for he is Lord of lords, and King of kings:
. . . And the woman which thou sawest is that great city,
which reigneth over the kings of the earth." (Rev. 17.)

The Vision of John

It is the faith of the Latter-day Saints that then
was made fact that other vision of John:

And I saw another angel fly in the midst of heaven,
having the everlasting gospel to preach unto them that dwell on
the earth, and to every nation, and kindred, and tongue, and
people,

Saying with a loud voice, Fear God, and give glory to him;
for the hour of his judgment is come: and worship him that
made heaven, and earth, and the sea, and the fountains of waters.

And there followed another angel, saying, Babylon is fallen, is fal'en, that great city, because she made all nations drink of the wine of the wrath of her fornication. (Rev. 14:6-8.)

It is the faith of the Latter-day Saints that the Gospel was restored through Joseph Smith, the Prophet, and that the restoration of that Gospel carried with it the restoration of the Holy Priesthoods, Aaronic and Melchizedek; that the Aaronic Priesthood was conferred upon Joseph Smith and Oliver Cowdery by John the Baptist at Harmony, Pennsylvania, on May 15, 1829, in the following words:

Upon you my fellow servants, in the name of Messiah I confer the Priesthood of Aaron, which holds the keys of the ministering of angels, and of the gospel of repentance, and of baptism by immersion for the remission of sins; and this shall never be taken again from the earth, until the sons of Levi do offer again an offering unto the Lord in righteousness. (D & C 13.)

It is the faith of the Latter-day Saints that later, Peter, James, and John, those upon whom the Savior, Moses, and Elias had conferred keys of the Melchizedek Priesthood at the time the Savior was transfigured, came and conferred upon Joseph Smith and Oliver Cowdery that same Priesthood; that Peter, James, and John later ordained and confirmed Joseph Smith and Oliver Cowdery to be Apostles in his Church and special witnesses of his name (*ibid.*, 27:12); that still later, in 1841, the Savior revealed unto Joseph Smith the officers belonging to the Priesthood after the "order of Melchizedek, which is after the order of mine Only Begotten Son." (*Ibid.*, 124:123.)

It is the faith of the Latter-day Saints that as in the days of Christ so in modern times, Seventy have been called "to preach the gospel, and to be especial witnesses unto the Gentiles and in all the world." (*Ibid.*, 107:25.)

To Go into All the World

It is the faith of the Latter-day Saints that in this day the Lord has instructed his servants to go into all the world and to preach the Gospel to every creature, acting under the authority of the Holy Priesthood given unto them by God, baptizing in the name of the Father and of the Son and of the Holy Ghost, and laying on hands for the reception of the Holy Ghost, even as the Apostles of old. (*Ibid.*, 35:6; 68:8.)

It is the faith of the Latter-day Saints that they who believe and are baptized shall be saved and they that believe not shall be damned. (*Ibid.*, 68:9.)

It is the testimony of the Latter-day Saints that their members, endowed with the Holy Priesthood of Melchizedek and holding the proper offices thereunder, have gone into the world to preach the Gospel and that the same signs which followed the Apostles of old have followed them. They have cast out devils; they have spoken with new tongues; they have taken up serpents; if they have drunk any deadly thing it has not harmed them; they have laid hands on the sick and they have recovered. And all this has come under and pursuant to the promise made to them by the Lord himself in these days when he said:

Therefore, as I said unto mine apostles I say unto you again, that every soul who believeth on your words, and is baptized by water for the remission of sins, shall receive the Holy Ghost.

And these signs shall follow them that believe—

In my name they shall do many wonderful works;

In my name they shall cast out devils;

In my name they shall heal the sick;

In my name they shall open the eyes of the blind, and unstop the ears of the deaf;

And the tongue of the dumb shall speak;

And if any man shall administer poison unto them it shall not hurt them;

And the poison of a serpent shall not have power to harm them. (*Ibid.*, 84:64-72.)

As Did the Primitive Church

It is the faith of the Latter-day Saints that God has established his work in these last days never again to be thrown down, that he has caused his Church to be established with the same officers and powers that existed in the Primitive Apostolic Church, for The Church of Jesus Christ of Latter-day Saints has prophets, apostles, patriarchs, high priests, seventy, elders, priests, teachers, and deacons as did the Primitive Church.

It is the faith of the Latter-day Saints that since through the apostasy, and by reason of it, the Holy Priesthood was taken away from the earth, and since through direct revelation and the administration of those ancient men who held the Priesthood, that Priesthood has been restored to the earth upon the heads of those who established and who have since carried on the work of The Church of Jesus Christ of Latter-day Saints, that therefore this Church, and this Church only, possesses the powers and authority which have from the beginning of time been exercised through the Holy Priesthood and which Christ himself exercised while he was on this earth and which he bestowed upon his Apostles and seventy as recorded by the Gospels, these powers and that authority which alone are the "power of God unto salvation."

Finally, there has been conferred upon Joseph Smith, and there has by him been transmitted to his successors in office down to the present day, the exact authority which was conferred by Christ upon the Apostles of old, in accordance with the promise given to Peter when he declared his first great testimony of the Messiahship of Jesus. The Lord, speaking to Joseph Smith, said:

For I have conferred upon you the keys and power of the priesthood, wherein I restore all things, and make known unto you all things in due time.

And verily, verily, I say unto you, that whatsoever you seal on earth shall be sealed in heaven; and whatsoever you bind on earth, in my name and by my word, saith the Lord, it shall be eterna'ly bound in the heavens; and whosoever sins you remit on earth shall be remitted eternally in the heavens; and whosesoever sins you retain on earth shall be retained in heaven.

And again, verily I say, whomsoever you bless I will bless, and whomsoever you curse I will curse, saith the Lord; for I, the Lord, am thy God. (*Ibid.*, 132:45-47.)

Thus the Latter-day Saints declare that they have the same power and authorities, the same Priesthood, which were possessed by the ancient servants of the Lord and by the Savior himself; that they received these powers and authorities under the direct administration of angels and by direct bestowal of Christ; that upon no other people have these powers and authorities been conferred; that by no other people are such powers and authorities now possessed.

As the Lord Has Declared

The Latter-day Saints believe that without the powers and authorities of that Holy Priesthood there is no real joy or happiness in this world, nor salvation and exaltation in the presence of God in the world to come. As the Lord has declared to his servant, the Prophet:

Which priesthood continueth in the church of God in all generations, and is without beginning of days or end of years.

[The lesser or Aaronic Priesthood] . . . also continueth and abideth forever with the priesthood which is after the holiest order of God.

And this greater priesthood administereth the gospel and holdeth the key of the mysteries of the kingdom, even the key of the knowledge of God.

Therefore, in the ordinances thereof, the power of godliness is manifest.

And without the ordinances thereof, and the authority of the priesthood, the power of godliness is not manifest unto men in the flesh;

For without this no man can see the face of God, even the Father, and live.

... For whoso is faithful unto the obtaining these two priesthoods of which I have spoken, and the magnifying their calling, are sanctified by the Spirit unto the renewing of their bodies. ...

And also all they who receive this priesthood receive me, saith the Lord;

For he that receiveth my servants receiveth me;

And he that receiveth me receiveth my Father;

And he that receiveth my Father receiveth my Father's kingdom; therefore all that my Father hath shall be given unto him.

And this is according to the oath and covenant which belongeth to the priesthood. (*Ibid.*, 84:17-22, 33, 35-39.)

Thus in these last days has God spoken unto us his children.

God grant to each of us, as in his infinite knowledge, mercy, and wisdom shall seem to him best and wise, a living, burning testimony, such as came to great-hearted Peter of old, that when the day of consuming trial shall come, we shall know that God is God, that Jesus is the Christ, the Lamb of God, the Redeemer of the world, that the Holy Priesthood is the authority of God delegated to man for the accomplishment of God's purposes on the earth, and that in and through the atoning blood of Jesus Christ all mankind may be saved by obedience to the laws and ordinances of the Gospel which has been again restored to the earth in all its fulness and glory.

". . . the principle of power which existed in the bosom of God, by which the worlds were framed, was faith; and that it is by reason of this principle of power existing in the Deity, that all created things exist; so that all things in heaven, on earth, or under the earth, exist by reason of faith, as it existed in him."

Lectures on Faith 1:15

Faith and the Priesthood

BRETHREN, [of the Priesthood], I refer again and for a moment only, to what the influence, the power of this Church would be, if we were united as one man. Then we might meet the principle announced in the prayer of the Great High Priest in the Garden, when he prayed that the disciples might be one, even as he and the Father were one, and as he declared in modern revelation: "I say unto you, be one; and if ye are not one ye are not mine." (D & C 38:27; and see John 17:21.)

As I have thought about what I might say I have thought I would like to say just a little bit about the Priesthood itself. We who are bearers of it, the Holy Priesthood after the Order of the Son of God, what is this Priesthood that we have? We have had our definitions. I will come to them, if I may, just a few minutes later. But I have thought that I would like to look first somewhat at the work of our Savior. His work was performed through faith. If you will examine a little bit carefully his life, you will find that in his miracles he performed many of the great functions of creation. He worked, I repeat, by the power of the Priesthood.

You will remember that he walked upon the water, thus defying and overruling, so far as we can see, the principle of gravity. You will remember that Peter asked to be bidden to come to him. Peter being so bidden, got out of the boat and walked a short distance on the water and then becoming fearful, he began to sink and called to the Lord for help, and the Lord said to him, "O thou of little faith...."

You will remember that on one occasion he was on the Sea of Galilee and a violent storm came up, so much so that those who were with him feared for the sinking of the ship. They awakened him and appealed to him and he stilled the tempest, having power over the forces that were involved in that.

You will recall that he fed a multitude with a few loaves and a few fishes, five thousand on one occasion, four thousand on another. You will recall that he also provided miraculous draughts of fish on two or three occasions. The whole world was under him.

You will recall that he cursed the barren fig tree. You will recall that he raised the dead to life again. Think of what was involved in that.

You will recall his thousands, almost (so far as we know), of healings of all sorts of diseases. These were manifestations of the power of faith. Sometimes it seems the faith was partially exercised by those whom he healed, as when the woman touched the border of his garment and was healed of an issue of blood. At other times it seemed as if the faith came from himself. Think of the blessing of faith exercised through the Priesthood.

As a Grain of Mustard Seed

On more than one occasion, he said: "If ye have faith as a grain of mustard seed...." (Matt. 17:20; Luke 17:6.) The commentators, I may add, make no explanation of this. The only statement I have found about that statement—faith is as a grain of mustard seed—is that the mustard seed is one of the smallest of seeds. And that was followed by, "... ye shall say unto this mountain, Remove hence to yonder place; and it shall remove." (*Ibid.*) And the commentators, who do not understand nor, apparently, believe in faith, say that this merely was an exaggerated imagery of the east; and that the expression "remove mountains" was common among Jewish preachers as indicating the impressiveness with which a man might speak, and referred only to *difficulty*. It is my judgment, my belief, my testimony, that the possible removal of a mountain is a sober statement of fact.

He told them at one time that if they had the faith, if they believed, they could say to a sycamine tree, "Be thou plucked up by the root, and be thou planted in the sea," and it would be done. (Luke 17:6.) I believe that. I believe that is literally true.

We have been given that Priesthood which carries in it this great power of faith. It has been given to us, you, me, and all who are listening in of the brethren holding the Priesthood.

Faith a Principle of Power

What about it? Paul said, ". . . faith is the assurance of things hoped for, the evidence of things not seen." (Heb. 11:1, Inspired Version.) I have never been able quite to understand that, but I can understand what has been said either by the Prophet Joseph or with his approval, found in the old "Lectures on Faith" in the Doctrine and Covenants. He said:

"By this we understand that the principle of power which existed in the bosom of God, by which the worlds were framed, was faith; and that it is by reason of this principle of power existing in the Deity, that all created things exist; so that all things in heaven, on earth, or under the earth, exist by reason of faith as it existed in Him." (Lectures on Faith, 1:15.)

As I think about faith, this principle of power, I am obliged to believe that it is an intelligent force. Of what kind, I do not know. But it is superior to and overrules all other forces of which we know. It is the principle, the force, by which the dead are restored to life.

I do not believe that the Lord, that God permits any man to have faith that would overrule *His* purposes. In that connection, I call to your attention the fact that the Savior, himself, pleaded that his crucifixion might be turned aside. Yet, on one occasion he said, when he asked that the hour might be passed on, ". . . but for this cause came I unto this hour." (John 12:27.) The Son of God was not given the necessary faith at that time to enable him to turn aside the purposes reached by himself and the Father before and still remembered by the Father. I repeat, I think that the Lord never gives faith to any individual to enable him to overturn the purposes of his will. Always we are subject to what he wishes.

I think that we should never administer to the sick, we should never pray, particularly when we pray for specific things, that we do not repeat and present to the Lord, even as Christ prayed in the Garden, "Nevertheless not my will, but thine, be done." (Luke 22:42.)

Magnify the Priesthood

You brethren, we brethren, have had this great power given unto us, this power of faith. What are we doing about it? Can you, can we, do the mighty things that the Savior did? Yes. They have been done by the members of the Church who had the faith and the righteousness so to do. Think of what is within your power if you but live the Gospel, if you but live so that you may invoke the power which is within you.

And I would like to add this as a sobering thought to myself and to you, each of you, and all of you: Remember the parable of the talents where the man who failed to improve the talent given him, had it taken from him? I ask you brethren, and myself, are we magnifying our Priesthood in such a way, are we living close enough to the Lord and in obedience to his commandments that we may exercise this power, or shall it be wholly or in part taken away from us? You would better think about it. It is worth thinking about. It is the greatest power that has been revealed to man.

God grant that we may all so live that we shall not lose that power, but that always it shall be available to us.

"Blessed are the merciful: for they shall obtain mercy."

Matthew 5:7

"Behold, verily I say unto you, there are hypocrites among you, who have deceived some, which has given the adversary power; but behold such shall be reclaimed;

"But the hypocrites shall be detected and shall be cut off, either in life or in death, even as I will; and wo unto them who are cut off from my church, for the same are overcome of the world."

Doctrine and Covenants 50:7-8

I Am the Law

M Y BROTHERS and sisters, fellow members of The Church of Jesus Christ of Latter-day Saints, the only true Church on the face of the earth at this time:*

The Lord has been good to me in giving me the physical strength to be with you this morning. I often facetiously say as long as you do not think with your heels, it does not make much difference what they do, it is only when the Lord or somebody begins to interfere with your head—I am uncertain on that point, personally. But I am grateful to be with you to mingle my testimony with the testimony of those who have gone before, that this is the work of God, that we are doing his service, that we are working under his plan, that we are instructing the world in general, and ourselves in particular, in the principles of his Gospel.

He said to the ancients on this continent, "I am the law," and such are his words. We need to look no further than to his words to get therefrom the guides and the principles which will lead us to eternal life. Time and time and time again, he said, sometimes involving the four principles, sometimes three of them, "I am the life, the light, the way, and the truth." And such is his message to us. Such are the principles by which our lives are to be guided.

I renew to you this morning the testimony I have given to you for over a quarter of a century, I believe every conference, a testimony that God lives, that Jesus is his Son and is the Christ, a testimony that the Father and the Son appeared to the Prophet, thus settling, so far as we are concerned, forever that the Father and the

---

*Last address in a General Conference by President J. Reuben Clark, Jr., October 9, 1960.

Son were personalities and that Jesus spoke truly when he said, "... he that hath seen me hath seen the Father. ..." (John 14:9.)

The Way Is Laid Down

My brothers and sisters, the way has been laid down for us. We have no choice and no necessity for anything beyond his words and the revelations of his mind and will which he makes known to his prophet, who is called, ordained and set apart, sustained by your vote to be the prophet, seer, and revelator of this Church. I renew again my testimony that the Savior with the Father came to the Prophet Joseph, that the Prophet and his associates through the assistance given to the associates, set up this Church, the only true Church, as I have already said, that exists upon the face of the earth.

How I wish we could carry this thought, this belief, this testimony in our hearts to the exclusion of all others. This is a time, nationally, when it happens that, so far as my memory goes, for the first time, the strictly religious problem has been thrown into the campaign. Be not disturbed. We are not concerned ecclesiastically. We have the truth. Ours is the Priesthood. We are the ones whom God has set up under a system of government which he revealed, where we have one man standing at the head, sustained as I have already said, by your vote, as the prophet, seer, and revelator of the Lord to his people. No one else has any right to declare the word of the Lord to this people.

I sometimes hear of persons, little groups, who undertake to direct us along lines that they think would be useful, politically. It is time for us to take notice and act when our prophet, seer, and revelator tells us what to do. We are not bound by any small group.

What a glorious thing it is to belong to the Lord's Church. As I have already said, it was the Lord who said, "I am the life, the light, the way, and the truth," and who said to the people on this continent, "I am the law," which meant, of course, that by his atoning sacrifice he fulfilled all that the law of Moses contemplated and provided for, and he alone is the one to whom we look.

Never forget those words of his to Martha, when she said, ". . . I know that he [Lazarus] shall rise again in the resurrection at the last day."

Christ said to her:

I am the resurrection, and the life: he that believeth in me, though he were dead [alluding, as I believe, to our ordinances for the dead], yet shall he live:

And whosoever liveth and believeth in me shall never die. (John 11:24-26.)

"This Is Life Eternal"

"And this is life eternal," said the Savior in the great prayer, "that they might know thee the only true God, and Jesus Christ, whom thou hast sent." (*Ibid.*, 17:3.)

And the great purposes of the Lord, the great purposes of the Father, were declared to Moses: ". . . this is my work and my glory—to bring to pass the immortality and eternal life of man." (Moses 1:39.)

How can we, as members of this Church, forget that great principle? How can we fail to keep his commandments and to go forward as he has directed, for that will bring to us the immortality and eternal life which God promised. And I would like to say—I was about to conclude, to the brethren of the Church, but unfortunately I fear I must include the sisters—someday, as a beginning to your transgression, you may have to determine whether a cigaret is worth more than what the Lord promised; someday, you will have to make the same determination about a drink of whiskey; someday, you may have to determine whether you prefer what the

Lord has promised, to an illicit date. You who have been through the temple of Almighty God, know your covenants, your obligations. Never forget them. Keep the commandments of the Lord.

The Sin of Hypocrisy

Very early in his ministry, the Savior, in that great conversation between him and Nicodemus, said that the Father sent the Savior to redeem the world, not to condemn it. The Lord never condemns the individual, except on rare occasions. He condemns the sin. And I can never forget that the most scathing denunciation that I know of in our literature, scriptural or otherwise, is that denunciation which the Savior made, and which is recorded in the latter chapters of Matthew, against hypocrisy. He leaves one almost with the persuasion that nothing is so bad as that.

And when you think what hypocrisy may do—lead you to following a life of falsehood, making you pretend to be what you are not, deceiving your fellow men, sometimes deceiving your wives and your children! But there is one whom you do not deceive, and that is Christ, our Lord. He knows all. Personally, I have felt that nobody need keep much of a record about me, except what I keep myself in my mind, which is a part of my spirit. I often question in my mind, whether it is going to require very many witnesses in addition to my own as to my wrongdoing, and I have frequently thought, in making funeral sermons—I wonder how many of us there are, who, if it became known that Jesus was out here at Wendover, and would be happy to see all who came to see him, Jesus our Lord, who knows all that we have done, all that we have thought, could read our minds as we would read a book—I wonder how many of us would have the courage to go out to Wendover and pay him a visit. And yet if we were not willing, had not the courage, it is because we have not lived and thought and believed as we should. To me, that is one great test of how well I am prepared to meet my Maker.

The Lord Is Merciful

The Lord helps us. He will give of his own Spirit even as much as we are prepared to accept. "I am the way, the truth, the life, and the light. I am the law," said the Savior.

Let us try always to learn what the Lord wants. If we are living the kind of lives we should live, that I hope we do live, we will find that no question ever arises in our minds for determination as to whether or not we should do a good deed, take a good course. The question comes only when we are thinking of doing something we should not do. And on that point, may I say just a word. "Prayer is the soul's sincere desire." And in praying, no matter what our words may be, there will be in the back of our minds the real prayer, the real desire, and that will be controlling.

The Lord is merciful. He overlooks much. He has to. Think of his life, what he did, what he said. That is your guide. We sometimes think that the Savior lived in a Palestine that was free from trouble, that there were no murders, no robbings, no thievings. Have you ever wondered a little why it was that Peter on that last night in the Garden happened to be armed with a sword? His Master's and his own message had never been to fight in that way. The Savior said he would make families fight among themselves, that their real enemy sometimes would be father or mother—but I have always understood that to mean the warfare between right and wrong, the warfare between his sayings and the sayings of the world.

Do you think of the Savior as living in a Roman civilization with all of the transgressions, all of the temptations, all of the evils of that great civilization? Yet so it was. And yet you will find nothing in the New Testament of any evils the Savior ever did of the many existing in the Roman Empire. I do not remember any reference, allusion, or statement given in the New Testament showing that the Savior patronized the Roman circus or the great amphitheaters which almost crowded the Palestine in which he lived.

Taking the New Testament alone, you will gain little idea of the kind of life the Romans led in Palestine, the kind of life that the Christ condemned, and yet as I have already said, it has seemed to me that the one sin that the Savior condemned as much as any other was the sin of hypocrisy—the living of the double life, the life we let our friends and sometimes our wives believe, and the life we actually live.

I repeat what I have already said, we may think nobody knows of our hypocrisy. As a matter of fact, I doubt if that assumption can be true. Somebody does know. But the Lord also knows, and we make up the record here in our minds—that part of us which I think is part of our eternal souls. We know, and we will never forget.

Power of the Priesthood

May the Lord give us strength and power to overcome evil. May he give to us men the power to magnify our Priesthood. May he give to us the knowledge that we hold in our hands through our Priesthood and the exercise of faith, the most powerful force of which we have any knowledge. It transcends the forces of nature, as the Lord showed on more than one occasion. It is the force by which the worlds were made. It is at our command, if we so live that we are entitled to it. But it is my faith and my belief that the Lord never gives anyone faith, it being his gift, that will defeat his purposes.

And when we pray, as I have said to you on many

occasions, I am sure, pray as he did in Gethsemane. And have you ever been struck with the thought that here was the Son praying to the Father to let the cup of crucifixion pass by, "... nevertheless not my will, but thine, be done." (Luke 22:42.) A few days before in the temple, he had said, "Father, save me from this hour: but for this cause came I unto this hour." (John 12:27.)

I have been struck with the fact that Deity himself, half mortal for the time, found himself asking that his destiny might be changed, but he finished his petition, "nevertheless not my will, but thine, be done."

In that spirit we should always approach our Heavenly Father in prayer. And when we go to our Heavenly Father for advice, let us not go to him with the request that he confirm us in our desires, but ask humbly and in full faith that he will give to us of our desires, no matter what they are or concerning whom they may be, that which accords with his will.

I am most grateful to be with you this morning, to mingle my voice with the voices of the other brethren who have testified to you during this conference. I have listened to you during the entire conference. I have enjoyed what has been said. I have regretted my absence. I am grateful that the Lord has permitted me to come this morning, and I thank President McKay for giving me the opportunity to say the few unpremeditated words I have said.

I pray the blessings of the Lord to be upon you and upon all of us. I pray the blessings of the Lord to be upon him, the prophet, seer, and revelator of the Church and the President thereof. I pray that we will give him the full measure of support that we have covenanted to give him when we sustained him by our uplifted hands. That is a marvelous covenant we make, and as we make it here, we bind the Church, for this is a constituent assembly speaking for the Church. God grant his blessings may be always with us, to help us, to build us up, to keep us in the straight and narrow path, even until the end of life, and may he enable us to bestow such an impress upon our families as will enable them in turn to follow his paths, never forgetting and applying strictly the great principle he announced, "I am the way, the truth, the life, and the light," and as to this continent, "I am the law," to the end that we ourselves and our families after us, may be saved and exalted and reunited in the hereafter.

"And Jesus said unto them, I am the bread of life: he that cometh to me shall never hunger; and he that believeth on me shall never thirst."

John 6:35

The Living Bread

LOOKING back across the nineteen hundred years that have gone, we marvel that of all of those who walked and talked with Jesus in Galilee and Judea, so few indeed understood or believed his message. And of the countless thousands who have lived and heard his message since his time, how scant the number that have really believed and walked in his way. It has been with great multitudes, even as with the Pharisees in their hypocrisy:

This people honoureth me with their lips, but their heart is far from me.
Howbeit in vain do they worship me, teaching for doctrines the commandments of men. (Mark 7:6-7; Matt. 15:8-9.)

The "Living Bread"

The multitudes flocked to him in Palestine, not for the spiritual truths he proclaimed, nor to follow the pattern of life he declared and led. They cared little for either of these. They came to him because he healed their sick, made whole their crippled, cast out from them their evil spirits. And yet because he cast out devils, they accused him of being in league with Beelzebub (Matt. 12:24 ff.; Mark 3:22 ff.; Luke 11:14-36); when he healed on the Sabbath day, they sought to kill him. (John 5:16 ff.)

They thronged in greatest mass to him when he fed them loaves and fishes without charge, and when, hot in their wild selfishness, they sought to make this free, generous Provider their king.

But Jesus declaring, "I am the living bread which came down from heaven: if any man eat of this bread, he shall live for ever" (John 6:51), his disciples

murmured and many of them thereafter walked no more
with him, for they understood him no more than did the
woman of Samaria at Jacob's Well when he discoursed
to her about the "well of water springing up into everlasting life" (*ibid.*, 4:14); he proclaiming his own mission, the Pharisees and chief priests sent officers to arrest
him (*ibid.*, 7:11 ff.); he declaring he was the Good Shepherd, they said he had a devil (*ibid.*, 10:1 ff.); he explain-
ing his oneness with the Father, they again sought first
to stone him and then to take him (*ibid.*, 10:22 ff.); he
affirming that "Before Abraham was, I am," they again
tried to stone him (*ibid.*, 8:55 ff.); he declaring his divine
Sonship, and the resurrection, they sought to kill him.
(*Ibid.*, 5:17 ff.)

Evil Powers Knew Him

At Nazareth, his friends and neighbors would have
cast him down headlong over a cliff for proclaiming a
universal salvation, save that he "passing through the
midst of them went his way." (Luke 4:16-30.)   Later,
rejected again by these and by his own kinsfolk and
household, his brothers and sisters (so runs the record),
he declared in comment and reproof:

A prophet is not without honour, but in his own country,
and among his own kin, and in his own house. (Mark 6:1-6.)

But the powers of evil knew him.   The Gadarene
demons proclaimed him, they knew his message and its
truth as they besought him not to cast them out into the
deep, bodiless (Matt. 8:28-34; Mark 5:1-20; Luke 8:26-
39); so knew him the demon in the synagogue in Capernaum (Mark 1:21-28; Luke 4:31-37), and the demons on
the day of miracles when Peter's mother-in-law was
healed. (Matt. 8:14-17; Mark 1:29-34; Luke 4:38-41.)
And Lucifer, the "son of the morning" (Isa. 14:12), he
who fell so far, to the very depths of hell, he knew him

on the Mount of Temptation and sought his destruction.
(Matt. 4:1-11; Mark 1:12-13; Luke 4:1-13.)

Rejected on the Cross

But his being cast off by the world and by his own
did not fill his cup of rejection. At the crucifixion, while
the passers-by and the soldiers mocked, scoffed, and re-
viled him (Matt. 27:39-44; Mark 15:29-32; Luke 23:
36-39), he hung on the cross alone, save for a thief on
either side, forsaken not only by the throngs of the idle
curious, but forsaken by the scores he had healed, by the
multitudes he had fed, by the greedy crowds that would
have made him king; he hung, forsaken by his disciples,
even by his Apostles who had boasted they would be devoted and loyal, even to death itself (Matt. 26:35; Mark
14:31), forsaken by all except his mother, her sister, and
Mary Magdalene, and John the Beloved (John 19:25-26),
and some women who stood afar off. (Matt. 27:55.) So
crucified and hanging in his infinite, forsaken loneliness,
his spirit about to go, his mighty grief burst forth in that
cry of mortal near-despair, "My God, my God, why hast
thou forsaken me?" (Matt. 27:46; Mark 15:34.)

So he died that by his death we and all other of
God's children, born since Adam, might live.

The Resurrected Lord

Then at the break of the third day, the stone was
rolled back from the mouth of the tomb, and the Christ
arose, a glorified, resurrected being, flesh and bone and
spirit reunited, making the perfect soul, the First Fruits
of the Resurrection.

Thus Christ's saying to Martha, "I am the resurrection," is an everlasting truth, as unchanging, as endur-
ing, as uncompromising as eternity itself.

To the pressing multitude he preached his great
sermon on "the bread of life":

> For the bread of God is he which cometh down from heaven, and giveth life unto the world. . . .
>
> I am the living bread which came down from heaven: if any man eat of this bread, he shall live for ever. . . . (John 6:33, 51.)

And speaking to his Apostles in the Passover chamber, Christ reiterated:

> I am the way, the truth, and the life: no man cometh unto the Father, but by me. (*Ibid.*, 14:6.)

And this fact exists and rules men and the universe whether men accept it or reject it. Eternal truth is not dependent for its existence upon the will or the understanding or the belief of man.

We declare as did Paul that in the resurrection, bodies arise in different glories, dependent upon the kind of lives lived on this earth. (1 Cor. 15:40-43; and see D & C 76 and 78.) We get hereafter that glory, that plane of existence, that status which our lives lived here fit us for. For a law has been given governing all things. If we would get a glory, a reward, we must live the law, do the things, that shall entitle us thereto. If we cannot abide the law, do the things, upon which the glory, the blessing is based, we cannot abide the glory itself. (D & C 88:13 ff.)

And "the way, the truth, the light, and the bread of life" of Jesus are for every one of God's children, freely given to every one who seeks.

The Sermon on the Mount

In the greatest sermon of all time, delivered on the Mount to the multitudes, he taught us some of the essential elements of "the way, the truth, the light, the bread of life," saying:

> Blessed are the poor in spirit: for their's is the kingdom of heaven.

Blessed are they that mourn: for they shall be comforted.

Blessed are the meek: for they shall inherit the earth.

Blessed are they which do hunger and thirst after righteousness: for they shall be filled.

Blessed are the merciful: for they shall obtain mercy.

Blessed are the pure in heart: for they shall see God.

Blessed are the peacemakers: for they shall be called the children of God. . . .

Ye have heard that it hath been said, Thou shalt love thy neighbour, and hate thine enemy.

But I say unto you, Love your enemies, bless them that curse you, do good to them that hate you, and pray for them which despitefully use you, and persecute you. (Matt 5:3-9, 43-44.)

Divine Command of Brotherly Love

This divine command of love gives the one and only remedy that will bring lasting peace out of the bloody tragedy that is now devastating the world. Hate is born of Satan; it fosters murder, the second crime in degree of all that God has listed. It strikes the friend of today and makes him the enemy of tomorrow. Once enkindled in a nation, it becomes a fiery furnace that consumes the people that lighted it. Hate-mongers brew a poison that makes victims of themselves. Hate, loosed and worldwide, breaks beyond direction or control. It eats away the righteousness of the nations, it corrodes their tolerance, it rots out brotherly love, it debauches the highest and the lowest, it prostitutes all that civilized man holds most dear, it attacks even the sacred relations of the family hearth.

We Christians professing the name of Christ and proclaiming his Gospel, give the lie to our professions and our proclamations, we "become as sounding brass, or a tinkling cymbal" (1 Cor. 13:1) if we do not live the brotherhood of man; if we do not ourselves obey this divine law of love. So sure as there is a God in heaven who decreed this law, just so surely is there no escape therefrom. But if we live the law, if we live the way of the Christ, we shall inherit the celestial glory, of which Paul spoke (1 Cor. 15:40); we shall be of them "whose bodies are celestial, whose glory is that of the sun, even the glory of God, the highest of all, whose glory the sun of the firmament is written of as being typical" (D & C 76:70), we shall be of them who "shall dwell in the presence of God and his Christ forever and ever." (*Ibid.*, v. 62.)

Gives a Prayer

In closing I voice a prayer:

Our Father in Heaven: Turn toward us, thy suffering children, thine listening ear. Heed our words of travail and sorrow. Lead us into paths of righteousness. Teach us the humility of thy Son. Grant us power to resist the Adversary. Keep us from temptation. Give to thine erring sons and daughters thy peace and thy comfort.

Bestow upon us in rich abundance the gift of faith, faith in the Gospel of the Christ, for that is a gift of thee, faith in thy goodness, thy mercy, thy love. Build in us the testimony of truth and grant us wisdom to know the truth, for that will make us free.

Cause that charity and patience and forbearance and love of fellow man, may come and abide with us. Banish from our hearts all hate, for where hate resides, thy spirit and righteousness cannot dwell.

We would be thine obedient sons and daughters, walking in the paths thou hast marked for us, keeping thy commandments, following the steps of the lowly Jesus, thine Only Begotten Son. We know our weaknesses and infirmities, we know the flesh is weak. But our desires are for thee and thy ways. Help our spirits to be strong for we would live thy word. Build in us an ever-growing testimony that Jesus is the Christ, thy Son, the Redeemer of the world.

Aid us to this end in our frailties and imperfections. Lead us so to live that we may inherit the celestial glory and abide with thee forever and ever.

And, O our Father: Work out thy divine purposes speedily among the nations, that peace—the world's peace and thy peace—may again fill the earth. And thine shall be the glory and the honor forever.

"But Jesus called them unto him, and said, Suffer little children to come unto me, and forbid them not: for of such is the kingdom of God."
Luke 18:16

He Blesses Little Children

I HAVE been asked to speak to you about our children, our grandchildren, our great-grandchildren, and those who are to come hereafter, down to the last generation. I have spoken to you before on these subjects, and today I have nothing new, or startling to tell you, really no new field to enter. I am not sure that you will enjoy, particularly, the things that I may have to say or to read. But after thinking over the matter of the request, I concluded perhaps it might be well for me to read to you what the scriptures say about the children and our relation to them. I found that these scriptures treated the matter of children from several points of view: one of them was from the relationship of the parent to the child; another, the relationship from the child to the parent; another, the relationship having to do with matters of discipline; another, the relationship of children to the Church; and finally, a relationship of children to the kingdom of God.

I thought perhaps it might be of value and interest to you if I were to take up a sort of history as disclosed in the more important passages of scripture, a history of the Lord's instructions regarding children. I have tried to follow along with reasonable accuracy the history as we have it in the scriptures from the beginning.

I am reading from the Old Testament period. I am reading from the period in the Book of Mormon before the time of the Savior. I am reading something of the things which the Savior said in Palestine. I am reading more of what the Savior said when he visited the people on this continent after his resurrection. I am reading something of what was said by the prophets thereafter on this hemisphere. And, lastly, I am trying to bring

together in some chronological order the things which
the Lord has said in our day to the Prophet Joseph Smith.

I hope you will bear with me. I shall not be able
to give you a full background, time will not permit, for
the various things about which I shall talk, and concerning which I shall read, but I will give some.

Old Testament Teachings

I will begin with the great commandment given on
Mount Sinai, the earliest, so far as I know, of any direction and command relating generally to the relationship
between child and parent.

"Honour thy father and thy mother . . ." declared
God on Sinai to Moses for the Children of Israel, ". . . that
thy days may be long upon the land which the Lord thy
God giveth thee." (Ex. 20:12.)

Couched in such general terms, as I take it, it applies not only to the Children of Israel traveling in the
wilderness, preparatory to going into the Promised Land,
but a commandment and a promise that come to every
people of God no matter where they are or in what time
they lived. It comes to us as it went to ancient Israel.

And in that connection I have in mind an application
of this principle which the Savior made during his ministry in Palestine. He condemned the Jews because they
had distorted this command, "Honour thy father and thy
mother . . ." so that they had come to the point where they
could, under the rabbinical rule, give to the parent a gift
called *Corban*, and by that gift relieve themselves of the
responsibility of that great commandment of Sinai which
the Savior then interpreted to mean that they should care
for their fathers and their mothers, in their material
needs; and the Savior condemned their practice in terms
that were most vigorous.

Now, there are some other expressions in the great
Book, in the Old Testament, which relate to the treatment

of children, and the attitude of ancient Israel towards children. I am going to read a few of those, taken primarily from Proverbs:

> Train up a child in the way he should go: and when he is old, he will not depart from it. (Prov. 22:6.)

That is a universal law, just as applicable today as it was the day it was written.

Then another one is given which does not quite comport with later commandments from the Lord. It says:

> Foolishness is bound in the heart of a child; but the rod of correction shall drive it far from him. (Prov. 22:15.)

Note, the rod. . . .

> Withhold not correction from the child: for if thou beatest him with the rod, he shall not die. (Prov. 23:13.)

—regarded perhaps as a comforting assurance.

Finally:

> The rod and reproof give wisdom: but a child left to himself bringeth his mother to shame. (Prov. 29:15.)

Those were the concepts of the Old Testament, in general.

Perhaps I might finish out this narration by noting the incident of Elisha and the little children at Bethel. They followed him out of the city, mocking him and saying unto him, "Go up, thou bald head; go up, thou bald head," whereupon he turned back, looked at them, and ". . . cursed them in the name of the Lord. And there came forth two she bears out of the wood, and tare forty and two children of them." (2 Kings 2:23-24.) Thus much for children in the Old Testament.

Book of Mormon Teachings before the Time of Christ

In his great farewell address to his people, King Benjamin, on this continent in Old Testament times, gave some great instructions regarding children, that I particularly wish to read to you. They cover a considerable area and contain instructions and comment that are just as pertinent today as they were the day Benjamin pronounced them. The whole concept is different from that of the Old Testament. In his address to his sons Mosiah, Helorum, and Helaman, he said:

"And ye will not suffer your children that they go hungry, or naked"—thus making a very clear declaration regarding the duty of these brethren and of the parents toward their children; ". . . neither will ye suffer that they transgress the laws of God"—they were to see that they lived righteously; "and [not] fight and quarrel one with another"—there was to be peace in the home; "and [not] serve the devil, who is the master of sin, or who is the evil spirit which hath been spoken of by our fathers, he [the devil] being an enemy to all righteousness. But ye will teach them to walk in the ways of truth and soberness; ye will teach them to love one another, and to serve one another." (Mosiah 4:14-15.)

The association of children together, the plane upon which that association should be placed and lived, the conduct, the whole realm of children's relationship in the family and with neighbors are given here.

Abinadi, preaching to the depraved King Noah and his corrupt priests, declared, first, "And little children also have eternal life,"—which seems to be the first recorded expression, which was later enlarged, showing that children, until they have reached the age of accountability, have no need for repentance. (*Ibid.*, 15:25.)

Alma, preaching to the humbled, poverty-stricken Zoramites, and declaring God is merciful to all who believe on his name, declared:

And now, he imparteth his word by angels unto men, yea, not only men but women also. Now this is not all; little children do have words given unto them many times which confound the wise and the learned. (Alma 32:23.)

Those of us who have had children and grandchildren and great-grandchildren know how frequently these little ones come to us with questions and comments which show a seeming profundity of reflection that makes us marvel.

But the words there spoken had a more literal fulfilment, as we shall later point out.

Teachings of the Savior in Palestine

Now, I come down to the time of the Savior, and, first as to his comments in Palestine, I will refer to two well-known incidents. In the great Galilean ministry, at Capernaum, the disciples came to the Savior and said:

. . . Who is the greatest in the kingdom of heaven? (Matt. 18:1.)

And the Savior replied:

. . . Verily I say unto you, Except ye be converted, and become as little children, ye shall not enter into the kingdom of heaven.

Whosoever therefore shall humble himself as this little child, the same is greatest in the kingdom of heaven.

And whoso shall receive one such little child in my name receiveth me.

But whoso shall offend one of these little ones which believe in me, it were better for him that a millstone were hanged about his neck, and that he were drowned in the depth of the sea. (*Ibid.*, 18:3-6.)

The care of children, the respect and consideration to be shown them, the position of those who ill-treat children are here poignantly described.

And here, for the first time in the Holy Writ of Palestine, we come into a larger view regarding the children. There is no suggestion here of the old adage, "Spare the rod and spoil the child." The spiritual position of children in the kingdom is declared. This is a message of love, of respect, of establishing an example of what all of us should be, if we would enter the kingdom. We must come even as a little child.

Later, during the Perean ministry, the Savior, you will remember, traveling along the way, the multitude came to him and wanted to bring little children to him. The disciples wished to prevent it, but he reproved his disciples in these words, beginning for the first time to give a place to children in the kingdom of God:

> But when Jesus saw it, he was much displeased, and said unto them, Suffer the little children to come unto me, and forbid them not: for of such is the kingdom of God.
>
> Verily I say unto you, Whosoever shall not receive the kingdom of God as a little child, he shall not enter therein.
>
> And he took them up in his arms, put his hands upon them, and blessed them. (Mark 10:14-16.)

Teachings of the Savior in America

These things happened and were spoken by the Savior regarding children in Palestine. I shall now come to the records of doings in America and point out some of the incidents that took place there.

Christ ministered to the people of America after his resurrection, he having been introduced to the inhabitants here by the Father, on an occasion of divine simplicity and exquisite tenderness and beauty. (3 Nephi 11.)

To appreciate the peace and calm of the account of Christ's visit to this continent, one should come to the record fresh from the reading of the record of the Gospels describing the Last Supper, the prayer in Gethsemane, the arrest, the trial and the crucifixion of Jesus, the Savior of the world; then the reading of the terrible destruction on this continent at the time of the crucifixion. And after this reading then turn to the record of Christ's work and ministry among those of this land who survived the awful days of the crucifixion, a record that is a holy benediction upon the mortal ministry of the Atoning Sacrifice, Jesus Christ of Nazareth.

We shall confine ourselves to repeating some of his sayings and doings about and concerning children. The record runs:

> And it came to pass that he commanded that their little children should be brought.
> So they brought their little children and set them down upon the ground round about him, and Jesus stood in the midst; and the multitude gave way till they had all been brought unto him. . . .
> And when he had said these words, he wept, and the multitude bare record of it, and he took their little children, one by one, and blessed them, and prayed unto the Father for them. (*Ibid.*, 17:11-12, 21.)

Thus he was repeating here on this land the incident (already noted, above) which took place in Palestine while he was on his way back to Jerusalem from Perea for the crucifixion. The account goes on:

> And when he had done this he wept again;
> And he spake unto the multitude, and said unto them: Behold your little ones.
> And as they looked to behold they cast their eyes towards heaven, and they saw the heavens open, and they saw angels descending out of heaven as it were in the midst of fire; and they came down and encircled those little ones about, and they were encircled about with fire; and the angels did minister unto them.
> And the multitude did see and hear and bear record; and they know that their record is true for they all of them did see and hear. . . .

Not a few of them saw, not an isolated individual here and there saw, but the whole multitude assembled beheld—they all saw.

> . . . every man for himself; and they were in number about two thousand and five hundred souls; and they did consist of men, women, and children. (*Ibid.*, 17:22-25.)

This shows how precious in the sight of the Lord are the children which we have. And may I remind you, these children did not come to you and ask you to give them bodies, they did not ask you sisters to become mothers and the men to become fathers of their earthly bodies. The Lord commanded, of course, that we should multiply and replenish the earth. But you, of your own volition, created the bodies for the spirits to take, and these little ones were gracious enough to come to the body you created. They are your guests. You, as hosts, owe to them all of the consideration, all of the love, all of the kindness, all of the patience and courtesy and all the other virtues that it is possible.for you to give. They are here because you invited them to come. Thank God for their presence.

May I reread a few words:

And he spake unto the multitude, and said unto them: Behold your little ones.

And as they looked to behold they cast their eyes towards heaven, and they saw the heavens open, and they saw angels descending out of heaven. . . .

And the multitude did see and hear and bear record; and they know that their record is true for they all of them did see and hear. . . . (*Ibid.*, 17:23-25.)

The record goes on:

And it came to pass that he did teach and minister unto the children of the multitude of whom hath been spoken, and he did loose their tongues. . . . (*Ibid.*, 26:14.)

Now I refer to the earlier statement about the wisdom that comes from children:

. . . he did loose their tongues, and they did speak unto their fathers great and marvelous things, even greater than he had revealed unto the people; and he loosed their tongues that they could utter.

And it came to pass that after he had ascended into heaven —the second time that he showed himself unto them, and had gone unto the Father, after having healed all their sick, and their lame, and opened the eyes of their blind and unstopped the ears of the deaf, and even had done all manner of cures among them, and raised a man from the dead, and had shown forth his power unto them, and had ascended unto the Father—

Behold, it came to pass on the morrow that the multitude gathered themselves together, and they both saw and heard these children; yea, even babes did open their mouths and utter marvelous things; and the things which they did utter were forbidden that there should not any man write them. (*Ibid.*, 26:14-16.)

I am rather persuaded that one of the reasons for forbidding them to write the things that were uttered was that they had no language to express the things which came into their minds and into their hearts by reason of the blessings and ministrations of our Lord and Master, just as we oftentimes have feelings come into our hearts for our loved ones that are beyond our powers to express; or things that come to us under the inspiration of the Spirit of the Lord. We have not the language, we have not the capacity really to think out the precise meaning of what so comes to us, what we feel, but we know of the great joy and the great happiness that come when we have these moments of high inspiration, even revelation.

Read Third Nephi

Then the Lord goes on here and talks about baptism for the dead and baptism for children.

I will close the recitation of what happened at the time that the Savior came here to the people of this land, precious above all other lands, by merely asking you to get your Book of Mormon when you get home and read the whole of Third Nephi. It is an incomparable record of the dealings of our Lord and Savior, Jesus Christ, with the children of our Father in Heaven, of whom Christ is our Elder Brother.

As I have indicated, I like to think of the Savior's

mission here on this land after his crucifixion, as the
benediction of his earthly life. I again ask you to read
first the account in the New Testament of all the woe,
of all the grief, of all the suffering, of all the anguish,
the trial, and the tribulation that came to our Savior,
and then pick up your Book of Mormon, turn to Third
Nephi, and read what happened here. Read, first, of
the marvelous introduction by which the Father introduced the Savior, how the voice came from heaven the
first time, and they did not understand it. It came the
second time; again they could not understand it. It came
the third time, and then they understood, for, finally
they had brought themselves into that spiritual condition where they could understand. (3 Nephi 11:1-7.) I
have always thought that there was a wonderful lesson
here. I wonder how often the Savior and the Father
would communicate with us if we but brought ourselves
into the frame of mind and the spiritual condition where
we could understand their words.

Teachings in the Book of Mormon After the Savior's Visit

After the Savior's visit to this continent following
his death and resurrection, Mormon wrote an epistle to
Moroni, in the course of which he said a few words about
children. He said:

Behold I say unto you that this thing shall ye teach—repentance and baptism unto those who are accountable and capable of
committing sin; yea, teach parents that they must repent and be
baptized, and humble themselves as their little children, and they
shall all be saved with their little children.

And their little children need no repentance, neither baptism.
Behold, baptism is unto repentance to the fulfilling the commandments unto the remission of sins.

But little children are alive in Christ, even from the foundation of the world; if not so, God is a partial God, and also a
changeable God, and a respecter to persons; for how many little
children have died without baptism!

Wherefore, if little children could not be saved without baptism, these must have gone to an endless hell. (Moroni 8:10-13.)

Then Mormon goes on and talks about baptism, but I will not read all of that, but he comes to this expression:

And I am filled with charity, which is everlasting love; wherefore, all children are alike unto me; wherefore, I love little children with a perfect love; and they are all alike and partakers of salvation.

For I know that God is not a partial God, neither a changeable being; but he is unchangeable from all eternity to all eternity.

Little children cannot repent; wherefore, it is awful wickedness to deny the pure mercies of God unto them, for they are all alive in him because of his mercy.

And he that saith that little children need baptism denieth the mercies of Christ, and setteth at naught the atonement of him and the power of his redemption. . . .

For behold that all little children are alive in Christ, and also all they that are without the law. For the power of redemption cometh on all them that have no law; wherefore, he that is not condemned, or he that is under no condemnation, cannot repent; and unto such baptism availeth nothing. (*Ibid.*, 8:17-20, 22.)

These words give clearly the position of children in the kingdom of God. They cannot sin; they have no need of baptism; they go to our Heavenly Father; and unless we become as little childen, we may not hope to come thus to our Father. Here is the first clear exposition that I have found in the scriptures, of the spiritual status of children, and their place in the kingdom of God.

Teachings Through the Prophet Joseph

We come now to strictly modern revelation, not only brought forth in modern times, as in the Book of Mormon, but actually revealed from heaven in our day.

The revelations given to the Prophet Joseph on the question of children began almost a year before the or-

ganization of the Church. The first one noted was in June
of 1829. A couple of months thereafter, according to
Brother Kirkham's computation, the copy for the Book
of Mormon went to the printers. I often think that these
early revelations may have come to the Prophet to settle
questions that had arisen in his mind because of the
teachings of the Book of Mormon; we know that certain
questions did so arise; he has told us so. But I think
that many other things were revealed that were the
result of questions raised by the Book of Mormon record,
and among such thought-provoking questions, as I am
inclined to believe, are these statements that I have read
to you of King Benjamin and others and then from the
Savior himself, and then from Mormon,—I say, I am
inclined to think that these principles and doctrines recorded in the Book of Mormon, had raised questions in
the Prophet's mind, and gradually the Lord answered
them.

I might say here, I am fully persuaded that the Lord
never at any time in the whole history of his dealings
with the human family, undertook to give all of his
commandments and reveal the principles of the Gospel
for that particular dispensation all at one time, at the
beginning of the dispensation. In all dispensations the
words of the Lord have come gradually as they are needed,
step by step, commandment upon commandment, direction upon direction, and that is the way the revelations
have come in this Last Dispensation of the Fulness of
Times.

Baptism of Children

I am reading now from the Doctrine and Covenants:

For all men must repent and be baptized, and not only men,
but women, and children who have arrived at the years of accountability. (D & C 18:42.)

We are not told what that age of accountability is. The Lord now begins to draw a distinction between the time when the child is not accountable and the time when the child is accountable.

Just about the time of the organization of the Church, the revelation was received, printed now as Section 20, that great section in the Doctrine and Covenants which relates to the organization of the Church. The Lord then said this:

> Every member of the church of Christ having children is to bring them unto the elders before the church, who are to lay their hands upon them in the name of Jesus Christ, and bless them in his name.
>
> No one can be received into the church of Christ unless he has arrived unto the years of accountability before God, and is capable of repentance. (*Ibid.*, 20:70-71.)

Here is a very clear statement about eligibility for Church membership, and inferentially the purpose and efficacy of baptism.

In September of that same year, five months later than the revelation I have just read, the Lord said this about little children:

> But behold, I say unto you, that little children are redeemed from the foundation of the world through mine Only Begotten;
>
> Wherefore, they cannot sin, for power is not given unto Satan to tempt little children, until they begin to become accountable before me;
>
> For it is given unto them even as I will, according to mine own pleasure, that great things may be required at the hand of their fathers. (*Ibid.*, 29:46-48.)

The Lord is again declaring the status of children before and after their accountability.

Instruction in Principles of the Gospel

The next that I wish to read to you occurred a year after the organization of the Church. This is a very interesting revelation. It shows how early the Lord instructed the Church in our day to give attention to the children. In June 1831, in a revelation through the Prophet, he said to William W. Phelps:

> And again, you shall be ordained to assist my servant Oliver Cowdery to do the work of printing, and of selecting and writing books for schools in this church, that little children also may receive instruction before me as is pleasing unto me. (*Ibid.*, 55:4.)

Thus in June 1831, the Lord revealed his care and concern for the instruction, the education, of little children, the little ones, in order that they might grow up understanding the principles of the Gospel.

In January of 1832, the Lord again spoke. The fathers of Jewish children had been desirous that their children be circumcised, and the Lord, speaking of this as an unholy tradition, said:

> But little children are holy, being sanctified through the atonement of Jesus Christ; and this is what the scriptures mean. (*Ibid.*, 74:7.)

Here is another statement regarding the spiritual status of children.

Before that (in November of 1831), as he was sending Orson Hyde, Luke S. Johnson, Lyman E. Johnson, and William E. M'Lellin on missions, he gave a revelation to them and in that revelation he touched upon this question of children. He declared that the words of missionaries spoken as moved upon by the Holy Ghost should be scripture; he sent them forth to baptize and to appoint more bishops, and declared the position in this relation of the literal descendants of Aaron. He then gave commandments concerning children that should be in our minds.

Age of Accountability

The Lord first sets out the duties of parents to teach their children the principles of the Gospel, and announces a penalty if the parents fail. He says:

And again, inasmuch as parents have children in Zion, or in any of her stakes which are organized, that teach them not to understand the doctrine of repentance, faith in Christ the Son of the living God, and of baptism and the gift of the Holy Ghost by the laying on of the hands, when eight years old, the sin be upon the heads of the parents.

For this shall be a law unto the inhabitants of Zion, or in any of her stakes which are organized. (*Ibid.*, 68:25-26.)

For the Whole Church

Thus this commandment is for the whole Church. The revelation continues:

And their children shall be baptized for the remission of their sins when eight years old, and receive the laying on of the hands. (*Ibid.*, 68:27.)

Thus parents are charged with the responsibility to see that their children shall become members of the Church at the time when they are eight years old; they are to be baptized. This is the first time observed in the revelations when the Lord fixes the age of accountability. Prior to this time, and speaking of the spiritual relationship of children to the kingdom, he spoke merely of the time while they were not accountable. Now he fixes the age.

Teach Children to Pray

The revelation then says:

And they shall also teach their children to pray, and to walk uprightly before the Lord. (*Ibid.*, 68:28.)

We seek our Heavenly Father through prayer. It seems that when the Lord was on the earth, he never

approached a great event or a seeming crisis in his earth-
life, without first going to his Father in prayer.

You will recall that Amulek, in his great sermon
to the multitude, told us the things about which we might
pray. This great message is worth reading and rereading,
and I would like to call your particular attention to the
admonition which he gave to the multitude when he recounted how vain would be their prayers if they turned
away the needy and the naked and visited not the sick
and afflicted and imparted not of their substance. (Alma
34:17 ff.)

And, as to this matter of prayer, remember also that
the Lord has told us that the Father knows what we need
even before we ask for it. (Matt. 6:8.) He knows what
would be wise for us to have with an infinite knowledge
of us and of our characters, our failings, our virtues. It
is not necessary, therefore, to give long and repetitious
prayers for the Father's sake or need. But yet he has
commanded us to pray, and pray we should.

Out of the many reasons and objects of prayer, there
may be this great function: it helps to bring our minds
upon ourselves; it helps us to make a sort of self-analysis
of ourselves so that we come to a knowledge of our weaknesses and imperfections and of those matters concerning
which we need the help of the Lord. We force ourselves
to screen our petitions; it helps us not to ask the Lord
for foolish, vain, or unnecessary things. The Lord is no
wiser when we finish the prayer than he was before we
began, but we, if we have prayed properly, have a better
appreciation of ourselves and of our needs.

Remember the Sabbath Day

The revelation goes on:

And the inhabitants of Zion shall also observe the Sabbath
day to keep it holy. (D & C 68:29.)

This, of course, refers to the children also, for they are among the inhabitants of Zion. The great commandment of Sinai, "Remember the sabbath day, to keep it holy," was given to all Israel, ancient and modern, and to all the inhabitants of the earth, children as well as adults.

The revelation next says:

And the inhabitants of Zion also shall remember their labors, inasmuch as they are appointed to labor, in all faithfulness; for the idler sha'l be had in remembrance before the Lord.

Now, I, the Lord, am not well pleased with the inhabitants of Zion, for there are idlers among them; and their children are also growing up in wickedness; they also seek not earnestly the riches of eternity, but their eyes are full of greediness. (*Ibid.*, 68:30-31.)

Idleness Condemned

You will note that the Lord calls attention to the duties of the laborer to perform his appointed tasks, and he calls attention to the idlers. I forego even citing to you the various commandments where the Lord in our day condemned idlers, but here, in this revelation, is one case in which he refers to the idleness of children, an idleness which quite obviously he regards as serious because he recognizes that the children of idlers are growing up in wickedness and intimates that they seek not earnestly the riches of eternity, but their eyes are full of greediness.

It would not be amiss if you were to look up the references to idleness in the Doctrine and Covenants and learn just what the Lord has said about it. Idleness is one of the great contributing causes for the taking away from Zion of the great principle of the United Order. All of these commandments are just as pertinent now as they were the day they were uttered.

We then come to the specific direction made to Oliver Cowdery, not specially mentioned earlier in the revelation. The Lord instructed him thusly:

These things ought not to be, and must be done away from among them; wherefore, let my servant Oliver Cowdery carry these sayings unto the land of Zion. (*Ibid.*, 68:32.)

These doctrines were to be broadcast to the Saints in Zion.

The Lord then returns to the matter of prayer and declares:

And a commandment I give unto them—that he that observeth not his prayers before the Lord in the season thereof, let him be had in remembrance before the judge of my people.

These sayings are true and faithful; wherefore, transgress them not, neither take therefrom.

Behold, I am Alpha and Omega, and I come quickly. Amen. (*Ibid.*, 68:33-35.)

Thus the Lord makes clear that the man who does not observe his prayers is to be taken before the judge, that is, before the bishop. Prayer is required.

All these commandments and directions, these expressions of rewards and punishments, have to do with parents, and, of course, with children after they have reached the age of accountability. And it appears clear that children before they reach the age of accountability are to be trained as herein directed in order that when they do so reach that age and are baptized, they will not depart from the righteousness of life which they theretofore lived.

Relationship of Child and Parent

Then, still later, the Lord gave that great revelation which deals with the conditions, in part, that we have today. This revelation dealt with the relationship of parent to child, child to parent, and of the Church to the widow and the orphan:

Verily, thus saith the Lord, in addition to the laws of the

church concerning women and children, those who belong to the church, who have lost their husbands or fathers:

Women have claim on their husbands for their maintenance, until their husbands are taken; and if they are not found transgressors they shall have fellowship in the church.

And if they are not faithful they shall not have fellowship in the church; yet they may remain upon their inheritances according to the laws of the land.

All children have claim upon their parents for their maintenance until they are of age.

And after that, they have claim upon the church, or in other words upon the Lord's storehouse, if their parents have not wherewith to give them inheritances.

And the storehouse shall be kept by the consecrations of the church; and widows and orphans shall be provided for, as also the poor. (*Ibid.*, 83:1-6.)

That revelation was given April 30, 1832, during the time the United Order was in operation in Zion— that is, in Missouri. This was over two years before the revelation given at Fishing River, which suspended the operation of the United Order. The present great welfare plan measurably meets the requirements of this revelation.

Homes to Be Set in Order

And then, finally, I come to the great revelation that was given on May 6, 1833. The First Presidency had recently been organized, and the Lord spoke to the First Presidency and to the bishop of Kirtland:

But I have commanded you to bring up your children in light and truth.

But verily I say unto you, my servant Frederick G. Williams, you have continued under this condemnation;

You have not taught your children light and truth, according to the commandments; and that wicked one hath power, as yet, over you, and this is the cause of your affliction. (*Ibid.*, 93:40-42.)

I want you to note that declaration: failure to teach and bring up your family in the right way may lead to afflictions. It brought them to Frederick G. Williams.

> And now a commandment I give unto you—if you will be delivered you shall set in order your own house, for there are many things that are not right in your house. (*Ibid.*, 93:43.)

To deliver ourselves from affliction, we must set our houses in order.

The Lord then speaks to Sidney Rigdon:

> Verily, I say unto my servant Sidney Rigdon, that in some things he hath not kept the commandments concerning his children; therefore, first set in order thy house. (*Ibid.*, 93:44.)

Again, is the command our houses must be set in order.

Then the Lord speaks to the Prophet Joseph, himself. I have always felt that this revelation was one evidence of the integrity and truthfulness of Joseph; he does not hesitate to record a reproof to himself.

"Verily, I say unto my servant Joseph Smith, Jun., or in other words, I will call you friends"—the Lord does not wish them to understand that he is chastizing too severely, he is pointing out the way to obtain blessings—"for you are my friends, and ye shall have an inheritance with me—I called you servants for the world's sake, and ye are their servants for my sake." (*Ibid.*, 93:45-46.) I call your attention to the lofty concept voiced in this sentence.

The Lord continues:

> And now, verily I say unto Joseph Smith, Jun.—You have not kept the commandments, and must needs stand rebuked before the Lord;
> Your family must needs repent and forsake some things, and give more earnest heed unto your sayings, or be removed out of their place.
> What I say unto one I say unto all; pray always lest that

wicked one have power in you, and remove you out of your place. (*Ibid.*, 93:47-49.)

If we do not live as the Lord commands, we shall be removed "out of our place."

Finally, to the bishop of Kirtland, the Lord addresses words of reproof and counsel:

My servant Newel K. Whitney also, a bishop of my church, hath need to be chastened, and set in order his family, and see that they are more diligent and concerned at home, and pray always, or they shall be removed out of their place. (*Ibid.*, 93:50.)

Once more, the command to set our homes in order.

These, so far as I have seen, are among the essential commandments that have been given in our day regarding children.

They clearly set forth the duties of parents to children, the position of children in the kingdom of God, and with equal clearness set forth that these children are ours to be cared for by us.

New Problems of This Generation

Now, may I add just a word or two to what I have already said. Always remember the devil is not asleep, nor is he dead. I wonder if you have considered, I know you have, the problems, the new problems which you of this generation now meet. There comes into the home of every one of you, practically, by radio, or by television, or both, and in the movies, at the theaters, words and pictures whereby your children have presented to them all of the allurements of the idle life, the life of the idle rich. Pictured in the finest pictures that can be made are the so-called pleasures of that life. Your children see and hear all these things.

Hour after hour they listen to or see, or both, the criminal side of our society. Do you appreciate that they are receiving an education in crime? Radio and television, particularly, picture great criminal incidents happening in our daily lives. Small children today know far more about crime and the way it is committed and how it is planned and how the law may be evaded and the criminals escape, than most of us who are mature.

I grant you that usually the end of the picture or radio story brings its moral, the guilty criminal meets his punishment, but in the meanwhile every child has seen what that criminal has done up to that point, to commit his crime, escape punishment, and has seen how the criminal worked out his criminal, even murderous designs.

And, lastly, your children see the pseudo-attractiveness of vice, the pleasures which allegedly vice can bring, they see the wayward life, the life not in harmony with our standards, the life that leads down to perdition. All are shown with an alluring glamour, a seductive persuasiveness that charms the children, the youth, the grown-ups, so that sometimes almost unconsciously they seek the ways of such a life.

I appreciate the problems which Sunday brings you because of your television and your radio. I can only hope and pray that the Lord will bless you and help you to meet this new threat to the standards lived by your children, and their conduct among themselves. I am quite aware of the great blessings that the radio and television bring to us, and the great service they may be brought to render in the cause of truth. But now I am not dwelling on the blessings. I am thinking of the ills, the criminal instincts that are fostered and displayed in all these things.

May the Lord bless you and help you to meet these things, help you to cope with them, give you wisdom of a different kind than has been called for in the past, wisdom as great as ever was bestowed upon any people to meet all these temptations. This I pray for you.

Prayer for Mothers of Israel

Mothers of Israel, in your hands primarily lie the rearing and guiding of the future generation, the one that follows ours; seek to guide your children aright that they may righteously carry on. But you cannot do this by lodging your child in some kind of a caretaking establishment while you go out to earn more money, perhaps to get a few more comforts or luxuries. Sometimes it may be necessary for a mother to leave her home and leave her children to a neighbor, to the older but immature brother or sister, or in so-styled nursery homes, but I beseech you mothers in Israel, make any of these courses your very last resort of necessity and be sure the reason for your action is one that would be recognized by our Heavenly Father as justifying your lack of care for the spirit which he has permitted to come to you at your invitation.

God bless you in the great work you have done and are doing. I believe I appreciate how great this organization [the Relief Society] is, and I appreciate how you are worked by the brethren. If it were not for the work which you do for the brethren, we brethren would be a pretty sad lot. I hope the brethren will try not to ruin your health and lives in doing the work which they ought to do.

God bless you.

"And a certain ruler asked him, saying, Good Master, what shall I do to inherit eternal life?"

Luke 18:18

The Rich Young Ruler

T HE young people of today are peculiarly blessed, and when I say peculiarly blessed, I mean that they are blessed in a peculiar way. Never before in the history, so far as we know, of the world, has there been such a wide diffusion of education among any great people, as exists today among the Latter-day Saints and the people of this nation. Never before in the history of the world, so far as we know, has a whole generation been nurtured in the luxury which has existed among the young for the past fifteen years, and there has been brought to us as servants everything which science could develop or discover.

But that is not the only heritage which the young people have. Not only this material blessing, if it shall prove so to be, have they possessed, but they have also had spiritual and intellectual blessings, more than have come to any other generation within the memory of man. And these heritages are for them carefully to guard.

Youth's Challenge

We sometimes hear the expression used: "A challenge to youth." To me the challenge to youth is the preservation of these heritages.

It is quite true that there have come along with the blessings some evil and some error. It is quite true that we are not entirely sure, perhaps, with reference to certain things, as to whether they are blessings or curses. One of the tasks which the young people will have to face, one of the problems which they will have to answer and solve, is to divide the good from the bad, and in that work I know of nothing that can be more beneficial than a true cultural development which shall develop and make grow the spiritual side of themselves, which will ennoble their thoughts and raise them above the ordinary vicissitudes and problems of life.

It would be a sad thing to me, indeed, if out of a situation of want—in some cases of distress—it would be sad, I say, to me, if out of that there should come to us only a consideration of the material things of life. Sad shall it be, indeed, if all that we shall think about shall be how much we can get of the riches of this life, and riches you know are just as attractive to the young as to the old.

The Rich Young Man

I want to refer here to that wonderful story of the Savior when he was on the road back from Judea through Perea, coming to Jerusalem for the tragic but glorious end. Many things happened on the way. Among them you will recall that he had them bring little children to him to bless, after which he apparently started out again on the road. I want to read to you from Mark, the story of the Savior and the rich young man:

And when he was gone forth into the way, there came one running, and kneeled to him, and asked him, Good Master, what shall I do that I may inherit eternal life?

That is the problem of every young man and young woman today.

And Jesus said unto him, Why callest thou me good? there is none good but one, that is, God.

Thou knowest the commandments, Do not commit adultery, Do not kill, Do not steal, Do not bear false witness, Defraud not, Honour thy father and mother.

And he answered and said unto him, Master, all these have I observed from my youth.

Then Jesus beholding him loved him. . . .

He seemed to have all the requirements; he seemed to be one whom even the Master himself might love. Then Jesus said unto him:

One thing thou lackest: go thy way, sell whatsoever thou hast, and give to the poor, and thou shalt have treasure in heaven: and come, take up the cross, and follow me.

That was not the first time that the Savior had used those words, "Follow me." On the shores of Galilee he had time and again spoken to those humble fishermen, and each time he had said, "Follow me," they had come after him.

And he [the young man] was sad at that saying, and went away grieved: for he had great possessions.

And Jesus looked round about, and saith unto his disciples, How hardly shall they that have riches enter into the kingdom of God! (Mark 10:17-23.)

Two Kinds of Riches

My brethren and sisters, there are two kinds of riches, those of which the Savior spoke here, and those which you young men and women may lay up so abundantly for yourselves in the work which you are doing in the Church, and I beseech you, do not let yourselves wander after the riches which this young man had, and which shut him out from following after the Master, whom all must follow and serve if they shall gain that which God has provided for them.

Do not forget the goodness and the mercy and the kindness of the Savior. Do not forget the blessings which the Gospel has for you. Do not overlook the joy of the Spirit, the joy which comes from living as the Savior has taught us to live.

Remember that when the Savior was here and bestowed the blessings which he, the Divine One, had to give, in no case did he give riches. He gave health, he gave strength, he restored sight, he made the dumb to speak, he pardoned sin, he led people from sin. The one thing that he did not do was to give of earthly riches, and in this conversation with the rich young man, he tells us why he did not make this gift.

And so, I would like to leave with you this thought, this message, that you will seek after the treasures of the Spirit, seek after the riches of goodness and mercy and righteous living. Go always after those things which are good. Follow along as you have been doing, seeking the finer cultural things of life. Discard the dross, cast it aside, trample it underfoot; cherish always and guard that which is beautiful in your lives.

Remember ever that Jesus is the Christ. He is not the mere teacher. He is the Messiah, the Redeemer of the world. His teachings and his works and his miracles were all ancillary to that. They were a part of the mission which he had, but nevertheless, he came to this earth the Only Begotten, the Redeemer and Savior of the world. Never overlook that. Never degrade him to the mere place of a teacher; believe in him, look to him always, worship him as the Redeemer of the world through whom alone salvation and exaltation may come.

Let all your activities, everything that you do in life, let them all lead unto this great fundamental fact, that Jesus is the Christ, the Messiah, the Only Begotten, and there shall come to you in this life joy and peace and happiness; there shall come to you more satisfaction in living and following this life than anything else you could do in this world; and in the life which is to follow after this there shall come eternal lives—the highest glory which can come to man.

"These words spake Jesus, and lifted up his eyes to heaven, and said, Father, the hour is come; glorify thy Son, that thy Son also may glorify thee:
"As thou hast given him power over all flesh, that he should give eternal life to as many as thou hast given him.
"And this is life eternal, that they might know thee the only true God, and Jesus Christ, whom thou hast sent.
"I have glorified thee on the earth: I have finished the work which thou gavest me to do.
"And now, O Father, glorify thou me with thine own self with the glory which I had with thee before the world was."
John 17:1-5

The Atoning Sacrifice

W HEN* the Savior came in through the gates of Jerusalem and moved on, on his lowly ass, to the temple, people looked to him and expected from him an announcement that he was the promised king for whom the Jews were looking. They expected him to proclaim himself a political power. I assume they did not know that more than three years before this time, Satan himself had taken Christ upon the high mountain and had offered to him the kingdoms of the world if he would bow down and worship Satan, and that the Savior pushed the crown aside. The Jews, groaning under oppression, smarting under political suppression, thought that he had come to give them a political life.

But such was not his mission. And as the week wore away and he finished his earthly mission, there came unto the multitudes of Jerusalem a feeling that they had been disappointed, perhaps misled.

The Savior's entire mission was devoted to the spiritual side of life and to the relieving of human suffering, physical and mental. His message is a spiritual message.

The reason for his coming was that he might redeem us from the Fall, that he might be the First Fruits of the Resurrection, that he might demonstrate to us that he was the Only Begotten of God in the flesh, that he might show to us he was the Redeemer of the world.

The Last Supper

For many years I have tried at this particular season of the year to have in mind some of the essentials of the great last three days of the Savior's mortality. I have tried to run over in my mind some of the chief events,

---

*A composite of several sermons delivered on Easter Sunday.

the death, the crucifixion, and the resurrection of him
who has given us the plan by which we may come back
into our Heavenly Father's presence.

Therefore I will go forward beginning on Thursday
night, the night of the Last Supper in the Upper Chamber, begun by an unseemly controversy as to precedence
and signalized by the institution of the Sacrament, which
occurred, I feel, after Judas had left the chamber to arrange to betray the Master. That was a great supper.
There were great sermons preached by the Master.

When they had finished they went out to the Mount
of Olives, where he preached again, and then a little later
they retired to the Garden, and the Savior, taking Peter,
James, and John, left the rest of the disciples and went
a little farther on.

Then the Savior left them and went still farther on
and asked them to wait and watch while he was gone.
I do not believe that you can understand, I know that I
cannot understand, the kind of agony that he went
through in the Garden of Gethsemane when he shed drops
of blood. I do not know, sometimes I have wondered if
anybody who is not a God could understand that. I repudiate, personally, the idea that his agony was caused
by any bodily suffering, any fear of death. There was
something deep and beyond that, and what it was I do
not know.

The burden of his prayer in the Garden was, "O my
Father, if it be possible, let this cup pass from me: nevertheless not my will, but thine, be done."

The Arrest and Trial

Shortly after that Judas returned with the crowd
that was to arrest the Savior and did arrest him.

He was taken first, in what they say was an illegal
examination, to Annas, the real high priest, the father-

in-law of Caiaphas, the titular high priest, who had been installed by the Roman government.

From Annas he went to Caiaphas, and it was Caiaphas, who, in an agony of fear and apprehension said, "I adjure thee by the living God, that thou tell us whether thou be the Christ, the Son of God." And the Savior said to him, "Thou hast said: nevertheless I say unto you, Hereafter shall ye see the Son of man sitting on the right hand of power."

From Caiaphas he was sent to the Sanhedrin (it was now nearly morning) and the Sanhedrin passed what apparently was a formal judgment that he was to be crucified.

Before Pilate and Herod

As the Jews could not impose the death penalty, from the Sanhedrin he was taken to Pilate, against whom Christendom has for nearly two thousand years vented its dislike, and yet, as I read the record, Pilate did practically all that the law under which he operated as stated in the Gospels, permitted him to do. Pilate came back to the multitude on at least five occasions and sought to secure the release of Jesus. At first he returned merely saying, "I find no fault in this man." And the multitude renewed their demand for his crucifixion.

Then Pilate sent him to Herod, and Herod sent him back, and Pilate began again the examination of Jesus. This time, and from then until the end, he pleaded that they take Barabbas and release Jesus. Three times at least this was done and each time they said, "Release unto us Barabbas"—and it was their right, apparently, to demand the release of one man on this occasion— "Crucify him,"—Jesus.

During this latter examination it was that Pilate's wife sent to Pilate a letter beseeching him not to do anything to this man. The result of one of the latest examinations was that Pilate took a basin and washed his hands and said, "I am innocent of the blood of this just person: see ye to it"; and the multitude cried, "His blood be on us, and on our children." It is my faith that this has been so for nearly two thousand years.

Pilate ordered that a title be placed on the cross written in Hebrew, Greek, and Latin, "The King of the Jews." He flatly refused to have the title either changed or removed.

The Crucifixion

Then Jesus was turned over to be crucified, he was scourged, had a wreath of thorns placed on his head. He was stripped of the royal trappings they had mockingly placed upon him; reclothed in his own raiment; then they started for the place of crucifixion.

Jesus was to have carried his own cross, but he was too weak. As he came to the place of crucifixion, they offered him a drink of vinegar and gall, an opiate. He refused it. He then went on to the crucifixion.

Having in mind the modesty which I am sure attached to him, recalling the experience of Peter on the lakeshore, how offensive it must have been when they stripped him naked and then laying the cross on the ground, they laid him upon the cross, the crosspiece under his shoulders, a peg protruding from the upright beam, which he straddled to support his body. They first nailed his hands and then his feet. Then as the next step in this, the cruelest death of which the ancients knew, they raised the cross and let it drop with a jolt into the pit which was dug to contain it, causing the one crucified to suffer excruciating agony.

First Words on the Cross

The first words the Savior uttered were, "Father, forgive them; for they know not what they do."

We can dimly perceive the loneliness which came to him. Apparently only John was present of the disciples, and the women from Galilee and the mother.

Second Words

Of the thieves, one began to upbraid him and the other to plead for mercy, and it was then that what was called the second outcry from the cross occurred, Jesus saying to the one who spoke kindly, "To day shalt thou be with me in paradise."

Third Words

As the Savior looked down into the multitude before him, he saw his mother and John. You recall that he saith unto his mother, "Woman, behold thy son!" Then saith he to the disciple, "Behold thy mother!"

Fourth Words

Then we come to his utter loneliness, when he repeated the words of the Psalm and that outcry of almost human desperation, "My God, my God, why hast thou forsaken me?"

Darkness Falls

It would seem that at about this time, which was midday, or the sixth hour, darkness fell over the land of Palestine.

Fifth, Sixth, and Seventh Words from the Cross

The Savior said, "I thirst," and those in attendance gave him the sponge saturated with vinegar and put it to his mouth.

A little later he cried out, "It is finished," apparently meaning that his earthly work was done. He had gone through his life. He had made the sacrifice.

Finally, just before his death, he cried out, "Father, into thy hands I commend my spirit."

Thus he became the true sacrifice for the Fall, ordained from the beginning of the world and before.

The Burial

I like to think of the Easter morning two thousand years ago, nearly. Christ, the Son of God, was buried without ostentation or pageantry, without anything but the humble worship of those who were immediately about him. He was carried to his rest and buried in a lent tomb, a newly hewn rock sepulchre belonging to Joseph of Arimathea, recognized as a follower of the Savior.

It is interesting to remember that the day he was buried was the day fixed under the Mosaic Law for the gathering of the first sheaf of the harvest, and as some commentators have noted, that while the women who were seated near the sepulchre returned sorrowful to their homes in the darkness, for their light had gone out, another group from across the Kedron returned joyously, carrying the sheaf, the first sheaf of the harvest.

That was Friday.

Saturday, the chief priests and the Pharisees went to Pilate and petitioned, saying, "We remember that that deceiver said, while he was yet alive, After three days I will rise again. Command therefore that the sepulchre be made sure until the third day, lest his disciples come by night, and steal him away, and say unto the people, He is risen from the dead: so the last error shall be worse than the first. Pilate said unto them, Ye have a watch: go your way, make it as sure as ye can."

Happenings in the Western Hemisphere

Meanwhile there was darkness on this [the American] continent.

You will remember that there was darkness in Palestine, and that there were some convulsions of nature, but nothing like that which happened on this continent, where the whole face of the land was changed. Apparently at the time the darkness came in Palestine, the convulsions began on this hemisphere.

Cities were sunk, mountains appeared where cities had been, cities were burned, there was widespread destruction which lasted, the historian tells us, only three hours, though many thought it lasted for a much longer time. Highways were broken, roadways were destroyed, whole cities were shaken by the earthquake. The historian tells us first of a storm and then of a tempest and of whirlwinds and of all manner of earthquakes, the cleaving of the rocks, and all the rest.

The Voice

At the conclusion of this, at the end of three hours, the people were mourning and howling, as the word is given in the Book of Mormon, and a voice was heard throughout the land, only a voice, which identified itself in the course of the talk, as the voice of Jesus Christ, the Son of God.

And he told them of the cities that had been destroyed, and how. He told them that he was responsible for the destruction. He told them why it was, and the historian tells us that the better part of those who lived righteously were saved, but the rest were destroyed.

Then the voice told them, as I see it, preparatory to the message that he was come to them after his ascension—this was a voice during the darkness—he told them he had come to fulfil the law of Moses and that thereafter burnt offerings were not acceptable to him, but that they should give to him humble hearts and contrite spirits. That was to be their sacrifice. So he told them,

this voice, that their old sacrifices were done away. He
ceased speaking, and there was silence.

The voice came the second time and told them how
often he would have gathered them, Israel—those where
he spoke and in Palestine—how often he would have
gathered them as a hen gathereth her chickens under her
wing, but they would not. Then the voice ceased.

There was silence, and then they began an outcry,
lamenting that they had not followed his commandments,
that they had broken them, and so had suffered.

That was one thing the Savior did while his body
was in the tomb—he came to America and gave them the
instructions and the report of the destruction to which
I have just referred.

The Dead Hear His Voice

But there is another apparent occupation of his
while he lay in the tomb. You will remember that at the
Second Passover, where he healed a man at the pool of
Bethesda and being reproved for doing that, he had told
them, "Verily, verily, I say unto you, The hour is coming,
and now is, when the dead shall hear the voice of the Son
of God: and they that hear shall live." That is all that
he said at that time.

Peter enlarges on this principle and tells us (as we
have interpreted it, though the exact text does not say
so, but at least it gives a clear implication thereof), that
during this period while he lay in the tomb, he preached
to the spirits in prison "which sometime were disobedient" in the time of Noah, and gave them another chance,
"that they might be judged according to men in the flesh,
but live according to God in the spirit."

To the condemned, believing thief on the cross,
Christ said, "To day shalt thou be with me in paradise."

Those are the two principal items about the activities of the spirit of Jesus Christ while he lay in the tomb:

coming to America to give instructions and report the destruction which had occurred on this continent, and, preaching to the spirits in prison.

Time, space, disappear when Deity moves; we do not see them in connection with the operations of our Heavenly Father, nor of his Son.

The Resurrection

Returning now to the morning of the resurrection—Sunday—no mortal eye, so far as I know or have read, saw Jesus emerge from the tomb. An angel came down and rolled the rock away from the door. It interests me as to why the Savior himself did not do it. But the record says an angel came.

Before daybreak in the morning, while it was still dark, a priest climbed to the topmost part of the great walls that enclosed the temple precincts and stood there looking southward. He stood four hundred and fifty feet above the valley floor. The priests below called out, "Is it yet light?" and the second question, "Is it light as far as Hebron?" And when the answer came back, "Yes," that was the signal for the beginning of the morning sacrifice in the temple.

At that same hour a solitary woman, half-running, half-walking, went out from the narrow streets of Jerusalem across the valley to Golgotha, where on Friday they had laid away in the tomb our Lord and Savior. She found the stone rolled back. Looking in, she perceived the body was not there. The tomb was empty. She hastened back to Peter and John, whom she had just left and told them.

To this point of time and for some time after, none of the Apostles seemingly had understood what we understand now so clearly, that Jesus was to die and be resurrected the Christ.

Peter and John, running, John outrunning Peter,

for he was younger, reached the sepulchre. John looked in but did not enter. Courageous Peter, coming up, strode in and saw the burial clothes lying about. The napkin was carefully folded and placed at one side. John believed. Peter seems not yet to have been convinced. They returned.

And then it would appear that Mary, coming alone, I suppose as fast as she could, came to the tomb the second time. She stood weeping. Within the tomb she saw two angels sitting, one at the head and one at the feet, where the body had lain. They asked why she wept. She answered that they had taken away her Lord, and she knew not where they had laid him. They told her he had risen.

The Resurrected Christ Appears to Mary

She turned about and saw someone, who she supposed was the gardener, and so she said to him, "Sir, if thou have borne him hence, tell me where thou hast laid him, and I will take him away." The figure spoke, calling her by name, "Mary."

Then, as it seems to have been the case all day, something happened and she recognized the Master, and would have rushed and embraced him, but the Savior said, "Touch me not; for I am not yet ascended to my Father... and your Father; and to my God, and your God."

Shortly after this, the two Marys came with other women, bringing with them a hundred pounds of sweet spices to be used for the preparation of the body for final burial. They did not understand, either. The women looked in and saw the two angels there. And the angel said to them, "Ye seek Jesus of Nazareth. He is not here. He is risen."

From then until now, the words of that angel stand a witness to us of the actuality of the resurrection.

Christ Appears to the Women at the Tomb

Christ appeared to the women at the tomb. They saw him. They heard his voice. They knew he was resurrected. While he forbade Mary to touch him, he permitted the women to hold his feet.

Christ Appears to the Disciples

Sometime during this first day, he showed himself to Peter, and, in the late afternoon, to the two on their way to Emmaus. "And beginning at Moses and all the prophets, he expounded unto them in all the scriptures the things concerning himself." As he sat at meat with them, "he took bread, and blessed it, and brake, and gave to them." Their eyes were opened, they knew him, and he vanished from their sight.

They returned to Jerusalem, met with the Twelve, except Thomas. The doors were shut. They told of their visit with the risen Lord. Even as they spoke, Jesus stood amongst them. He reproved and calmed their fears. "Behold my hands and my feet, that it is I myself: handle me, and see; for a spirit hath not flesh and bones, as ye see me have." He asked for food. They gave him and he ate a piece of broiled fish and honeycomb.

Eight days later, the Twelve being again in a room with the doors shut, Thomas now being with them, Jesus again suddenly stood in their midst. He bade Thomas to look at and touch his hands; to thrust his finger into the spear wound in his side, and then, said he, "be not faithless, but believing."

On the shores of the Sea of Galilee, he appeared to Peter, and Thomas and Nathanael of Cana, to the sons of Zebedee and two others, who had gone fishing. "After that, he was seen of above five hundred brethren at once," and of James. Eleven of the disciples visited him on a mountain in Galilee, where he had appointed them to come.

The Ascension

Finally, after forty days, he assembled them together in Jerusalem, and then leading them out as far as Bethany, where Mary and Martha and Lazarus lived, and while they still beheld him, "a cloud received him out of their sight." Two men stood before them in white apparel, and said to them: "Ye men of Galilee, why stand ye gazing up into heaven? this same Jesus, which is taken up from you into heaven, shall so come in like manner as ye have seen him go into heaven."

Christ had risen. He had made the great Atoning Sacrifice for our sins.

How glorious is the resurrection (planned from before the foundation of the world) of the Christ, designated in some scriptures, even as of that time, as the Lamb of God. I cannot comprehend what the resurrection did. I have read nothing that explains to my mind what the resurrection, biologically or physiologically, is. I feel quite convinced that if it were explained, that it would be in language and invoking principles that I would not understand. The Lord has given us all that we need to know—that Christ is our Savior, the Redeemer of the world, the One through whom we attain that destiny which is marked out as possible for all of God's children who earn it.

Eternal progression is brought about through that Atonement. We may go on and on forever. That is our destiny through the Atonement of Jesus Christ.

May God bring this fact, this principle, this opportunity, and this destiny into the minds and hearts of all of us, and may we, so knowing and so believing, live his principles and obey his commandments.

"Hear, O ye heavens, and give ear, O earth, and rejoice ye inhabitants thereof, for the Lord is God, and beside him there is no Savior.

"Great is his wisdom, marvelous are his ways, and the extent of his doings none can find out.

"His purposes fail not, neither are there any who can stay his hand.

"From eternity to eternity he is the same, and his years never fail."

Doctrine and Covenants 76:1-4

Faith, Belief, and Knowledge of This Church Concerning Jesus Christ

I WISH to state the faith, the belief, and the knowledge of the Latter-day Saints regarding Jesus of Nazareth.

We accept literally the words of John concerning the Christ: "In the beginning was the Word, and the Word was with God, and the Word was God." The Christ has declared in our own day: "I was in the beginning with the Father, and am the Firstborn."

We also accept John's declaration that Jesus Christ was the Creator of the world, that "all things were made by him; and without him was not any thing made that was made."

We believe that in the Great Council in Heaven held before the world was, Satan proposed one plan for creation and ruling the world and its progeny, and that Christ proposed another; that Satan's plan was rejected, as taking away the agency of man, and Christ's was accepted as keeping man's agency.

We believe that in obedience to the plan, Christ created the world and all that in it is, first spiritually, then temporally, and that in this work of creation he acted as one of the Great Trinity of three distinct Personages, the Godhead, the Father, the Son, and the Holy Ghost.

We believe that following this creation, the Lord from time to time showed himself to man, either in person or in vision, or dream, or by speech, beginning even with Adam, and later to Enoch, Noah, Abraham, Moses, Samuel, Daniel, and others on the eastern hemisphere, and to many prophets on the western continents; that on this hemisphere, in one of the most glorious theophanies of all time, the Lord showed himself, before his birth, to the brother of Jared, the man of greatest faith to his time, saying: "Because of thy faith thou hast seen that I shall take upon me flesh and blood. . . . Behold, this body, which ye now behold, is the body of my spirit . . . and even as I appear unto thee to be in the spirit will I appear unto my people in the flesh."

We believe that in the Meridian of Time, Mary the Virgin gave birth to Jesus, the Only Begotten of the Father, in very deed and fact the Son of God; that Jesus was crucified upon the cross; that he was buried and lay in the tomb till the morning of the third day when he was verily resurrected from the dead—that is, his spirit and his body reunited, and he rose from the tomb a perfect, glorified, living soul; that thus Christ atoned for Adam's Fall from which man is so redeemed, and that all men will by reason of that Atonement be resurrected—that is, the body and the spirit of every person born into the world will at some time after death, and in the due course of the Lord, be reunited, thus fulfilling Paul's saying: "As in Adam all die, even so in Christ shall all be made alive."

We believe that except for this Atonement of Christ for the Fall of Adam, man would, through all the eternities, have remained under the penalty of the mortal and spiritual death brought upon the human family by Adam.

We thus believe Christ to be in the full, true, and most literal sense, the Creator of the world, one of the Godhead, the Only Begotten of the Father, the Son of God, the promised Messiah, the First Fruits of the Resurrection, the Redeemer of the world.

We believe that some eighteen hundred years after the Son's death and resurrection, the Father and the Son, two glorified Personages having human form, appeared to a boy fourteen years of age, even as the Lord came of old to the child Samuel in the temple; that the Father, pointing to the Son, said: "This is My Beloved Son; Hear Him"; and that the Son, responding to the lad's inquiry as to which of the many sectarian creeds were right, told the lad that none of them was right, and that he should join none of them.

We believe that through the instrumentality of this same lad, Joseph Smith, grown to maturity, the Lord restored to earth the true Gospel and the Priesthood of God which had been taken from the earth because of the transgressions of men.

Hundreds of thousands of Latter-day Saints, living and dead, have proclaimed their absolute knowledge of the truth of every declaration I have made; some of them have sealed their testimonies with a martyr's blood. To the testimony of the humblest of all these, I wish in humility to add my own.

". . . are called to be the Twelve Apostles, or special witnesses of the name of Christ in all the world."
Doctrine and Covenants 107:23

The Witness of an Apostle of the Lamb

God declared his work and his glory are to "bring to pass the immortality and eternal life of man";—a resurrected being, each in the image of God himself, with eternal progress before him. Jesus declared our destiny to the multitude on the Mount: "Be ye therefore perfect, even as your Father which is in heaven is perfect."...

How blessed are we for our own credo: "We believe that through the atonement of Christ, all mankind may be saved by obedience to the laws and ordinances of the Gospel", — all mankind may be saved, those that have lived from the beginning, through our work for the dead, those now living and those to be born in the future through our spread of the Gospel, till God's plan is completely fulfilled,

How blessed are we to have this never dimming, always glowing hope, and the eternal knowledge that belongs to us, to comfort us and to urge us on through life, that we may add to God's declared work and glory by gaining for ourselves, and for all believers and doers, the priceless destiny of immortality and eternal life.

May God grant us the power so to live is my prayer for you.

J Reuben Clark Jr

Index